Ovid's *Metamorphoses*

Ovid's Metamorphoses is a Latin reader designed to partner existing elementary Latin textbooks.

The book features thirty compelling stories, graduated in difficulty and adapted from Ovid's epic *Metamorphoses* into prose. The original poem contains many different stories united thematically by the transformation which occurs in all of them; the epic features romance, seduction, humour, violence, monsters, and misbehaving gods.

Each chapter contains:

- a Latin passage adapted from the epic
- an accompanying vocabulary list
- a short commentary to help with translation
- a concise review of the specific grammar covered
- a brief comment on a literary aspect of the poem, or featured myth.

Suitable for college students studying Latin at the elementary level, *Ovid's Metamorphoses* is designed to be used alongside elementary Latin textbooks. Preserving Ovid's language and highly vivid descriptions, this reader introduces students to the epic masterpiece, allows them to consolidate their understanding of Latin prose, and offers opportunities for literary discussion.

Christine L. Albright is Assistant Professor and Elementary Languages Program Coordinator at the University of Georgia, USA.

Ovid's *Metamorphoses*
A Reader for Students in Elementary College Latin

Christine L. Albright

Routledge
Taylor & Francis Group

LONDON AND NEW YORK

First published 2018
by Routledge
2 Park Square, Milton Park, Abingdon, Oxon OX14 4RN

and by Routledge
711 Third Avenue, New York, NY 10017

Routledge is an imprint of the Taylor & Francis Group, an informa business

British Library Cataloguing in Publication Data
A catalogue record for this book is available from the British Library

Library of Congress Cataloging in Publication Data
Names: Ovid, 43 B.C.-17 A.D. or 18 A.D., author. | Albright, Christine L., editor.
Title: Ovid's Metamorphoses: a reader for students in elementary college Latin/ Christine L. Albright.
Description: Abingdon, Oxon: Routledge, 2017. | Includes bibliographical references and index.
Identifiers: LCCN 2017012612 | ISBN 9781138291171 (harback: alk. paper) | ISBN 9781138291188 (pbk.: alk. paper) | ISBN 9781315265605 (ebook)
Subjects: LCSH: Latin language–Readers.
Classification: LCC PA6519.M5 A537 2017 | DDC 873/.01–dc23
LC record available at https://lccn.loc.gov/2017012612

ISBN: 978-1-138-29117-1 (hbk)
ISBN: 978-1-138-29118-8 (pbk)
ISBN: 978-1-315-26560-5 (ebk)

Typeset in Times New Roman
by Sunrise Setting Ltd., Brixham, UK

FILIO CARISSIMO

Contents

Acknowledgements

Many people have assisted with the production of this reader, and I am indebted to each one of them. I thank my colleagues in the Department of Classics at the University of Georgia, including especially Thomas Biggs, Keith Dix, Erika Hermanowicz, Naomi Norman, and Peter O'Connell. John Nicholson and Charles Platter read drafts of stories and offered excellent suggestions and very helpful advice. I am grateful to both of them for their input. I also owe much to my anonymous reviewers, whose comments resulted in a very-much-improved reader. Any mistakes which remain are of course my own. I should thank several graduate research assistants who have helped with the project, including Silvio Curtis, Alex Karsten, and Aaron Ivey. Kelly Dugan, with her endless energy and meticulous organizational and editing skills, made enormous contributions to the project in its final stages. Carrie Cabe and Lori Gibbons of the University of Georgia's Information Technology team helped with many technical matters. I would like to thank my parents, George and Carol Albright, for their support and for the many hours they have spent entertaining my young son so I could work. Finally, I would like to thank the students in my elementary Latin classes at the University of Georgia, for whom I undertook this project in the first place.

Abbreviations

abl.	ablative
acc.	accusative
adj.	adjective
adv.	adverb
conj.	conjunction
dat.	dative
defect.	defective
demonst.	demonstrative
f.	feminine
gen.	genitive
impers.	impersonal
indecl.	indeclinable
inf.	infinitive
interj.	interjection
interrog.	interrogative
m.	masculine
Met.	*Metamorphoses*
n.	neuter
nom.	nominative
numer.	numeral/numerical
pl.	plural
poss.	possessive
prep.	preposition
pron.	pronoun
reflex.	reflexive
rel.	relative
sing.	singular

Introduction

Publius Ovidius Naso, commonly known as Ovid, was born on March 20, 43 BCE at Sulmo, a town located about 100 miles east of Rome. He was born to a family of equestrian rank, and he received an excellent education which was meant to prepare him for a legal career. Although he did hold some minor public offices, Ovid instead felt compelled to write poetry. In *Tristia* 4.10.17–26, Ovid recalls his early devotion to poetry:

> frater ad eloquium viridi tendebat ab aevo,
> fortia verbosi natus ad arma fori;
> at mihi iam puero caelestia sacra placebant,
> inque suum furtim Musa trahebat opus.
> saepe pater dixit "studium quid inutile temptas?
> Maeonides nullas ipse reliquit opes."
> motus eram dictis, totoque Helicone relicto
> scribere temptabam verba soluta modis.
> sponte sua carmen numeros veniebat ad aptos,
> et quod temptabam scribere versus erat.

My brother tended towards oratory from a young age; he was born for the strong weapons of the wordy forum. But for me already as a boy heavenly worship was pleasing, and the Muse stealthily was drawing me into her work. Often my father said: "Why do you attempt a useless pursuit? Homer himself left no wealth." I was moved by his words, and, with Helicon altogether left behind, I tried to write words freed from meter. Of its own accord, song came to fitting numbers, and whatever I tried to write was verse.

Ovid enjoyed poetic success as a young man and eventually published many works in elegiac meter, including *Amores* (love poems), *Heroides* (letters from heroines to heroes), *Medicamina Faciei Femineae* (a poem about cosmetics), *Ars Amatoria* (a didactic poem about erotic pursuits), *Remedia Amoris* (a poem about how to disentangle oneself from relationships), *Fasti* (a poem about the Roman calendar), *Tristia* (poems written from exile), *Epistulae ex Ponto* (letters written from exile), and *Ibis* (a curse-poem).

In 8 CE, at the height of his career, Ovid was exiled to Tomis on the Black Sea by the emperor Augustus. His sentence was *relegatio*, which meant that he was banished from Rome but allowed to keep his property and citizenship. The exact cause for the punishment is not known, although in his later poetry Ovid himself tells his audience that his banishment was due to a *carmen* (poem) and an *error* (mistake). It is generally assumed that the *carmen* was the *Ars Amatoria*, although it had been published almost a decade before Ovid's relegation.

The *Metamorphoses*, which was almost finished in the year Ovid's sentence was passed down, seems just as likely to have offended Augustus.

The *Metamorphoses* is Ovid's only surviving work in dactylic hexameter, the meter of Greek and Roman epic. It is organized in 15 books, and it contains a multitude of mythological stories from various cultures. The poem begins with a description of the creation of the universe and ends with a celebration of the political order of Rome under Augustus, so in general there is some sense of linear progression through the course of the text. The structure is quite complicated, however. Ovid embeds stories within other stories, allows stories to bleed from one book into the next, and uses multiple internal narrators. Transformation serves as a unifying theme, and Ovid's characters change into animals, birds, watery springs, constellations, and plants, for example.

This reader offers 30 stories which have been adapted from Ovid's verse into Latin prose. The reader is intended to complement elementary Latin textbooks and aims to help bridge the often wide gap between the elementary and intermediate reading levels by providing compelling, challenging passages. The reader has been designed as a supplementary text; ideally, students will attempt these stories after translating simpler passages in a primary textbook. The stories are graduated in difficulty and introduce grammatical topics typically covered during the first year of studying college Latin. In general, the length of the stories increases as the reader progresses, although a few shorter examples are found in the middle chapters which reflect the concise nature of Ovid's own narratives. As they work their way through the reader, students will encounter elements of Latin which tend to be difficult to negotiate when they first begin to read actual texts, such as relative pronouns which begin sentences, epithets, and plural words used when singular words are expected. The stories feature much of Ovid's own vocabulary and syntax.

The reader also aims to introduce students to Ovid's epic masterpiece. Thus, Ovid's poetic language and highly vivid descriptions have been preserved wherever possible. His graphic presentation of the mythical material has been retained. Sexual situations and raw violence are pervasive in the epic, and the content of Ovid's stories has not been sanitized. Most of the stories in the reader appear in the first half of the epic, but the last five stories are taken from Books 14 and 15. Like the epic itself, the reader begins with the story of creation and ends with the story of the apotheosis of Julius Caesar. Thus, if read from beginning to end, the reader will provide a sense of the structure and linear progression of the *Metamorphoses* and offer opportunities for robust literary discussion.

Each chapter includes a Latin passage adapted from the epic, an accompanying vocabulary list, a short commentary to help with translation, a concise review of the specific grammar covered, and a comment about a literary aspect of the poem or the featured myth. Students should note that vocabulary words are glossed the first time they appear but are not glossed in subsequent chapters. Some commonly used words such as *nōn* and *sed* appear only in the final glossary. Participles are glossed as adjectives until Chapter 18, when participles are introduced. After Chapter 18, vocabulary lists include the verbs from which participles are derived. Comparative and superlative adjectives and adverbs appear in vocabulary lists and the final glossary in their comparative or superlative forms.

1   Creation begins

(*Met.* 1.5–150)

At the beginning of Book 1, Ovid offers an account of creation. He calls this primordial state "Chaos," borrowing the term from the Greek poet Hesiod.

1   Ante terrās et aquās, nātūra est ūna sphaera. Sphaera nōn ordināta est. Massa
2   indīgesta est. Nōn sunt stellae. Nōn est lūna. Terra, aqua, et aura sunt, sed terrae,
3   aquae, et aurae sine formā sunt. Nōn sunt silvae. Nōn sunt āreae. Nōn sunt bestiae.
4   Nōn sunt casae. Nōn sunt undae. Nōn rīpae sunt. Nōn piscīnae sunt. Nōn nāviculae
5   sunt. Nōn Eurus, Zephyrus, Boreās vel Auster. Nōn sunt muscae. Chaos est. Nihil
6   suam formam servat. Aliud aliīs obstat. Tum aliquis inordinātam māteriam ordinat.

Commentary

4 *Nōn sunt undae. Nōn rīpae sunt*: Notice that the subject of the sentence can appear in various positions with respect to the verb. That they are in the nominative case indicates that *undae* and *rīpae* are the subjects of these sentences.

5 *Nōn Eurus, Zephyrus, Boreās vel Auster*: The names of the winds are all in the nominative case.

5–6 *Nihil suam formam servat*: The Latin word *suus, a, um* is a reflexive adjective, which means that it reflects back to the subject of the sentence and takes its meaning from that. Thus, it can mean *his own*, *her own*, *its own*, or *their own*. Like any adjective, it agrees with the noun it modifies in case, number, and gender, but you must determine what the subject is to translate it correctly. Here, the subject is *nihil*, so it should be translated *its own*.

aliquis, aliquid: someone, something

aliud ... aliīs: one thing (nom.) ... the others (dat.)

ante: (adv. and prep. + acc.) before

aqua, ae f.: water

ārea, ae f.: open space, plain, threshing floor

aura, ae f.: air, breeze, wind

Auster, Austrī m.: Auster, the south wind

bestia, ae f.: beast, animal

Boreās, ae m.: Boreas, the north wind

casa, ae f.: cottage, cabin, house

Chaos n.: Chaos, boundless empty space

Eurus, ī m.: Eurus, the east wind

forma, ae f.: form, shape

indīgestus, a, um: confused, unarranged

inordinātus, a, um: disordered, confused

lūna, ae f.: the moon

massa, ae f.: a mass, lump

māteria, ae f.: matter, material

musca, ae f.: a fly

nātūra, ae f.: nature

nāvicula, ae f.: little ship, boat

nihil n.: (indecl.) nothing

obstō, obstāre, obstitī, obstātum: to stand against, oppose (+ dat.)

ordinātus, a, um: ordered, organized

ordinō, ordināre, ordināvī, ordinātum: to put in order, arrange

piscīna, ae f.: a fishpond, reservoir

rīpa, ae f.: river bank, shore

servō, servāre, servāvī, servātum: to keep, save, preserve

silva, ae f.: wood, forest

sine: (prep. + abl.) without

sphaera, ae f.: globe, sphere

stella, ae f.: star

sum, esse, fuī, futūrum: to be

suus, a, um: (reflex. poss. adj.) his, her, its own

terra, ae f.: land

tum: (adv.) then, at that time

unda, ae f.: water, wave

ūnus, a, um: one, single

vel: (conj.) or

Zephyrus, ī m.: Zephyr, the west wind

NOUN AND VERB BASICS

First declension

	Singular	Plural
Nominative	terra	terrae
Genitive	terrae	terrārum
Dative	terrae	terrīs
Accusative	terram	terrās
Ablative	terrā	terrīs

First conjugation present indicative active

	Singular	Plural
1st Person	obstō	obstāmus
2nd Person	obstās	obstātis
3rd Person	obstat	obstant

Present indicative of *esse*

	Singular	Plural
1st Person	sum	sumus
2nd Person	es	estis
3rd Person	est	sunt

Ovid introduces his epic with a short statement about his poetic agenda. He says: "My mind compels me to tell of forms changed into new bodies. Gods (for you all also have changed those forms), breathe favorably upon my beginnings and draw out an everlasting song which runs from the first origin of the universe to my own time." The opening statement thus highlights the theme of the epic: transformation. Change occurs within each story included in the poem, and the opening account of creation, in which an ordered universe develops from a state of chaos, certainly is in keeping with Ovid's stated theme. If read from beginning to end, the entire epic may be interpreted as a political cosmogony which celebrates the grand political metamorphosis of Rome under Augustus.

2 Creation continues

(*Met.* 1.5–150)

Ovid continues his account of creation by describing how one god brings order to the universe by arranging things in their proper place. Various living things occupy their respective habitats, and man is born.

1   Subitō deus mundum fabricat. Quid fabricat? Sunt terrae. Sunt tumulī et campī.
2   Sunt silvae. Est herba. Cicādae et muscae sunt. Arāneae sunt. Cervae, ursae,
3   cunīculī sunt. Caprae sunt. Aquae sunt. Pontus est. Rīpae et stāgna sunt. Pluvia est.
4   Sunt conchae et delphīnī. Cocleae, salamandrae, et anguillae sunt. Caelum est.
5   Sunt stellae. Est lūna. Virgō, Capricornus, Aquārius, Piscēs, Leō, Ariēs, Geminī,
6   Taurus, Lībra, Sagittārius, Cancer, et Scorpiō sunt. Est orbis lacteus. Ventī et aurae
7   sunt. Eurus, Zephyrus, Boreās, et Auster sunt. Hūmānī autem nōn sunt. Tum virī
8   sunt—sīve deus sīve terra virōs creat.

9   Sunt quattuor aeva mundī. Prīmum aevum aureum est. Terra ipsa multa sine rastrō
10   dat. Nōn est tuba. Nōn galeae, nōn gladiī. Flāvum mel stillat. Tum aevum argenteum
11   est. In aevō argenteō prīmum virī casās optant. Cultūra terrae est. Tertium aevum
12   aēneum est. Multa arma sunt, sed aevum tamen nōn est scelerātum. Ultimum
13   aevum dē dūrō ferrō est. Virī vēla ventīs dant, et ad terrās novās nāvigant. Bella
14   sanguinea sunt. Virī dīs nōn sacrificant. Iuppiter nōn beātus est.

Commentary

5–6 *Virgō, Capricornus, Aquārius, Piscēs, Leō, Ariēs, Geminī, Taurus, Lībra, Sagittārius, Cancer, et Scorpiō sunt*: You will no doubt recognize these signs of the zodiac. In Latin, the names mean *The Virgin, The Goat, The Water Carrier, The Fish, The Lion, The Ram, The Twins, The Bull, The Scales, The Archer, The Crab*, and *The Scorpion*. You will see these signs again in the story of Phaethon, where they are represented both on a work of art and as giant forms in the sky.

9–10 *Terra ipsa multa sine rastrō dat*: The word *ipse, ipsa, ipsum* is an intensive pronoun or adjective which is used to add emphasis or to focus attention on a word, so its meaning depends on what it is intensifying. Here, it agrees with *terra*, so it should be translated *itself*. Ovid means here that the land produces food easily without agriculture.

10 *Flāvum mel stillat*: *mel, mellis n.* is a noun of the third declension and is in the nominative.

14 *Virī dīs nōn sacrificant*: *dīs* is dative plural of *deus*.

ad: (prep. + acc.) to, towards
aēneus, a, um: bronze
aevum, ī n.: age, period of time
anguilla, ae f.: eel
arānea, ae f.: spider, web
argenteus, a, um: of silver
arma, ōrum n. pl.: arms, weapons
aureus, a, um: golden
autem: (conj.) but, however
beātus, a, um: happy
bellum, ī n.: war
caelum, ī n.: heaven, sky
campus, ī m.: field
capra, ae f.: goat
cerva, ae f.: deer
cicāda, ae f.: cicada
coclea, ae f.: snail
concha, ae f.: sea-shell, shell-fish
creō, creāre, creāvī, creātum: to create, make
cultūra, ae f.: cultivation, tilling
cunīculus, ī m.: rabbit
dē: (prep. + abl.) from, down from, about
delphīnus, ī m.: dolphin
deus, ī m.: a god
dō, dare, dedī, datum: to give
dūrus, a, um: hard
fabricō, fabricāre, fabricāvī, fabricātum: to make, construct
ferrum, ī n.: iron
flāvus, a, um: blonde, yellow
galea, ae f.: helmet
gladius, ī m.: sword
herba, ae f.: herb, grass
hūmānus, a, um: human
in: (prep. + abl.) in, on; (prep. + acc.) into

ipse, ipsa, ipsum: himself, herself, itself
Iuppiter, Iovis m.: Jupiter/Jove, ruler of the gods
mel, mellis n.: honey
multus, a, um: many
mundus, ī m.: world, universe
nāvigō, nāvigāre, nāvigāvī, nāvigātum: to sail
novus, a, um: new, young
optō, optāre, optāvī, optātum: to desire, wish for
orbis lacteus: Milky Way
pluvia, ae f.: rain
pontus, ī m.: sea, ocean
prīmum: (adv.) at first, first
quattuor: (indecl. numer. adj.) four
quis, quid: (interrog. pron.) who, what
rastrum, ī n.: rake, hoe
sacrificō, sacrificāre, sacrificāvī, sacrificātum: to offer sacrifice
salamandra, ae f.: salamander
sanguineus, a, um: bloody
scelerātus, a, um: wicked, profane
sīve/seu ... sīve/seu: (conj.) whether ... or
stāgnum, ī n.: standing water, pond
stillō, stillāre, stillāvī, stillātum: to drip
subitō: (adv.) suddenly
tamen: (conj.) however, nevertheless
tertius, a, um: third
tuba, ae f.: military horn
tumulus, ī m.: hill, burial mound
ultimus, a, um: last, final
ursa, ae f.: bear
vēlum, ī n.: sail, covering
ventus, ī m.: wind
vir, virī m.: a man

SECOND DECLENSION

Masculine

	Singular	Plural
Nominative	ventus	ventī
Genitive	ventī	ventōrum
Dative	ventō	ventīs
Accusative	ventum	ventōs
Ablative	ventō	ventīs

Neuter

	Singular	Plural
Nominative	caelum	caela
Genitive	caelī	caelōrum
Dative	caelō	caelīs
Accusative	caelum	caela
Ablative	caelō	caelīs

Ovid presents the creation of the universe in terms of an artist fashioning a work of art, although he is vague about which god serves as the cosmic fabricator. An obvious choice would be Vulcan, who is a craftsman-god. Art and artists figure prominently throughout Ovid's *Metamorphoses*. In fact, some scholars believe that, by focusing on the fates of so many mythological artists in the poem (many of whom suffer unpleasant outcomes), Ovid is making a statement about the role of artists in Augustan Age Rome.

3 Lycaon

(*Met.* 1.163–252)

At a meeting of the gods, Jupiter tells the story of how he punished impious Lycaon, king of Arcadia.

1   Iuppiter, plēnus īrae, concilium deōrum vocat. Deī et deae ad magna tecta et
2   rēgiam Iovis volant, et in sellīs marmoreīs sedent. Iuppiter fābulam dīs narrat:
3   "Infāmia mē movet, et dē summō Olympō volō. Deus sub simulācrō hūmānō terrās
4   lustrō. Ad tecta inhospita tyrannī Arcadiī appropinquō, cum crepusculum tenebrās
5   portat. Signa deī dō, et vulgus mihi supplicat. Lycāōn, tyrannus Arcadius, pia vōta
6   inrīdet. Avet vērum: estne advena deus vel vir? Lycāōn experientiam excōgitat.
7   Lycāōn iugulum victimae hūmānae secat, et carnōsa in flammā torret. Tum,
8   tyrannus carnōsa quasi cēnam mihi dat. Iniūria īram meam auget. Animus meus mē

Commentary

3 *Infāmia mē movet, et dē summō Olympō volō*: The story Jupiter is telling has already happened, but he is using the present tense to make the story especially vivid for his audience.

3–4 *Deus sub simulācrō hūmānō terrās lustrō*: *Deus* agrees with the subject of *lustrō*, which is first person singular. Translate: *I, a god, traverse the lands under a human image.*

4 *Ad tecta inhospita*: Latin often uses a plural noun when a singular idea is intended.

advena, ae m. or f.: stranger
animus, ī m.: spirit, mind
**appropinquō, appropinquāre, appro-
  pinquāvī, appropinquātum:** to approach
Arcadius, a, um: of Arcadia, a region in
  central Greece
augeō, augēre, auxī, auctum: to make grow
aveō, avēre: to desire, long for
carnōsus, a, um: fleshy, meaty
cēna, ae f.: dinner
concilium, ī n.: meeting, assembly, council
crepusculum, ī n.: the twilight
cum: (conj.) when, since, although,
  (prep. + abl.) with
dea, ae f.: a goddess
**excōgitō, excōgitāre, excōgitāvī,
  excōgitātum:** to devise, invent
experientia, ae f.: trial, testing
fābula, ae f.: story, tale
flamma, ae f.: flame, fire
infāmia, ae f.: negative report, dishonor
inhospitus, a, um: inhospitable, uninviting
iniūria, ae f.: injury, harm
inrīdeō, inrīdēre, inrīsī, inrīsum: to mock,
  jeer at
īra, ae f.: anger, rage
iugulum, ī n.: throat
lustrō, lustrāre, lustrāvī, lustrātum: to go
  place to place, traverse, purify
Lycāōn Lycāonis m.: Lycaon, mythical ruler
  of Arcadia
magnus, a, um: big, great
marmoreus, a, um: of marble
meus, a, um: (poss. adj.) my, mine

moveō, movēre, mōvī, mōtum: to move,
  set in motion
narrō, narrāre, narrāvī, narrātum: to tell,
  relate
Olympus, ī m.: Mt. Olympus, home of the
  gods
pius, a, um: dutiful, devoted to the gods
plēnus, a, um: full
portō, portāre, portāvī, portātum: to bring,
  carry
quasi: (conj. and adv.) as if
rēgia, ae f.: palace, royal house
secō, secāre, secuī, sectum: to cut
sedeō, sedēre, sēdī, sessum: to sit
sella, ae f.: seat
signum, ī n.: sign, mark, statue
simulācrum, ī n.: image, likeness
sub: (prep. + abl.) under
summus, a, um: highest
**supplicō, supplicāre, supplicāvī,
  supplicātum:** to worship, entreat (+ dat.)
tectum, ī n.: roof, building
tenebrae, ārum f. pl.: shadows, shade,
  darkness
torreō, torrēre, torruī, tostum: to burn, roast
tyrannus, ī m.: an absolute ruler, tyrant
vērum, ī n.: the truth
victima, ae f.: a sacrificial victim
vocō, vocāre, vocāvī, vocātum: to call,
  summon
volō, volāre, volāvī, volātum: to fly, move
  quickly
vōtum, ī n.: prayer, wish
vulgus, ī m.: common people, crowd

9   movet, et iactō flammās dē caelō. Lycāōn territus cursat. In labiīs spūmat. Agnōs
10   videt, et cruentāre terga nivea avet. Formāre verba frūstrā temptat, et tantum
11   exululat. Vestīmenta in villōs mūtant. Lacertī in crūra mūtant. Nunc trucīdāre
12   gaudet. Lupus est, sed vestīgia formae servat. Capillī sunt cānī. Oculī lūcent.
13   Lycāōn poenās multās dat!"

14   Aliī verba probant, aliī in silentiō nūtant. Iuppiter castīgāre virōs optat. Auster
15   pluvius volat, et Neptūnus undīs magnīs iuvat. Est dīluvium immensum! Sīc īra
16   Iovis est.

Commentary

11 *Lacertī in crūra mūtant*: *crūra* is accusative plural.
13 *Lycāōn poenās multās dat*: The phrase *dare . . . poenās* is an idiom which means *to pay the penalty*.

agnus, ī m.: lamb

aliī ... aliī: some ... others

alius, alia, aliud: (adj. and pron.) another, other, different

cānus, a, um: white, grey

capillus, ī m.: hair

castīgō, castīgāre, castīgāvī, castīgātum: to punish

cruentō, cruentāre, cruentāvī, cruentātum: to make bloody

crūs, crūris n.: leg

cursō, cursāre, cursāvī, cursātum: to run to and fro

dīluvium, ī n.: flood

exululō, exululāre, exululāvī, exululātum: to howl loudly

formō, formāre, formāvī, formātum: to form, shape, fashion

frūstrā: (adv.) in vain

gaudeō, gaudēre, gāvīsus sum: to rejoice, be glad

iactō, iactāre, iactāvī, iactātum: to throw, hurl

immensus, a, um: huge

iuvō, iuvāre, iūvī, iūtum: to help, aid, please, delight

labia, ae f.: lip

lacertus, ī m.: arm

lūceō, lucēre, luxī: to be bright, gleam

lupus, ī m.: a wolf

mūtō, mūtāre, mūtāvī, mūtātum: to change

Neptūnus, ī m.: Neptune, god of the sea

niveus, a, um: snowy, white

nunc: (adv.) now

nūtō, nūtāre, nūtāvī, nūtātum: to nod

oculus, ī m.: eye

pluvius, a, um: rainy

poena, ae f.: punishment

probō, probāre, probāvī, probātum: to approve

sīc: (adv.) thus

silentium, ī n.: silence

spūmō, spūmāre, spūmāvī, spūmātum: to foam

tantum: (adv.) only, to such a degree

temptō, temptāre, temptāvī, temptātum: to attempt, try

tergum, ī n.: back

territus, a, um: thoroughly scared

trucīdo, trucīdāre, trucīdāvī, trucīdātum: to slaughter

verbum, ī n.: word

vestīgium, ī n.: footprint, trace

vestīmentum, ī n.: garment

videō, vidēre, vīdī, vīsum: to see

villus, ī m.: shaggy hair

SECOND CONJUGATION PRESENT
INDICATIVE ACTIVE

	Singular	*Plural*
1st Person	torreō	torrēmus
2nd Person	torrēs	torrētis
3rd Person	torret	torrent

Lycaon, whose name probably comes from the Greek word for wolf, is sometimes considered to be the first werewolf. Ovid follows the tradition that Lycaon offended the gods by serving human flesh to them, but other sources report that the king of Arcadia sacrificed a human infant to Zeus Lycaeus. In the *Republic*, Plato alludes to men becoming wolves—a transformation known as lycanthropy—after eating human flesh at a human sacrifice on Mt. Lycaeon in Arcadia. The ancient Greek geographer Pausanias says that these men would return to human form after nine years, provided that they abstained from eating human flesh.

4 Deucalion and Pyrrha

(*Met.* 1.313–415)

One man and one woman, both pious and good, are saved from the flood by Jupiter and must repopulate the land.

1   Dīluvium adhūc immēnsum est. Phōcis Āoniam ab Oetaeīs arvīs sēparat. Ibi est
2   mōns Parnāsus. Deucaliōn cum consorte in parvā rate nāvigat, et hūc appropinquat.
3   Prīmum nymphās et nūmina montis adōrant. Tunc Themin, deam fātidicam,
4   adōrant. Ibi dea ōrāculum tenet. Deucaliōn bonus est, et Pyrrha, uxor eius, casta
5   est. Semper dīs supplicant. Iuppiter hominēs bonōs videt, et īra eius nōn manet.
6   Undae removent. Orbis terrārum redditus est. Deucaliōn dēsōlātās terrās videt, et
7   uxōrem cum multīs lacrimīs appellat: "Ō fēmina, nōs duo turba sumus! Aqua
8   cētera possidet. Exempla hominum manēmus." Duo flent. Tum, deae supplicant, et
9   vōta multa dant: "Themi, signa nōbīs dā! Quōmodo terrās sānāmus? Quōmodo

Commentary

3–4 *Tunc Themin ... adōrant*: *Themin* is a Greek accusative singular.

6 *Orbis terrārum redditus est*: *orbis terrārum* means *the world*.

7 *Ō fēmina, nōs duo turba sumus*: Think of this sentence as *Ō fēmina, nōs duo sumus turba!* *Ō* can remain untranslated. Ovid's use of *turba* is comic since there are only two humans left in the world.

8 *Exempla hominum manēmus*: *Exempla* is in the nominative. Translate: *We remain as examples of humans*.

9 *Themi, signa nōbīs dā*: *Themi* is in the vocative.

ā/ab: (prep. + abl.) from, away from

adhūc: (adv.) still

adōro, adōrāre, adōrāvī, adōrātum: to entreat, worship

Āonia, ae f.: Aonia, part of the region of Boeotia in Greece

appellō, appellāre, appellāvī, appellātum: to address, name

arvum, ī n.: field

bonus, a, um: good

castus, a, um: clean, chaste, pious

cēterī, ae, a: others, rest

consors, consortis m. or f.: one who has an equal share, partner, wife

dēsōlātus, a, um: desolate, forsaken

Deucaliōn, Deucaliōnis m.: Deucalion, a son of Prometheus

duo, duae, duo: two

exemplum, ī n.: example

fātidicus, a, um: speaking fate, prophetic

fēmina, ae f.: woman

fleō, flēre, flēvī, flētum: to weep

homō, hominis m.: man, human being

hūc: (adv.) to this place

ibi: (adv.) there, in that place

is, ea, id: (third person pron.) eius (gen.) he, she, it, this, that

lacrima, ae f.: tear

maneō, manēre, mansī, mansum: to remain, stay

mōns, montis m.: mountain

nūmen, nūminis n.: divinity, divine spirit

nympha, ae f.: nymph

Oetaeus, a, um: of Oeta, the mountain range between Thessaly and Macedonia

ōrāculum, ī n.: oracle, divine utterance, place of prophecy

orbis, orbis m.: circle, coil

Parnāsus, ī m.: Parnassus, a mountain in Phocis sacred to Apollo

parvus, a, um: small, little

Phōcis, Phōcidis f.: Phocis, a district in central Greece

possideō, possidēre, possēdī, possessum: to possess, hold

Pyrrha, ae f.: Pyrrha, a daughter of Epimetheus

quōmodo: (adv.) in what manner, how

ratis, ratis f.: raft, boat

redditus, a, um: given back, restored

removeō, removēre, remōvī, remōtum: to move back, withdraw

sānō, sānāre, sānāvī, sānātum: to cure, restore to health

semper: (adv.) always

sēparō, sēparāre, sēparāvī, sēparātum: to disjoin, sever, separate

teneō, tenēre, tenuī, tentum: to hold

Themis, Themis f.: Themis, a Greek goddess of the earth and justice

tunc: (adv.) then

turba, ae f.: crowd, mob

uxor, uxōris f.: wife

10   fēminās et virōs fabricāmus?" Vōta deam movent, et dea sortem dat: "Ē templō
11   ambulāte, et ossa mātris post tergum iactāte!" Deucaliōn et Pyrrha stupent. Diū in
12   silentiō stant. Nōn iactāre ossa mātrum mortuārum avent. Deinde Deucaliōn
13   adsevērat: "Māter est terra, et lapidēs sunt ossa mātris!" Statim lapidēs post
14   vestīgia iactant. Subitō lapidēs mollitiam habent, et fōrmās paene hūmānās habent,
15   ut statuae coeptae dē marmore inconditae sunt. Pars ūmida et terrēna lapidis
16   carnōsa est, et pars solida os est. Fēminae et virī sunt!

Commentary

15 *ut statuae coeptae dē marmore inconditae sunt*: Ovid compares the rocks which change into human bodies to statues which are in the process of being carved from a block of marble.

adsevērō, adsevērāre, adsevērāvī, adsevērātum: to assert with confidence

ambulō, ambulāre, ambulāvī, ambulātum: to walk

coeptus, a, um: begun

deinde: (adv.) from that place, next, then

diū: (adv.) for a long time

ē/ex: (prep. + abl.) out of, from

habeō, habēre, habuī, habitum: to have, hold

inconditus, a, um: disorderly, not clearly arranged, hidden in

lapis, lapidis m.: a stone

marmor, marmoris n.: marble

māter, mātris f.: mother

mollitia, ae f.: softness

mortuus, a, um: dead

os, ossis n.: bone

paene: (adv.) almost

pars, partis f.: a part, portion

post: (prep. + acc.) behind, after

solidus, a, um: solid

sors, sortis f.: a lot, fortune, oracular response

statim: (adv.) immediately

statua, ae f.: statue, image

stō, stāre, stetī, statum: to stand

stupeō, stupēre, stupuī: to be struck dumb, be stunned

templum, ī n.: temple

terrēnus, a, um: earthen, of the earth

ūmidus, a, um: moist

ut: (adv.) as, just as

THIRD DECLENSION

Masculine/feminine

	Singular	Plural
Nominative	uxor	uxōrēs
Genitive	uxōris	uxōrum
Dative	uxōrī	uxōribus
Accusative	uxōrem	uxōrēs
Ablative	uxōre	uxōribus

Neuter

	Singular	Plural
Nominative	os	ossa
Genitive	ossis	ossum
Dative	ossī	ossibus
Accusative	os	ossa
Ablative	osse	ossibus

i-stem masculine/feminine

	Singular	Plural
Nominative	orbis	orbēs
Genitive	orbis	orbium
Dative	orbī	orbibus
Accusative	orbem	orbēs
Ablative	orbe	orbibus

i-stem neuter

	Singular	Plural
Nominative	animal	animālia
Genitive	animālis	animālium
Dative	animālī	animālibus
Accusative	animal	animālia
Ablative	animālī	animālibus

Ovid's description of a great flood resonates with accounts of floods in *Genesis* and in the Near Eastern *Epic of Gilgamesh*. The appearance of similar material in multiple texts is known as intertextuality. The story about Deucalion's and Pyrrha's recovery from the flood is particularly notable for its description of how people grow from the rocks which the two elderly people throw. The explicit comparison of the changing rocks to statues in the beginning stages of carving is reflective of the poet's general focus on art and artists in the poem, readily apparent earlier in the story of creation.

5 Apollo and Python

(*Met.* 1.416–451)

Apollo, the god of music and poetry, athletics, and prophecy, slays the monstrous serpent Python and establishes athletic games to commemorate his victory.

1   Nunc sunt novī virī et fēminae, atque terra ipsa cētera animālia dat. Antīquus ūmor
2   igne sōlis percalescit. Sīc Nīlus septemfluus agrōs madidōs dēserit, et in alveō fluit.
3   Agricolae plūrima animālia sub glaebīs versīs vident. Ubi ūmor et calor miscent, est
4   anima. Partim terra figūrās antīquās dat, et partim monstra nova creat. Terra
5   quoque tē, maxime Pȳthōn, creat. Pȳthōn est immēnsa serpēns, incognita. Est
6   terror novīs populīs. Tantum spatiī dē monte tenet. Deus arcitenēns monstrum
7   multīs sagittīs perdit. Apollō mille tēla iactat, et pharetra est paene exhausta.
8   Venēnum magnae serpentis per vulnera nigra effundit. Sīc deus monstrum vincit.
9   Apollō tenēre fāmam victōriae in memoriā optat. Lūdōs magnōs instituit, et
10 certāmina "Pȳthia" ā nōmine magnae serpentis victae vocat. In lūdīs, iuvenēs
11 pugnīs, pedibus, et rotā certant. Victōrēs honor aesculeae frondis capiunt.
12 Laurea nōndum est.

Commentary

1–2 *Antīquus ūmor igne sōlis percalescit:* When the waters of the great flood start to subside, the moisture held in the soil heats up and causes the seeds of various forms of life to grow. *igne* is an ablative of means. Translate: *by means of the fire* or *with the fire*.

4 *Partim terra figūrās antīquās dat*: These are the species which existed before the great flood.

4–5 *Terra quoque tē, maxime Pȳthōn, creat*: Ovid varies his narrative style by addressing the Python directly.

6 *Tantum spatiī dē monte tenet:* The word *tantus, a, um* is used here as a neuter substantive, and it governs the genitive *spatiī*. Thus, the phrase is translated *such a great space*. The Python covers a large expanse of land on Mt. Parnassus.

10–11 *In lūdīs, iuvenēs pugnīs, pedibus, et rotā certant:* The words *pugnīs*, *pedibus*, and *rotā* are ablatives of means and indicate boxing matches, foot races, and chariot races.

aesculeus, a, um: of oak
ager, agrī m.: field
agricola, ae m.: farmer
alveus, ī m.: a hollow, cavity, bed of a stream
anima, ae f.: life, breath, soul
animal, animālis n.: animal
antīquus, a, um: old, ancient
Apollō, Apollinis m.: Apollo, god of music, athletics, and prophecy
arcitenēns, arcitenentis: bow-holding, epithet of Apollo
atque: (conj.) and, and indeed
calor, calōris m.: heat
capiō, capere, cēpī, captum: to seize, take
certāmen, certāminis n.: contest, competition
certō, certāre, certāvī, certātum: to compete
dēserō, dēserere, dēseruī, dēsertum: to leave, abandon, forsake
effundō, effundere, effūdī, effūsum: to pour out
exhaustus, a, um: empty, exhausted
fāma, ae f.: fame, reputation, story
figūra, ae f.: form, figure, shape
fluō, fluere, fluxī, fluxum: to flow
frons, frondis f.: leaf, foliage
glaeba, ae f.: a lump of earth, clod, ball
honor, honōris n.: honor, prize
ignis, ignis m.: fire
incognitus, a, um: unknown
instituō, instituere, instituī, institūtum: to put in place, establish
iuvenis, iuvenis m. or f.: young person, youth
laurea, ae f.: the laurel tree
lūdus, ī m.: game
madidus, a, um: wet
maximus, a, um: greatest
memoria, memoriae f.: memory
mille: (indecl. numer.) a thousand
misceō, miscēre, miscuī, mixtum: to mingle, mix

monstrum, ī n.: monster, supernatural thing or event, wonder
niger, nigra, nigrum: black, dark
Nīlus, ī m.: Nile, a river in Egypt
nōmen, nōminis n.: name
nōndum: (adv.) not yet
partim ... partim: (adv.) in part ... in part
per: (prep. + acc.) by, through, because of
percalescō, percalescere, percaluī: to become warm
perdō, perdere, perdidī, perditum: to ruin, destroy
pēs, pedis m.: the foot
pharetra, ae f.: quiver
plūrimus, a, um: very much, very many
populus, ī m.: people
pugnus, ī m.: the fist
Pȳthia, Pȳthiōrum n.: the Pythian Games
Pȳthōn, Pȳthōnis m.: Python, a huge serpent
quoque: (conj.) also, too
rota, ae f.: wheel
sagitta, ae f.: arrow
septemfluus, a, um: flowing sevenfold, seven-mouthed
serpēns, serpentis f. or m.: creeping thing, snake
sōl, sōlis m.: sun
spatium, ī n.: space, extent
tantus, a, um: so much, so great
tēlum, ī n.: dart, arrow, spear
terror, terrōris m.: fright, dread, object which causes fear
ubi: (adv.) when, where
ūmor, ūmōris m.: moisture, fluid
venēnum, ī n.: poison, venom
versus, a, um: turned over
victor, victōris m.: victor, winner
victōria, ae f.: victory
victus, a, um: conquered
vincō, vincere, vīcī, victum: to conquer
vulnus, vulneris n.: a wound

THIRD CONJUGATION

Present indicative active

	Singular	Plural
1st person	instituō	instituimus
2nd person	instituis	instituitis
3rd person	instituit	instituunt

-io present indicative active

	Singular	Plural
1st person	faciō	facimus
2nd person	facis	facitis
3rd person	facit	faciunt

The *Homeric Hymn to Apollo*, which may date to as early as the eighth century BCE, tells the story of Apollo's birth on Delos and subsequent founding of his sanctuary at Delphi. In that Greek poem, Hera entrusts the monster Typhaon to the care of a she-serpent, but Apollo slays the giant snake and leaves the corpse to rot in the sun. Thus, the Python takes its name from the Greek verb "pythein," meaning "to rot." Delphi itself was also called Pytho, and the panhellenic games held there in honor of Apollo were called the Pythian Games. The laurel tree was sacred to Apollo, so victors at these games received crowns of laurel leaves as prizes. Ovid goes on to explain how the laurel becomes sacred to Apollo in the next story.

6   Apollo and Daphne

(*Met.* 1.452–567)

Ovid describes Apollo's first experience with erotic pursuit in wonderful comic detail. Here, he loses Daphne but gains a sacred tree.

1   Prīmus amor Phoebī erat Daphnē Pēnēia. Daphnē formam bellam habēbat. Dēlius
2   Cupīdinem cum sagittīs vidēbat, et Apollō glōriōsus deum amōris dērīdēbat. "Quid
3   tibi est, lascīve puer, lūdere cum armīs? Arma umerōs meōs decent. Pȳthōn est
4   mortuus, et factum est meum. Ego sōlus vincere tanta monstra possum. Irrītāre
5   tantum amōrēs dēbēs." Cupīdō plēnus īrae saevae est. Deus amōris dīcit: "Sagitta
6   tua cētera fīgere potest, sed sagitta mea tē fīgere potest!"

7   Cupīdō duo tēla ē pharetrā prōmit. Sagitta aurea amōrem facit; tēlum plumbeum
8   amōrem fugat. Apollinem aureā sagittā vulnerat, et Daphnēn plumbeā sagittā
9   vulnerat. Prōtinus alter amat, altera nōmen amantis fugit. Deus nympham amat, et
10   cōnūbium Daphnēs cupit. Utque stipulae conflagrant, ut saepēs ardent cum forte
11   viātor vel facēs nimis admovet vel facēs sub lūce relinquit, sīc deus in flammās
12   abit. Sua ōrācula deum fallunt. Apollō capillōs et oculōs nymphae videt. Osculum
13   videt, et nōn satis vidēre osculum. Cupit bāsiāre nympham. Deus digitōs et lacertōs
14   nūdōs laudat. Daphnē, territa, currit.

Commentary

1 *Prīmus amor … Daphnē*: *Daphnē* is a Greek name meaning *laurel*. The genitive is *Daphnēs*, and the accusative is *Daphnēn*.

2–3 *Quid tibi est … lūdere cum armīs:* Apollo's question is an expression in which a dative of reference is used with the interrogative word *quid* to mean *what use is it for you?*

10–12 *Utque stipulae conflagrant … sīc deus in flammās abit*: Ovid uses the images of stalks of grain and hedges burning when a torch comes too close to capture the intensity of Apollo's urgent desire. The comparison is relatively common in Latin poetry. *sub lūce* means, literally, *under the light* but indicates *at dawn*.

12 *Sua ōrācula deum fallunt*: Apollo is a god of prophecy. Here, he is so overcome with desire for Daphne that he cannot console himself in the way he might console someone visiting his oracle.

abeō, abīre, abivī or abiī, abitum: to go away, pass into a state

admoveō, admovēre, admōvī, admōtum: to move towards

alter ... altera: the one ... the other

alter, altera, alterum: one of two

amāns, amantis m. or f.: lover

amor, amōris m.: love

ardeō, ardēre, arsī: to burn, glow

bāsiō, bāsiāre, bāsiāvī, bāsiātum: to kiss

bellus, a, um: beautiful

conflagrō, conflagrāre, conflagrāvī, conflagrātum: to catch fire, burn up

cōnūbium, ī n.: marriage

Cupīdo, Cupīdinis m.: Cupid, the god of love (**cupīdo, cupidinis f.:** desire)

cupiō, cupere, cupīvī, cupītum: to desire, yearn for

currō, currere, cucurrī, cursum: to run

Daphnē, ēs f.: Daphne, a nymph

dēbeō, dēbēre, dēbuī, dēbitum: to owe, ought

decet, decēre, decuit: (often impers. verb) it is proper, seemly, fitting (+ acc. of thing fitted)

Dēlius, ī m.: of Delos, epithet of Apollo

dērīdeō, dērīdēre, dērīsī, dērīsum: to laugh at, mock

dīco, dīcere, dixī, dictum: to say, speak

digitus, ī m.: finger

faciō, facere, fēcī, factum: to make, do

factum, ī n.: deed, act

fallō, fallere, fefellī, falsum: to deceive, lead astray, disappoint

fax, facis f.: torch

fīgō, fīgere, fixī, fixum: to fix, fasten, thrust a weapon

fors, forte (abl.) f.: luck, chance

fugō, fugāre, fugāvī, fugātum: to cause to flee, chase away

fugiō, fugere, fūgī, fugitum: to flee

glōriōsus, a, um: haughty, boastful, famous

irrītō, irrītāre, irrītāvī, irrītātum: to stir up, incite

lascīvus, a, um: playful, insolent

laudō, laudāre, laudāvī, laudātum: to praise

lūdō, lūdere, lūsī, lūsum: to play, frolic, trick

lux, lūcis f.: light

nimis: (adv.) too much

nūdus, a, um: naked

osculum, ī n.: lips, mouth, kiss

Pēnēius, a, um: of Peneus, a river-god

Phoebus, ī m.: Phoebus, epithet of Apollo

plumbeus, a, um: made of lead

possum, posse, potuī: to be able, have in one's power

prīmus, a, um: first, foremost

prōmō, prōmere, prompsī, promptum: to bring forth, produce

prōtinus: (adv.) further, immediately

puer, puerī m.: boy

relinquō, relinquere, relīquī, relictum: to leave behind

saepes, is f.: a hedge

saevus, a, um: savage, fierce

satis: (indecl. adj. and adv.) enough

sōlus, a, um: alone, only

stipula, ae f.: stalk of grain, grain-stubble

tuus, a, um: (poss. adj.) your

umerus, ī m.: upper arm, shoulder

viātor, viātōris m.: a traveler

vulnerō, vulnerāre, vulnerāvī, vulverātum: to wound

15   "Manē, nympha!" Apollō inquit, "Tē amō! Nōn hostis sum. Nōn agricola, et hīc
16   horridus armenta nōn observō. Nōn sine fāmā sum! Deus poētārum et athlētārum
17   sum. Amor mihi causa studiī est." Daphnē fugit et ōrat: "Pater, opem fer!" Sine
18   mōrā, forma nymphae mūtat. Torpor membra occupat. Forma nymphae frondōsa
19   est, et bracchia in rāmōs crescunt. Subitō Daphnē est laurea. Adhūc Apollō
20   nympham amat. Deus bāsia laureae dat, et laurea abhorret. Deus dīcit: "Sī mea
21   puella esse nōn potes, dēbēs esse arbor mea." Procul Cupīdō rīdet.

Commentary

15 *Nōn hostis sum*: Apollo tries to convince Daphne that he is not a threat to her here, but later in the epic the god is portrayed as a rapist.

17 *Pater, opem fer*: *fer* is an irregular second person singular imperative.

20–1 *Sī mea puella esse nōn potes*: In English, the word order would be *sī nōn potes esse mea puella*.

abhorreō, abhorrēre, abhorruī: to shrink back from, shudder at

amō, amāre, amāvī, amātum: to love

arbor, arboris f.: tree

armentum, ī n.: herd, flock

athlēta, ae m.: athlete, contender

bāsium, ī n.: kiss

bracchium, ī n.: arm

causa, ae f.: cause, reason

crescō, crescere, crēvī, crētum: to grow

ferō, ferre, tulī, lātum: to bear, carry, endure

frondōsus, a, um: leafy

hīc: (adv.) here, in this place

horridus, a, um: unkempt, rough, uncouth, horrible

hostis, hostis m.: enemy

inquit, inquiunt: he, she, it says, they say

membrum, ī n.: limb

mora, ae f.: delay, pause

observō, observāre, observāvī, observātum: to watch, regard, attend to

occupō, occupāre, occupāvī, occupātum: to take hold of, seize, master

ops, opis f.: resource, help, assistance

ōrō, ōrāre, ōrāvī, ōrātum: to speak, beg, pray

pater, patris m.: father

poēta, ae m.: poet

procul: (adv.) far away, at a distance, from afar

puella, ae f.: girl

rāmus, ī m.: branch

rīdeō, rīdēre, rīsī, rīsum: to smile, laugh at

sī: (conj.) if

studium, ī n.: eagerness, pursuit

torpor, torpōris m.: sluggishness, dullness

IMPERFECT INDICATIVE ACTIVE

First conjugation

	Singular	Plural
1st person	basiābam	basiābāmus
2nd person	basiābās	basiābātis
3rd person	basiābat	basiābant

Second conjugation

	Singular	Plural
1st person	dērīdēbam	dērīdēbāmus
2nd person	dērīdēbās	dērīdēbātis
3rd person	dērīdēbat	dērīdēbant

Third conjugation

	Singular	Plural
1st person	fallēbam	fallēbāmus
2nd person	fallēbās	fallēbātis
3rd person	fallēbat	fallēbant

Third conjugation *-io*

	Singular	Plural
1st person	faciēbam	faciēbāmus
2nd person	faciēbās	faciēbātis
3rd person	faciēbat	faciēbant

esse

	Singular	Plural
1st person	eram	erāmus
2nd person	erās	erātis
3rd person	erat	erant

Apollo was an important deity in Augustan Age Rome. After his victory over Mark Antony and Cleopatra at the Battle of Actium in 31 BCE, Augustus, then known as Octavian, embraced Apollo as a patron god. He built a temple to the god on the Palatine Hill which was connected to his own palace. Subsequently, many references to Apollo appeared in artistic images of the age. Augustus' doorposts were garlanded with the god's sacred laurel leaves as an honor, and this image was celebrated on coins from the period. Here, Apollo is depicted comically as he burns with lust for Daphne. He is also depicted as a potential rapist. Indeed, his role as a rapist is confirmed later in the epic on a tapestry which Arachne weaves featuring the exploits of male gods such as Jupiter, Apollo, Neptune, and Bacchus. One wonders how the emperor would have viewed Ovid's playful and even irreverent portrait of an amorous Apollo.

7 Phaethon

(*Met.* 2.1–400)

Phoebus' son by Clymene, Phaethon, visits his father for the first time and foolishly tries to drive the chariot of the Sun.

1   Phaethōn fīlius Phoebī est, sed puer numquam vidēre patrem potest. Phaethōn
2   mātrem rogat: "Quis meus pater est?" Clymenē, māter Phaethōntis, dīcit: "Per
3   iubar sōlis, nāte, ā Sōle satus es. Sī animus tē movet, pete vērum ā deō ipsō!"
4   Phaethōn laetus ēmicat post verba mātris, et dīcit: "Ambulābō ad rēgiam Sōlis!"

5   Rēgia Sōlis erat alta sublīmibus columnīs. Rēgia clāra aurō et pyrōpō erat. Ebur
6   nitidum summa fastīgia tegēbat. Valvae lūmine argentī radiābant. Opus māteriam
7   superābat. In valvīs ars caelāta Mulciberis erat: terrae, aquae, et caelum sunt. Terra
8   silvās, ferās, nymphās habet. Unda caeruleōs deōs habet. In foribus dextrīs et
9   sinistrīs, caelum bis sex signa habet: Virgō, Capricornus, Aquārius, Piscēs, Leō,
10   Ariēs, Geminī, Taurus, Lībra, Sagittārius, Cancer, et Scorpiō. Phaethōn rēgiam
11   Sōlis intrat. Vestīgia ad patriam faciem vertit, sed procul constat. Nōn ferre iubar
12   potest. Phoebus, vēlātus veste purpureā, in soliō sedet. Solium smaragdīs clārīs
13   radiat. Ā dextrā et laevā Diēs et Mensis et Annus et Saecula stant. Hōrae sunt. Vēr
14   novum cinctum corōnā flōrum est. Aestās spīcea serta gerit. Autumnus sordidus
15   ūvīs calcātis stat, et Hiems hirsūta cānōs capillōs habet.

Commentary

5 *Rēgia Sōlis erat alta sublīmibus columnīs*: The ablative is used here to qualify the adjective *alta*. Translate: *high with lofty columns*.

6–7 *Opus māteriam superābat*: The doors are constructed out of precious metals, but the craftmanship of the engraved artwork is even more impressive than the shining metals.

11 *Vestīgia ad patriam faciem vertit*: *faciem* is accusative singular.

13–15 *Vēr novum cinctum . . . capillōs habet*: Each personified season is adorned with its own attributes.

Aestās, Aestātis f.: Summer, divine representation of the summertime
altus, a, um: high, lofty
Annus, ī m.: Year, divine representation of a year
argentum, ī n.: silver
ars, artis f.: skill, art, work of art
aurum, ī n.: gold
Autumnus, ī m.: Autumn, divine representation of the fall
bis: (adv.) in two ways, double
caelātus, a, um: carved, engraved
caeruleus, a, um: greenish blue
calcātus, a, um: stamped down, crushed
cinctus, a, um: circled, encompassed
clārus, a, um: clear, shining, brilliant
Clymenē, ēs f.: Clymene, a nymph
columna, ae f.: column, pillar
constō, constāre, constitī, constātum: to stand, stand firm, stand unchanging
corōna, ae f.: garland, wreath, crown
dexter, dextra, dextrum (or dextera, dexterum): right, on the right
Diēs, Diēī m. or f.: Day, divine representation of a day
ebur, eboris n.: ivory
ēmicō, ēmicāre, ēmicuī, ēmicātum: to spring out, break forth
faciēs, faciēī f.: form, shape, face
fastīgium, ī n.: gable, pediment
fera, ae f.: wild animal, beast
fīlius, ī m.: son
flōs, flōris m.: flower
foris, foris f.: door, gate
gerō, gerere, gessī, gestum: to bear, carry, carry out, display
Hōrae, ārum f.: Hours, goddesses of time and seasons
Hiems, Hiemis f.: Winter, divine representation of the winter
hirsūtus, a, um: rough, shaggy, bristly
intrō, intrāre, intrāvī, intrātum: to walk into, enter
iubar, iubaris n.: light, brightness, sunshine

laetus, a, um: joyful, happy, delighted
laevus, a, um: left side
lūmen, lūminis n.: light
Mensis, Mensis m.: Month, divine representation of a month
Mulciber, Mulciberis m.: epithet of Vulcan, god of craftsmanship
nātus, ī m.: son
nitidus, a, um: shining, bright
numquam: (adv.) never
opus, operis n.: work, art, workmanship
patrius, a, um: fatherly, paternal
petō, petere, petīvī, petītum: to seek, demand, beg
Phaethōn, Phaethōntis m.: Phaethon, son of Clymene and Sōl
purpureus, a, um: purple, crimson
pyrōpus, ī m.: bronze
radiō, radiāre, radiāvī, radiātum: to shine, radiate
rogō, rogāre, rogāvī, rogātum: to ask
Saeculum, ī n.: Generation, divine representation of a generation
satus, a, um: sprung, born, sown
sertum, ī n.: wreath, woven garland
sex: (indecl. numer.) six
sinister, sinistra, sinistrum: left, on the left
smaragdus, ī m.: emerald
solium, ī n.: seat
sordidus, a, um: dirty, foul, sordid
spīceus, a, um: of corn
sublīmis, e: lofty, exalted, elevated
superō, superāre, superāvī, superātum: to overcome, prevail, be greater than
tegō, tegere, texī, tectum: cover, surround
ūva, ae f.: grape
valvae, ārum f. pl.: doors
vēlātus, a, um: wrapped, covered, concealed
Vēr, Vēris n.: Spring, divine representation of the springtime
vertō, vertere, vertī, vertus: to turn, turn around
vestis, vestis f.: garment, clothing

16   Deus iuvenem videt, et dīcit: "Quae est tibi causa viae?" Phaethōn dīcit: "Sī
17   Clymenē culpam sub falsā imāgine nōn cēlat, pignora dā, pater." Phoebus rogat:
18   "Quid optās?" Phaethōn stultus dīcit: "Agere quadrīgās tuās cupiō." Sōl clāmat:
19   "Stulte! Agere quadrīgās Sōlis est officium deōrum, nōn virōrum. Perīculum erit
20   magnum. Agere equōs Sōlis nōn poteris!" Phaethōn dīcit: "Sī pater meus es, dā
21   votum meum!" Sine morā, deus quadrīgās aureās fīliō monstrat. Quadrīgae
22   gemmīs radiant. Habēnās fīliō dat, et monet: "Habē habēnās, et nōlī agere nimium
23   equōs."

24   Aurōra appāret, et stellās fugat. Phaethōn habēnās habet, sed equī per sē festīnant.
25   Ut nāviculae curvae sine saburrā labant per undās, sīc quadrīgae, sine magistrō
26   solitō, per nimbōs labant. Phaethōn pavet. Puer equōs ferōs nōn temperat. Equī in
27   viā solitā nōn currunt, et perīculum magnum mundō est! Gelidae zōnae radiīs sōlis
28   calescunt, et nimbī ambustī fūmant. Herba, flōrēs, et pābula ardent. Silvae et rīpae
29   ardent. Radiī sōlis aquās siccant. Helicon, Aetna, et Parnāsus in flammīs sunt.
30   Ostia septem pulverulenta Nīlī perterritī vacant. Nēreus et Dōris et nātae sē in
31   antrīs tepidīs cēlant. Phaethōn valdē timet. Iuppiter quadrīgās effrēnātās videt, et
32   timet. Exitium terrārum erit. Iuppiter remedium flammārum optat. Deus tonat, et
33   fulmen deī Phaethōntem necat. Terrae superant. Nāiades corpusculum Phaethōntis
34   in tumulum pōnunt, et signum in saxō faciunt: HĪC SITUS EST PHAETHŌN.
35   QUADRĪGĀS PATERNĀS NŌN TENĒRE POTERAT, SED MAGNA
36   TEMPTĀBAT.

Commentary

19 *Agere quadrīgās Sōlis est officium deōrum*: The infinitive *agere* serves as the subject of the verb *est*. Because it is an infinitive, it also takes the object *quadrīgās*.

22–3 *nōlī agere nimium equōs*: *nōlī* plus an infinitive indicates a negative command. Translate: *do not drive*.

30–1 *Nēreus et Dōris et nātae sē in antrīs tepidīs cēlant*: The word *se* in this sentence is a reflexive pronoun in the accusative case. Like the reflexive adjective *suus, a, um*, it derives its meaning from the subject. Here, since *Nēreus et Dōris et nātae* is the subject, translate: *Nereus and Doris and their daughters conceal themselves in tepid caves*.

Aetna, ae f.: Etna, a volcano in Sicily

agō, agere, ēgī, actum: to drive, do, set in motion

ambustus, a, um: burnt

antrum, ī n.: cave, grotto

appāreō, appārēre, appāruī, appāritum: to appear, become visible

Aurōra, ae f.: Dawn, divine representation of dawn

calescō, calescere: to grow warm

cēlō, cēlāre, cēlāvī, cēlātum: to hide, conceal, cover

clāmō, clāmāre, clāmāvī, clāmātum: to shout, make a loud noise, call to or upon

corpusculum, ī n.: a small body

culpa, ae f.: fault, blame

curvus, a, um: curved, bent, arched

Dōris, Dōridos f.: Doris, a sea nymph

effrēnātus, a, um: ungoverned, unrestrained

equus, ī m.: horse

exitium, ī n.: destruction, ruin

falsus, a, um: false, fake, deceitful

ferus, a, um: untamed, wild, rough

festīnō, festīnāre, festīnāvī, festīnātum: to hurry, make haste

fulmen, fulminis n.: lightning, thunderbolt

fūmō, fūmāre, fūmāvī, fūmātum: to smoke, fume

gelidus, a, um: cold, frozen, icy

gemma, ae f.: jewel, gem

habēna, ae f.: strap, rein

Helicon, Helicōnis m.: Helicon, a mountain in Greece

imāgō, imāginis f.: image, likeness

labō, labāre, labāvī, labātum: to waver, totter

magister, magistrī m.: master, teacher

moneō, monēre, monuī, monitum: to warn, admonish

monstrō, monstrāre, monstrāvī, monstrātum: to show, point out, indicate

Nāias, Nāiadis f.: a Naiad, water nymph

nāta, ae f.: daughter

necō, necāre, necāvī, necātum: to kill, slay

nōlō, nōlle, nōluī: to be unwilling (nōlī = imperative)

Nēreus, ī m.: Nereus, a god of the sea

nimbus, ī m.: vapor, cloud

nimium: (adv.) excessively, too much

officium, ī n.: duty, position, service

ostium, ī n.: door, entrance, mouth

pābulum, ī n.: food, nourishment

paternus, a, um: fatherly, paternal

paveō, pavēre, pāvī: to be afraid, quake

perīculum, ī n.: danger, risk

perterritus, a, um: frightened, terrified

pignus, pignoris n.: pledge, assurance

pōnō, pōnere, posuī, positum: to place, put, put aside

pulverulentus, a, um: dusty

quadrīgae, ārum f. pl.: four-horse chariot

quī, quae, quod: (interrog. adj.) which? what? what kind of?

radius, ī m.: ray, spoke, shuttle for weaving

remedium, ī n.: remedy, relief

saburra, ae f.: sand, ballast

saxum, ī n.: rock, crag

septem: (indecl. numer.) seven

situs, a, um: situated, buried

siccō, siccāre, siccāvī, siccātum: to dry, dry up

solitus, a, um: accustomed, usual

stultus, a, um: foolish, silly

temperō, temperāre, temperāvī, temperātum: to govern, manage

tepidus, a, um: lukewarm, tepid

timeō, timēre, timuī: to fear

tonō, tonāre, tonuī, tonitum: to thunder

vacō, vacāre, vacāvī, vacātum: to be empty

valdē: (adv.) intensely, greatly

via, ae f.: road, way, journey

zōna, ae f.: zone, region, girdle

FUTURE INDICATIVE ACTIVE

First conjugation

	Singular	Plural
1st person	radiābō	radiābimus
2nd person	radiābis	radiābitis
3rd person	radiābit	radiābunt

Second conjugation

	Singular	Plural
1st person	sedēbō	sedēbimus
2nd person	sedēbis	sedēbitis
3rd person	sedēbit	sedēbunt

Third conjugation

	Singular	Plural
1st person	petam	petēmus
2nd person	petēs	petētis
3rd person	petet	petent

Third conjugation *-io*

	Singular	Plural
1st person	faciam	faciēmus
2nd person	faciēs	faciētis
3rd person	faciet	facient

esse

	Singular	Plural
1st person	erō	erimus
2nd person	eris	eritis
3rd person	erit	erunt

Ovid offers a detailed description of the carved artwork which adorns the doors of the Sun-god's palace in this story. This kind of rhetorical description is known as *ekphrasis*, which in Greek means "a speaking out." The rhetorical device is a convention of epic poetry and is used by earlier poets such as Homer, Apollonius Rhodius, Catullus, and Vergil. Notice how Ovid's description of the images on the doors recalls his earlier description of creation, which also features lands, bodies of water, and the heavens. Thus, the ekphrasis here is a microcosm of the more detailed version of creation which he offers at the beginning of the epic. Notice also how Ovid vividly describes the vision of the Sun surrounded by his attendants, which Phaethon first sees when he enters the palace, as if it is a carefully arranged work of art. Ovid thus blurs the boundaries between the ekphrasis and the primary narrative, again revealing his interest in visual art.

8 Cadmus and the founding of Thebes

(*Met.* 3.1–137)

When Jupiter abducts Europa from Phoenicia, her father King Agenor tells his son Cadmus to find her. Cadmus is unsuccessful in finding his sister, who gives birth to King Minos on Crete, but he founds his own city in Boeotia. Thebes is where Oedipus will eventually rule as king.

1   Eurōpa erat fīlia Agēnoris, rēgis Tyriōrum. Quandō Eurōpa Crētam in tergō taurī nat,
2   Agēnōr iubet fīlium lustrāre terrās. Agēnōr exilium poenam addit. Cadmus, fīlius
3   Agēnoris, cum comitibus orbem terrārum frūstrā pererrat (quis enim dēprendere
4   furta Iovis potest?). Cadmus Eurōpam nōn videt. Sīc Cadmus patriam et īram patris
5   vītat. Supplex ōrāculum Phoebī consulit, et deus dīcit: "Bōs tibi in arvīs occurret.
6   Post vestīgia bovis ambulā, et, quā in herbā requiescit, fac moenia urbis, et vocā
7   loca "Boeōtiam."

8   Cadmus ex antrō Castaliō dēscendit. Bovem videt. Bōs lentē movet; Cadmus
9   vestīgia bovis legit. Taciturnus Phoebum adōrat. Iuvenca multās hōrās adambulat.
10 Bōs dēnique in herbā recubat. Cadmus est valdē beātus, et grātēs agit. Tunc
11 Cadmus sacrificāre Iovī optat, et iubet virōs petere aquās ē vīvīs fontibus. Silva
12 vetus, violāta nullīs secūribus, prope stābat, et in mediā silvā erat spēlunca densa
13 virgīs et vīminibus. Erat arcus, factus compāgine lapidum, et aqua fēcunda. In
14 antrō erat anguis Martius praesignis cristā. Oculī igne micant, et omne corpus
15 venēnō tumet. Trēs linguae vibrant, et dentēs triplicēs in ordine stant. Ubi Tyriī virī
16 lūcum tangunt et urnās in undīs dēmittunt, sonant. Serpēns caeruleus ex antrō caput

Commentary

1 *Quandō Eurōpa Crētam in tergō taurī nat*: *Crētam* is an accusative of place to which. The accusative is used without a preposition with cities, small islands, *domus*, and *rūs*.

2 *Agēnōr exilium poenam addit*: That is, Cadmus will suffer exile if he does not find his sister Europa. Understand *exilium* to be in apposition to *poenam*. Translate: *Agenor adds exile as a punishment*.

5 *Supplex ōrāculum Phoebī consulit*: The noun *supplex* here is in the nominative and stands in apposition to Cadmus, who is understood as the subject. Translate: *As a suppliant, he consults the oracle*.

6 *fac moenia urbis*: The word *fac* is an irregular second person singular present imperative of the verb *facere*.

9 *Iuvenca multās hōrās adambulat*: *multās hōrās* is an example of an accusative of extent of time. Translate: *for many hours*.

adambulō, adambulāre, adambulāvī, adambulātum: to walk near, walk about

addō, addere, addidī, additum: to add, join to

Agēnor, Agēnoris m.: Agenor, a king of Phoenicia

anguis, anguis m. or f.: serpent, snake

arcus, ūs m.: bow, arch

Boeōtia, ae f.: Boeotia, a region of Greece

bōs, bovis m. or f.: cow, ox

Cadmus, ī m.: Cadmus, son of Agenor

Castalius, a, um.: of Castalia, a fountain on Mt. Parnassus

caput, capitis n.: head

compāgo, compāginis f.: a joining together, structure

consulō, consulere, consuluī, consultum: to consider, consult

corpus, corporis n.: a body

Crēta, ae f.: Crete, an island in the Mediterranean Sea

crista, ae f.: crest

dēmittō, dēmittere, dēmīsī, dēmissum: send down, drop

dēnique: (adv.) finally, at last

dens, dentis m.: tooth

densus, a, um: thick, dense

dēprendō, dēprendere, dēprendī, dēprensum: to catch hold of, detect, discover

dēscendō, dēscendere, dēscendī, descensum: to go down, descend

enim: (conj.) indeed, in fact

Eurōpa, ae f.: Europa, daughter of the Phoenician King Agenor

exilium, ī n.: banishment, exile

fēcundus, a, um: fruitful, fertile

fīlia, ae f.: daughter

fōns, fontis m.: spring, fountain

furtum, ī n.: trick, deceit, secret love

grātēs, ium f. pl.: thanks

iubeō, iubēre, iussī, iussum: to order, command

iuvenca, ae f.: cow

legō, legere, lēgī, lectum: to pick out, choose, read

lentē: (adv.) slowly

lingua, ae f.: tongue

loca, ōrum n. pl.: region

lūcus, ī m.: wood, grove

Martius, a, um: sacred to Mars, the god of war

medius, a, um: middle

micō, micāre, micuī: to vibrate, move rapidly, flicker

moenia, ium n. pl.: walls

nō, nāre, nāvī: to swim

nullus, a, um: none, not any

occurrō, occurrere, occurrī, occursum: to meet, appear (often + dat.)

omnis, e: every, all

ordo, ordinis m.: row, line, order

pererrō, pererrāre, pererrāvī, pererrātum: to wander through

praesignis, e: remarkable, illustrious

prope: (adv.) nearby, near

quā: (adv.) where

quandō: (adv.) when

recubō, recubāre, recubāvī, recubātum: to lie back, recline

requiescō, requiescere, requiēvī, requiētum: to rest

rēx, rēgis m.: king

secūris, is f.: an axe, hatchet

sonō, sonāre, sonuī, sonitum: to make a noise, sound

spēlunca, ae f.: cave

supplex, supplicis m.: a suppliant, petitioner

taciturnus, a, um: quiet, silent

tangō, tangere, tetigī, tactum: to touch, reach, arrive at

trēs, tria: three

triplex, triplicis: triple

tumeō, tumēre, tumuī: to swell, be puffed up

Tyrius, a, um: of Tyre, a Phoenician city, purple

urbs, urbis f.: city

urna, ae f.: water jar, urn

vetus, veteris: old, ancient

vibrō, vibrāre, vibrāvī, vibrātum: to shake, quiver, vibrate

vīmen, vīminis n.: branch, twig

violātus, a, um: broken, injured

virga, ae f.: branch, twig

vītō, vītāre, vītāvī, vītātum: to escape, avoid

vīvus, a, um: living

17   trūdit, et sībila horrenda mittit. Urnae dē manibus virōrum effluunt, et sanguis
18   corpus relinquit. Tremor membra occupat. Serpēns orbēs squāmōsōs in volūbilibus
19   nexibus torquet. Ērēctus in aurās levēs stat, et omne nemus dēspicit. Statim
20   Phoenīcēs necat, sīve tēla sīve fugam parant. Virōs Cadmī dentibus, orbibus longīs,
21   et tābe fūnestā venēnī necat.

22   Intereā Cadmus virōs exspectat. Ubi sōl altissimus in caelō est, virōs vestīgat.
23   Tegumen eius est pellis leōnis; tēlum est lancea cuspide ferreā; et animus est fortis.
24   Silvam intrat, et antrum videt. Tunc corpora lētāta et serpentem ingentem videt.
25   Anguis vulnera sanguinea virōrum lambit. Cadmus, plēnus furōris, magnum
26   lapidem iactat, sed serpēns sine vulnere manet. Cadmus tunc necāre immēnsum
27   serpentem lanceā temptat, sed tēlum corium squāmōsum nōn vincit. Nunc serpēns
28   plēnus īrae est. Post multās plāgās, Cadmus īrātus dēnique anguem Martium necat.

29   Dum victor spatium hostis victī consīderat, subitō vōx sonat. Vōx dīcit: "Quid
30   serpentem victum spectās? Tū serpēns eris, et virī tē spectābunt." Cadmus pavet
31   timōre. Sed Pallas adest. Pallas Cadmum arāre terram et suppōnere dentēs vīpereōs
32   iubet. Cadmus deae pāret, et dentēs ut sēmina spargit. Terra movēre incipit, et virī
33   armātī ā dentibus sparsīs surgunt. Virī inter sē pugnant. Quinque virī superant, et
34   Cadmus quīnque virōs comitēs habet. Iam Thēbae stant.

Commentary

18–19 *Serpēns orbēs squāmōsōs in volūbilibus nexibus torquet*: *orbēs* here means *coils*. Ovid's poetic language creates a vivid image of the snake's twisted body.

19 *Ērēctus in aurās levēs stat*: The phrase *in aurās levēs* should be translated *into the light breezes*. Ovid suggests here that when the huge serpent raises its neck, it touches the upper air. Thus, it is very tall.

20–1 *Cadmī dentibus, orbibus longīs, et tābe fūnestā venēnī necat*: The ablatives here are all ablatives of means.

29–30 *Vōx dīcit ... virī tē spectābunt*: The voice is divine and prophesies that Cadmus himself will become a snake, which is a transformation which occurs later in the epic.

34 *Cadmus quinque virōs comitēs habet*: The noun *comitēs* stands in apposition to the noun *virōs* and is best translated as *companions*. The five armed soldiers who remain after the battle become the founders of the noble families of Thebes and, together with Cadmus, establish the city.

adsum, adesse, adfuī, adfutūrum: to be at a place, be present

altissimus, a, um: highest

armātus, a, um: armed

arō, arāre, arāvī, arātum: to plow, till

comes, comitis m. or f.: companion, comrade, partner

consīderō, consīderāre, consīderāvī, consīderātum: to look at closely, consider, reflect

corium, ī n.: skin, hide

cuspis, cuspidis f.: a point, spear

dēspiciō, dēspicere, dēspexī, dēspectum: to look down on, despise, disregard

dum: (conj.) while

effluō, effluere, effluxī: to flow out, run out

ērēctus, a, um: raised up, erect

exspectō, exspectāre, exspectāvī, exspectātum: to await, look for, expect

ferreus, a, um: made of iron

fortis, e: strong, powerful

fuga, ae f.: flight, escape

fūnestus, a, um: deadly, fatal, destructive

furor, furōris m.: raging, madness, fury

horrendus, a, um: dreadful, terrible, horrible

iam: (adv.) now, already

incipiō, incipere, incēpī, inceptum: to begin

ingēns, ingentis: huge

inter: (prep. + acc.) among, between

intereā: (adv.) meanwhile

īrātus, a, um: angered, enraged

lambō, lambere, lambī, lambitum: to lick, lap

lancea, ae f.: lance, spear

lētātus, a, um: murdered

levis, e: light, swift

longus, a, um: long, extended

manus, ūs f.: hand, band

mittō, mittere, mīsī, missum: to send

nemus, nemoris n.: wood, grove

nexus, ūs m.: a joint, entwining, connection

Pallas, Palladis f.: epithet of Athena/Minerva, the goddess of weaving, wisdom, and battles

pāreō, pārēre, pāruī, pāritum: to be obedient to, submit to (+ dat.)

parō, parāre, parāvī, parātum: to prepare

pellis, pellis f.: skin, hide

Phoenīcēs, um m. pl.: Phoenicians

plāga, ae f.: a blow, wound

pugnō, pugnāre, pugnāvī, pugnātum: to fight

quid: (interrog. adv.) why

quinque: (indecl. numer.) five

sanguis, sanguinis m.: blood, vigor, strength

sēmen, sēminis n.: seed, child

sībilus, a, um: hissing, whistling

spargō, spargere, sparsī, sparsum: to sprinkle, strew, scatter

sparsus, a, um: strewn, scattered

spectō, spectāre, spectāvī, spectātum: to look at, observe, behold

squāmōsus, a, um: scaly

suppōnō, suppōnere, supposuī, suppositum: to place under, bury, sow

surgō, surgere, surrexī, surrectum: to elevate, rise, arise

tābēs, tābis f.: a wasting away, melting, pestilence

tegumen, teguminis n.: covering

Thēbae, ārum f. pl.: Thebes, a city in Boeotia

timor, timōris m.: fear, dread

torqueō, torquēre, torsī, tortum: to twist, turn

tremor, tremōris m.: shaking, quivering, tremor

trūdō, trūdere, trūsī, trūsum: to thrust, push forth

vestīgō, vestīgāre, vestīgāvī, vestīgātum: to track down, trace out

vīpereus, a, um: of a snake

volūbilis, e: turning, spinning, whirling

vōx, vōcis f.: voice

THIRD DECLENSION ADJECTIVES

Masculine/feminine adjectives

	Singular	*Plural*
Nominative	praesignis	praesignēs
Genitive	praesignis	praesignium
Dative	praesignī	praesignibus
Accusative	praesignem	praesignēs
Ablative	praesignī	praesignibus

Neuter adjectives

	Singular	*Plural*
Nominative	praesigne	praesignia
Genitive	praesignis	praesignium
Dative	praesignī	praesignibus
Accusative	praesigne	praesignia
Ablative	praesignī	praesignibus

The armed soldiers who spring from the planted teeth of the serpent are known as the *Spartoi*, which in Greek means "Sown Men," and the five men who remain after the battle become the founders of the noble families of Thebes. Thus, the Thebans considered themselves *autochthonous*, or "sprung from the earth." In myth, Athena gives some of the serpent's teeth to King Aeëtes of Colchis. Later, the hero Jason fights the armed soldiers which grow from those teeth when he contends for the golden fleece.

9   Actaeon

(*Met.* 3.138–252)

The grandson of Cadmus, Actaeon, accidentally sees Diana naked while he is hunting, and the angry goddess punishes him by turning him into prey for his own hounds.

1   Erat mōns infectus caede ferārum variārum. Iuvenis vēnātor, Actaeōn nomine, cum
2   comitibus per lustra vagābat. Actaeōn clāmat: "Līna nostra et ferrum nostrum
3   cruōre ferārum madent. Vēnātus satis fortūnae habet. Cum Aurōra sē redūcet, opus
4   repetēmus." Comitēs labōrem intermittunt.

5   Erat vallis densa piceīs et cupressū acūtā. Sacra Diānae erat. In recessū extrēmō
6   antrum erat, labōrātum nullā arte. Ibi nātūra suō ingeniō artem simulābat. Fōns
7   perlūcidus ā dextrā sonābat. Hīc dea fessa vēnātū ferārum perfundere virgineōs artūs
8   solēbat. Nunc dea tēlum pharetramque arcumque ūnī nymphārum trādit, et alia
9   nympha pallam habet. Duae nymphae vincla pedibus dēmunt. Alia nymphārum
10   capillōs sparsōs in nōdum colligit, quamvīs capillī nymphae ipsīus solūtī erant.
11   Cēterae aquam dē urnīs capācibus fundunt.

12   Dum Diāna sē in stāgnō solitō lavat, nepōs Cadmī per nemus ignōtum passibus nōn
13   certīs errat, et in lūcum intrat. Simul atque antrum rōrāns fontibus intrat, nymphae
14   nūdae sua pectora percutiunt, et vīsū virī multum ululant. Clāmor antrum implet.
15   Nymphae Diānam circumfundunt, et deam corporibus suis tegunt. Dea tamen
16   omnēs superēminet. Vultus deae vīsae sine vestamentō rubens est, ut Aurōra est
17   purpurea in caelō.

Commentary

3 *Vēnātus satis fortūnae habet*: The indeclinable word *satis* often takes a partitive genitive. Translate: *enough luck*. In other words, the men have enjoyed success in their hunting.
6–7 *Fōns perlūcidus ā dextrā sonābat*: *ā dextrā* is best translated *on the right*.
12–13 *nepōs Cadmī ... passibus nōn certīs errat*: *passibus* is an ablative of means with *errat*.

Actaeōn, Actaeonis m.: Actaeon, a grandson of Cadmus

acūtus, a, um: sharp, pointed

artus, ūs m.: joint, limb

caedēs, is f.: a cutting down, a killing

capāx, capācis: able to hold much material, capacious

certus, a, um: determined, fixed, certain

circumfundō, circumfundere, circumfūdī, circumfūsum: to pour around, surround

clāmor, clāmōris m.: a loud shouting

colligō, colligere, collēgī, collectum: to gather together, collect

cruor, cruōris m.: blood from a wound, gore

cupressus, ūs f.: cypress tree

dēmō, demere, dempsī, demptum: take away, withdraw, remove

Diāna, ae f.: Diana, goddess of the hunt

errō, errāre, errāvī, errātum: to wander

extrēmus, a, um: extreme, last, farthest

fessus, a, um: tired, exhausted

fortūna, ae f.: luck, fortune

fundō, fundere, fūdī, fūsum: to pour

ignōtus, a, um: unknown

impleō, implēre, implēvī, implētum: to fill up

infectus, a, um: (inficiō) stained, dyed

ingenium, ī n.: nature, genius, character

intermittō, intermittere, intermīsī, intermissum: to discontinue, interrupt, suspend

labor, labōris m.: work, labor

labōrātus, a, um: made, manufactured

lavō, lavāre, lāvī, lautum: to wash

līnum, ī n.: linen, thread, hunter's net

lustrum, ī n.: a den, lair, bog, woodland

madeō, madēre, maduī: to be wet

multum: (adv.) much, very much

nepōs, nepōtis m.: grandson, descendant

nōdus, ī m.: knot

noster, nostra, nostrum: (poss. adj.) our

palla, ae f.: long garment, cloak

passus, ūs m.: step, pace

pectus, pectoris n.: breast, chest

percutiō, percutere, percussī, percussum: to strike, beat

perfundō, perfundere, perfūdī, perfūsum: to steep, pour over, fill, spread

perlūcidus, a, um: shining, bright, transparent

picea, ae f.: spruce-fir tree

quamvīs: (conj.) although

recessus, ūs m.: a recess

redūcō, redūcere, reduxī, reductum: to draw backwards, lead back

repetō, repetere, repetīvī, repetītum: to seek again, begin again, repeat

rōrāns, rōrantis: causing dew, dripping, being moist

rubens, rubentis: red

sacer, sacra, sacrum: sacred

simul atque: (conj.) as soon as

simulō, simulāre, simulāvī, simulātum: to make like

soleō, solēre, solitus sum: to be accustomed

solūtus, a, um: loose, loosened, unbound

superēmineō, superēminēre, supereminuī: to overtop, stand above

trādō, trādere, trādidī, trāditum: to hand over

ululō, ululāre, ululāvī ululātum: to howl

vagō, vagāre, vagāvī, vagātum: to wander, ramble

vallis (valles), vallis f.: valley

varius, a, um: diverse, manifold

vēnātor, vēnātōris m.: a hunter, sportsman

vēnātus, ūs m.: the chase, hunting

vinclum, ī n.: bond, binding, sandal strap

vīsus, a, um: seen, looked upon

vīsus, ūs f.: a sight, appearance

virgineus, a, um: maiden, virgin

vultus, ūs m.: face, expression, appearance

18   Quamquam turba nymphārum suārum stīpat, dea in latus oblīquum stat et ōs retrō
19   flectit. Tunc aquās in vultum Actaeonis iactat, et capillōs iuvenis undā spargit.
20   Diāna dīcit: "Nunc fābulam deae vīsae nūdae narrā, sī potes!"

21   Dea cornua cervī capitī Actaeonis dat, spatium collō dat, aurēs cacūminat, manūs
22   cum pedibus mūtat, bracchia cum crūribus mūtat, et corpus vellere maculōsō vēlat.
23   Actaeōn territus fugit. Ubi vultum et cornua in undā videt, temptat dīcere: "Mē
24   miserum!" Cupit dīcere, sed nulla vōx est. Tantum mēns pristina manet. Quid
25   faciet? Repetetne domum, vel latēbit in silvīs?

26   Dum dubitat, canēs cervum vident. Actaeōn mūtātus fugit per loca solita, et canēs
27   post vestīgia currunt. Cupit clāmāre: "Sum Actaeōn; dominum vestrum
28   cognoscite!" Verba cupīdinī verbōrum dēsunt. Undique canēs circumstant, et rostra
29   in corpus mergunt. Dominum sub imāgine falsā cervī dīlacerant. Īra deae
30   pharetrātae satiāta est.

Commentary

18 *dea in latus oblīquum stat*: The goddess stands in a position turned away from Actaeon to shield herself but still looks back at him.

23 *Ubi vultum et cornua in undā videt*: Actaeon sees his reflection in the pool of water.

28 *Verba cupīdinī verbōrum dēsunt*: The verb *dēesse* takes a dative of the thing failed here, which is the impulse to speak. Translate: *Words fail the desire for words*. That is, he wants to speak but cannot.

auris, auris f.: ear
cacūminō, cacūmināre, cacūmināvī, cacūminātum: to make pointed, point
canis, canis m. or f.: dog
cervus, ī m.: stag
circumstō, circumstāre, circumstetī: to stand around, encircle
cognoscō, cognoscere, cognōvī, cognitum: to become acquainted with, know, recognize
collum, ī n.: neck
cornū, ūs n.: horn
dēsum, dēesse, dēfuī, dēfutūrum: to fail, be lacking
dīlacerō, dīlacerāre, dīlacerāvī, dīlacerātum: to tear in pieces
dominus, ī m.: master
domus, ūs f.: house, home
dubitō, dubitāre, dubitāvī, dubitātum: to hesitate, be doubtful
flectō, flectere, flexī, flexum: to bend, turn
lateō, latēre, latuī: to lie concealed
latus, lateris n.: side

maculōsus, a, um: spotted
mēns, mentis f.: mind, reason, intellect
mergō, mergere, mersī, mersum: to sink, plunge, immerse
miser, misera, miserum: poor, wretched, pitiable
mūtātus, a, um: changed, transformed
oblīquus, a, um: indirect, on one side, slanting
ōs, ōris n.: mouth, face
pharetrātus, a, um: wearing a quiver
pristinus, a, um: former, earlier, of yesterday
quamquam: (conj.) although
retrō: (adv.) backwards
rostrum, ī n.: beak, snout, muzzle
satiātus, a, um: satisfied, sated
stīpō, stīpāre, stīpāvī, stīpātum: to press around, crowd
undique: (adv.) from everywhere
vellus, velleris n.: fleece, hide
vēlō, vēlāre, vēlāvī, vēlātum: to cover, hide
vester, vestra, vestrum: (poss. adj.) your

FOURTH DECLENSION

Masculine/feminine

	Singular	Plural
Nominative	arcus	arcūs
Genitive	arcūs	arcuum
Dative	arcuī	arcibus
Accusative	arcum	arcūs
Ablative	arcū	arcibus

Neuter

	Singular	Plural
Nominative	genū	genua
Genitive	genūs	genuum
Dative	genū	genibus
Accusative	genū	genua
Ablative	genū	genibus

Actaeon is ripped apart by his own hunting dogs in this story, which resembles *sparagmos*, a ritual tearing apart of flesh associated with the worship of Dionysus/Bacchus. In an Orphic myth, Actaeon's cousin Dionysus is torn apart and eaten by the Titans. Zeus later eats the child-god's heart, which has been saved by Athena from the Titans. When Zeus impregnates Semele, Dionysus is reconstituted in Semele's womb and reborn as Dionysus Zagreus. Unlike Dionysus, Actaeon is mortal and thus does not recover from his dogs' attack.

10 Semele

(*Met.* 3.253–315)

When Semele, one of Cadmus' daughters, becomes pregnant by Jove, Juno disguises herself as Semele's nurse and tricks the young woman into destroying herself.

1   Quandō fāma mortis Actaeōnis aurēs Iūnōnis tangēbat, uxor Iovis gaudēbat.
2   Memoriam Eurōpae, sorōris Cadmī et amōris Iovis, in animō habēbat. Nunc fāma
3   nova deae dolēbat. Semelē, fīlia Cadmī, gravida dē sēmine Iovis magnī erat.
4   Dum linguam ad iurgium cum Iove solvit, sibi dīcit: "Quōmodo iurgia mē
5   iuvant? Semelē poenās dabit! Fīliam Cadmī perdam, sī mē tenēre sceptrum
6   gemmāns decet. Rēgīna caelī et coniunx et certē soror Iovis sum. At, putō, Semelē
7   furtō contenta est, et iniūria meī thalamī brevis est. Gravida tamen est, et ego māter
8   dē Iove esse cupiō. Ipsa māter dē rēge deōrum nōn sum! Nōn Sāturnia sum, nisi
9   ista fēmina in undās Stygiās penetrābit, mersa ab Iove ipsō!"

10   Surgit, et sē nūbe fulvā circumfundit. Tunc venit ad tecta Semelēs. Ante nūbem
11   removet, anum simulat. Capillōs cānōs ad tempora pōnit, et cutem rūgīs sulcat.
12   Vōcem anīlem facit, et nunc nūtrix Semelēs est. Sermo multus est, et fēminae ad
13   nōmen Iovis veniunt. Iūnō suspīrat et dīcit: "Multī falsī sē deōs appellant et
14   intrāre thalamōs pudīcōs possunt. Nōn satis est habēre nōmen Iovem. Pignus
15   postulā. Quantus Iūnōnem amat, tantus tē amāre dēbet. Omnia insignia Iovis
16   postulā. Complexūs Iūnōnis postulā."

Commentary

5 *Semelē poenās dabit*: The idiom *poenās dare* means *to pay the penalty.*

5–6 *sī mē tenēre ... decet*: The impersonal verb *decet* takes an accusative-infinitive construction. Translate: *if it is fitting for me to hold ...*

6–7 *Semelē furtō contenta est*: The ablative is used here with *contenta* for the thing with which one is contented. Juno starts her internal dialogue by telling herself that Jupiter's affair with Semele is not that offensive, but she decides to punish the daughter of Cadmus when she considers how Semele is pregnant by Jupiter while she herself is not.

15 *Quantus Iūnōnem amat, tantus tē amāre dēbet*: The words *quantus* and *tantus* work together in this sentence and agree with the subject *Iuppiter*. Translate: *As great as he is when he loves Juno, in such greatness he ought to love you.*

anīlis, e: like an old woman, aged

anus, ūs f.: an old woman

at: (conj.) but, at least, moreover

brevis, e: brief

certē: (adv.) certainly

complexus, ūs m.: an embrace

coniunx, coniugis m. or f.: spouse, wife, husband

contentus, a, um: content, satisfied

cutis, cutis f.: skin

doleō, dolēre, doluī, dolitum: to grieve, suffer pain, cause pain (+ dat.)

fulvus, a, um: yellow, golden

gemmāns, gemmantis: set with jewels

gravidus, a, um: heavy, laden, pregnant

insigne, insignis n.: a distinguishing mark, sign

iste, ista, istud: (demonst. pron.) that, those

Iūnō, Iūnōnis f.: Juno, wife of Jupiter, goddess of marriage

iurgium, ī n.: argument, quarrel

mersus, a, um: sunk, overwhelmed

mors, mortis f.: death

nūbes, nūbis f.: cloud

nūtrix, nūtrīcis f.: nurse

nisi: (conj.) unless, if not

penetrō, penetrāre, penetrāvī, penetrātum: to pass through, sink deep into

postulō, postulāre, postulāvī, postulātum: to demand, claim, request

pudīcus, a, um: chaste, modest

putō, putāre, putāvī, putātum: to think

quantus, a, um: of what size, how great, how much

rēgīna, ae f.: queen

rūga, ae f.: wrinkle

Sāturnia, ae f.: Saturnia, epithet of Juno, daughter of Saturn

sceptrum, ī n.: scepter, royal staff

Semelē, Semelēs f.: Semele, a daughter of Cadmus

sermo, sermōnis m.: talk, conversation

solvō, solvere, solvī, solūtum: to loosen, dissolve, set free

soror, sorōris f.: sister

Stygius, a, um: Stygian, of Styx

sulcō, sulcāre, sulcāvī, sulcātum: to furrow, wrinkle

suspīrō, suspīrāre, suspīrāvī, suspīrātum: to take a deep breath, sigh

tempus, temporis n.: temple, brow, time

thalamus, ī m.: bedroom, marriage bed

veniō, venīre, vēnī, ventum: to come

17   Iūnō tālibus verbīs animum fīliae Cadmī format. Ubi Iuppiter ad tecta Semelēs
18   venit, Semelē Iovem mūnus rogat. Deus dīcit: "Ēlige! Iūro per Stygem." Semelē
19   laeta nimis gaudet et dīcit: "Quālem Sāturnia tē sentīre solet, ubi thalamum deae
20   intrās, tālem tē mihi dā!" Deus ingemit. Iūrāta revocāre nōn potest!

21   Iuppiter maestissimus aethera altum conscendit, et nūbēs, ventōs, fulmina, et
22   tonitrūs colligit. Tunc rēgiam Semelēs intrat. Corpus mortāle tolerāre vīrēs Iovis
23   nōn potest. Corpus Semelēs ardet! Iuppiter infantem imperfectum ab uterō mātris
24   ēripit, et (sī fāma est digna) infantem in femur insuit. Deus māterna tempora
25   complet, et posteā Bacchus nātus est. Furtim Īnō, soror mātris, infantem prīmīs
26   cūnīs ēducat, et inde nymphae Nȳsaeae in antrō occulunt et lacte alunt.

Commentary

18 *Semelē Iovem mūnus rogat*: The verb *rogāre* takes an accusative object of the person asked and also an accusative object of the thing requested.

19–20 *Quālem Sāturnia tē sentīre solet ... tālem tē mihi dā!*: The words *quālem* and *tālem* agree with the pronouns *tē*. Translate: *As Saturnia is accustomed to feel you ... give me yourself in such form!*

21 *Iuppiter maestissimus aethera altum conscendit*: *aethera* is accusative singular.

25–6 *Furtim Īnō ... prīmīs cūnīs ēducat*: The phrase *prīmīs cūnīs* means *in earliest childhood*. Here, Ovid refers to the story of Dionysus' upbringing in Asia Minor. The god eventually returns to Thebes.

aether, aetheris m.: the upper air (aethera = acc. sing.)

alō, alere, aluī, altum: to nourish, support

Bacchus, ī m.: Bacchus, the god of wine and intoxication

compleō, complēre, complēvī, complētum: to fill up, fulfill

conscendō, conscendere, conscendī, conscensum: to mount, climb up, go up to

cūnae, ārum f. pl.: cradle

dignus, a, um: worthy, deserving of (+ abl.)

ēducō, ēducāre, ēducāvī, ēducātum: to rear, bring up

ēligō, ēligere, ēlēgī, ēlectum: to choose, pluck out

ēripiō, ēripere, ēripuī, ēreptum: to snatch away, tear out, rescue

femur, femoris n.: thigh

furtim: (adv.) secretly

imperfectus, a, um: unfinished, incomplete

inde: (adv.) from there

infāns, infantis m. or f.: speechless one, baby

ingemō, ingemere, imgemuī: to groan

Īnō, ūs f.: Ino, a daughter of Cadmus

insuō, insuere, insuī, insūtum: to sew in, sew up

iūrātus, a, um: sworn to

iūrō, iūrāre, iūrāvī, iūrātum: to swear

lac, lactis n.: milk

maestissimus, a, um: very sad, very gloomy

māternus, a, um: of the mother, maternal

mortālis, e: mortal, human

mūnus, mūneris n.: office, charge, favor, gift

nātus, a, um: born

Nȳsaeus, a, um: of Nysa, a region in Asia Minor

occulō, occulere, occuluī, occultum: to cover, hide

posteā: (adv.) afterwards

quālis, e: of what sort, like

revocō, revocāre, revocāvī, revocātum: to call back, recall

sentiō, sentīre, sensī, sensum: to feel, experience, perceive

Styx, Stygis f.: Styx, a river in the Underworld

tālis, e: such, of such a kind

tolerō, tolerāre, tolerāvī, tolerātum: to endure, withstand

tonitrus, ūs m.: thunder

uterus, ī m.: belly, womb

vīs, vis f.: strength, power, force

FOURTH CONJUGATION

Present

	Singular	Plural
1st person	veniō	venīmus
2nd person	venīs	venītis
3rd person	venit	veniunt

Imperfect

	Singular	Plural
1st person	veniēbam	veniēbāmus
2nd person	veniēbās	veniēbātis
3rd person	veniēbat	veniēbant

Future

	Singular	Plural
1st person	veniam	veniēmus
2nd person	veniēs	veniētis
3rd person	veniet	venient

In this story, Semele burns up when Jupiter has intercourse with her as he would with Juno, but the fetus she is carrying is saved from the fire. The king of the gods sews the fetus into his own thigh, where it continues to gestate. Later, Bacchus is born from his father's thigh. In another story, the king of the gods swallows his first wife, Metis, to prevent her from giving birth to a son who will challenge his power. When he swallows her, Metis is pregnant with the goddess Athena, who eventually is born out of her father's head. These two myths demonstrate how the king of the gods manages to exhibit feminine procreative power while at the same time displaying traditional characteristics of masculinity.

11 Tiresias

(*Met.* 3.316–38)

Ovid tells a brief story of how Tiresias loses his sight when he offends Juno but gains the ability to see the future.

1 Ubi cūnae Bacchī tūtae erant, forte Iuppiter iocōs cum Iūnōne agēbat. Rex deōrum
2 uxōrī dīcit: "Ubi miscent, voluptās uxōrum, putō, maior quam voluptās
3 marītōrum est." Illa negat. Rēgīna deōrum dīcit: "Marītī maiōrem voluptātem
4 capiunt quam uxōrēs." Quaerere sententiam Tīresiae constituunt. "Tīresiās
5 utrōsque amōrēs noscit," Iuppiter dīcit. Rex deōrum fābulam narrat:

6 "Tīresiās ictū baculī duo corpora serpentum magnōrum coeuntium in silvā viridī
7 violat. Mīrābiliter hic corpus virīle āmittit. Tīresiās fēmina est! Septem annōs
8 formam fēmineam habet. Octāvō annō, rursus eōsdem serpentēs videt, et dīcit:
9 'Quoniam, sī vōs feriō, mūtare in formam contrāriam potest, nunc quoque vōs
10 feriam.' Dīcit haec verba, et anguēs percutit. Statim forma virīlis et imāgō genetīva
11 revenit."

12 Hic igitur arbiter in līte iocōsā deōrum erat. Tīresiās dicta Iovis firmat. Sāturnia
13 multum dolet. Illa nōn iustē dolet, et oculōs iūdicis damnat. Pater omnipotēns
14 Tīresiae miserescit. Cuiquam enim deō facere inritum factum alterīus nōn licet.
15 Iuppiter prō oculīs illī scīre futūra dat. Sīc poenam honōre levat.

Commentary

2–3 *Ubi ... maior quam voluptās marītōrum est*: The word *quam* follows the comparative adjective *maior* and means *than*.

9 *Quoniam ... mūtare in formam contrāriam potest*: *potest* is used here impersonally. Translate: *Since ... it is possible to change into the opposite form*.

14 *Cuiquam enim deō facere inritum factum alīus nōn licet*: The impersonal verb *licet* takes a dative of the person given permission and an infinitive of what is granted. Translate: *Indeed it is not allowed for any god to make invalid the deed of another god*.

15 *Iuppiter prō oculīs illī scīre futūra dat*: The verb *dat* should be translated *grants* here, and the infinitive phrase *scīre futūra* is its object.

āmittō, āmittere, āmīsī, amissum: to send away, lose

arbiter, arbitrī m.: judge

baculus, ī m.: staff, walking stick

coiēns, coeuntis: coming together, mating

constituō, constituere, constituī, constitūtum: to cause to stand, settle, decide

contrārius, a, um: opposite

damnō, damnāre, damnāvī, damnātum: to condemn, cause loss or injury to

dictum, ī n.: something said

fēmineus, a, um: feminine, of a woman

feriō, ferīre: to strike, knock

firmō, firmāre, firmāvī, firmātum: to make firm, strengthen, prove

futūrus, a, um: future, yet to come

genetīvus, a, um: innate, inborn

hic, haec, hoc: (demonst. pron.) this, these

honos, honōris n.: honor, distinction

ictus, ūs m.: blow, strike

īdem, eadem, idem: the same

igitur: (conj.) therefore

ille, illa, illud: (demonst. pron.) that, those

inritus, a, um: void, invalid

iocōsus, a, um: jocular, playful

iocus, ī m.: joke

iūdex, iūdicis m.: judge

iustē: (adv.) justly

levō, levāre, levāvī, levātum: to raise up, lift, make light, ease

licet, licēre, licuit: (impers. verb) it is allowed (+ inf.)

līs, lītis f.: legal controversy, suit, quarrel, contention

maior, ius: greater

marītus, ī m.: husband

mīrābiliter: (adv.) miraculously, wonderfully

miserescō, miserescere: to pity, have compassion for (+ gen.)

negō, negāre, negāvī, negātum: to deny

noscō, noscere, nōvī, nōtum: to become acquainted with, know

octāvus, a, um: eighth

omnipotēns, omnipotentis: all powerful

prō: (prep. + abl.) in place of, on behalf of

quaerō, quaerere, quaesīvī, quaesītum: to search for, seek

quam: (adv.) than, as, how

quisquam, quaequam, quidquam or quicquam: anyone, anything

quoniam: (conj.) since, because

reveniō, revenīre, revenī, reventum: to come back, return

rursus: (adv.) again

sciō, scīre, scīvī, scītum: to know

sententia, ae f.: opinion, thought

Tīresiās, ae m.: Tiresias, a man known for wisdom

tūtus, a, um: safe

uterque, utraque, utrumque: each of two, both

violō, violāre, violāvī, violātum: to treat with violence, outrage, rape

viridis, e: green

virīlis, e: manly, masculine

voluptās, voluptātis f.: pleasure, enjoyment

DEMONSTRATIVES

hic, haec, hoc: this, these

	Singular			Plural		
	Masculine	Feminine	Neuter	Masculine	Feminine	Neuter
Nominative	hic	haec	hoc	hī	hae	haec
Genitive	huius	huius	huius	hōrum	hārum	hōrum
Dative	huic	huic	huic	hīs	hīs	hīs
Accusative	hunc	hanc	hoc	hōs	hās	haec
Ablative	hōc	hāc	hōc	hīs	hīs	hīs

ille, illa, illud: that, those

	Singular			Plural		
	Masculine	Feminine	Neuter	Masculine	Feminine	Neuter
Nominative	ille	illa	illud	illī	illae	illa
Genitive	illīus	illīus	illīus	illōrum	illārum	illōrum
Dative	illī	illī	illī	illīs	illīs	illīs
Accusative	illum	illam	illud	illōs	illās	illa
Ablative	illō	illā	illō	illīs	illīs	illīs

is, ea, id: this, that (as a pronoun: he, she, it, they)

	Singular			Plural		
	Masculine	Feminine	Neuter	Masculine	Feminine	Neuter
Nominative	is	ea	id	eī/iī	eae	ea
Genitive	eius	eius	eius	eōrum	eārum	eōrum
Dative	eī	eī	eī	eīs	eīs	eīs
Accusative	eum	eam	id	eōs	eās	ea
Ablative	eō	eā	eō	eīs	eīs	eīs

iste, ista, istud: that, those

	Singular			Plural		
	Masculine	Feminine	Neuter	Masculine	Feminine	Neuter
Nominative	iste	ista	istud	istī	istae	ista
Genitive	istīus	istīus	istīus	istōrum	istārum	istōrum
Dative	istī	istī	istī	istīs	istīs	istīs
Accusative	istum	istam	istud	istōs	istās	ista
Ablative	istō	istā	istō	istīs	istīs	istīs

īdem, eadem, idem: the same

	Singular			Plural		
	Masculine	*Feminine*	*Neuter*	*Masculine*	*Feminine*	*Neuter*
Nominative	īdem	eadem	idem	eīdem/īdem	eaedem	eadem
Genitive	eiusdem	eiusdem	eiusdem	eōrundem	eārundem	eōrundem
Dative	eīdem	eīdem	eīdem	eīsdem	eīsdem	eīsdem
Accusative	eundem	eandem	idem	eōsdem	eāsdem	eadem
Ablative	eōdem	eādem	eōdem	eīsdem	eīsdem	eīsdem

Tiresias appears in Greek literature as a figure known for his great wisdom and forethought. In Homer's *Odyssey*, Odysseus travels to the Underworld to seek Tiresias' advice. In tragedies such as Sophocles' *Antigone* and Euripides' *Bacchae*, Tiresias is a character who tries to deter the protagonists from their destructive behavior. In another Sophoclean tragedy, *Oedipus the King*, Tiresias' physical blindness draws attention to his remarkable inner vision. In that play, Oedipus ignores Tiresias' advice and ends up blinding himself upon realizing the horrible truth about his identity, highlighting the connection between vision and knowledge. The fact that Tiresias spends time both as a woman and as a man no doubt contributes to his great wisdom.

12 Bacchus and Pentheus

(*Met.* 3.511–733)

Pentheus, Cadmus' grandson, refuses to recognize that Semele's son Bacchus is divine and suffers horribly for the outrage.

1   Fāma Tīresiae per urbēs crēscēbat, et nōmen magnum erat. Penthēus, nepōs Cadmī,
2   sōlus fāmam huius spernēbat. Penthēus, contemptor deōrum, verba praesāga
3   rīdēbat et oculōs āmissōs senis dērīdēbat. Ille senex autem caput album mōvit et
4   dixit: "Erit deus novus; tempus nōn procul est. Līber, fīlius Semelēs, hūc veniet.
5   Nisi illum venerābis, māter tua et sorōrēs tē dīlacerābunt et tē in mille locīs
6   spargent. Silvās sanguine foedābis. Verba mea audīre dēbēs, et venerāre deōs
7   dēbēs." Nātus ab Echīone tālia verba dērīsit, sed verba vātis vēra erant.

8   Mox Līber adest, et agrī ululātibus fēstīs fremunt. Turba ruit, fēminae cum virīs,
9   nōbilēs cum vulgō; omnēs ad sacra Bacchī currunt. Penthēus īrātus clāmāvit: "Quī
10   furor, anguigenae, prōlēs Māvortia, vestrās mentēs attonuit? Puer inermis Thēbās
11   capiet! Aerane, tībia, fraudēs magicae, et vōcēs fēmineae vincere mīlitēs possunt?
12   Minimē!" Penthēus mīlitēs iūssit: "Īte, sine morā ducem turbae ululantis hūc
13   attrahite." Cadmus et aliī hunc verbīs corripuērunt, et inhibēre hunc frūstrā
14   labōrāvērunt. Mīlitēs discessērunt.

Commentary

5 *māter tua et sorōrēs tē dīlacerābunt*: Cadmus has four daughters: Agave, Ino, Autonoë, and Semele. Semele is dead at this point.

8 *Mox Līber adest, et agrī ululātibus fēstīs fremunt*: Bacchus embodies an embracing of the "other" and freedom from rules. His worship thus included running in the wild, drinking, dancing, singing, and ululating loudly.

aes, aeris n.: bronze, something made of bronze, bronze cymbal

albus, a, um: white

anguigena, ae m.: snake-born man

attonō, attonāre, attonuī, attonitum: to strike with thunder, make senseless

attrahō, attrahere, attraxī, attractum: to drag, lead

audiō, audīre, audīvī, audītum: to hear, listen to

contemptor, contemptōris m.: a despiser

corripiō, corripere, corripuī, correptum: to seize violently, attack, blame, rebuke

discedō, discedere, discessī, discessum: to depart, go away, separate

dux, ducis m.: leader

Echīōn, Echīonis m.: Echion, one of the Thebans sprung from the serpent's teeth

eō, īre, īvī or iī, itum: to go

fēstus, a, um: having to do with a holiday or festival

foedō, foedāre, foedāvī, foedātus: to make foul, make filthy

fraus, fraudis f.: deceit, deception, fraud

fremō, fremere, fremuī, fremitum: to roar, murmur

inermis, e: unarmed

inhibeō, inhibēre, inhibuī, inhibitum: to hold in check, restrain

labōrō, labōrāre, labōrāvī, labōrātum: to work at

Līber, Līberī m.: Liber, an Italian deity associated with Bacchus

magicus, a, um: relating to magic

Māvortius, a, um: of Mars, having to do with Mars

mīles, mīlitis m.: soldier

minimē: (adv.) not at all

mox: (adv.) soon

nōbilis, e: well-known

Penthēus, ī m.: Pentheus, a grandson of Cadmus

praesāgus, a, um: foreboding, predicting

prōlēs, prōlis f.: offspring, descendants

ruō, ruere, ruī, rutum: to rush

senex, senis m.: old man

spernō, spernere, sprēvī, sprētum: to put away, reject, scorn, despise

tībia, ae f.: flute, pipe

ululāns, ululantis: producing howls, yelling loudly

ululātus, ūs f.: a howling, shrieking

vātēs, vātis m. or f.: seer, prophet

venerō, venerāre, venerāvī, venerātum: to worship, entreat

15   Mīlitēs cruentātī revēnērunt. Penthēus rogāvit: "Ubi Bacchus est?" Mīlitēs:
16   "Illum nōn vīdīmus. Hunc tamen, comitem eius famulumque sacrōrum, cēpimus."
17   Mīlitēs nōn sentiunt, sed famulus est Līber ipse. Penthēus hunc oculīs spectāvit, et
18   īra magna fuit. Dixit: "Mīlitēs, hunc rapite, corpus eius cruciāte, et in noctem
19   Stygiam dēmittite!" Penthēus perstitit. Posteā, dum mīlitēs instrūmenta cruciātūs
20   parant, famulus catēnās āmīsit, iūtus ā nullō. Famulus discessit.

21   Nunc Penthēus ipse ad Cithaerōnem vādit. Penthēus famulum quaerit. Mōns
22   cantibus et vōce clārā Baccharum sonābat. In monte ferē mediō campus pūrus erat,
23   spectābilis undique. In hōc locō Penthēus ambulābat. In hōc locō Bacchae sacra
24   etiam faciēbant. Hīc māter prīma illum, cernentem sacra oculīs profānīs, vīdit.
25   Māter, dēmēns, clāmāvit: "Sorōrēs, maximus aper est! Errat in nostrīs agrīs. Illum
26   ferīre dēbeō!" Omnis turba furēns ruit, et Pentheum dīlacerant. Agāvē, māter
27   Pentheī, ululat et caput scindit. Agāvē dīcit: "Iō comitēs, hoc opus est victōria
28   nostra!" Verba Tīresiae vera sunt. Nunc populus Thēbānus sacra nova frequentat,
29   et semper ārās Bacchī colit.

Commentary

18–19 *et in noctem Stygiam dēmittite*: Ovid uses poetic language here to tell the slaves to kill their captive, who is actually Bacchus himself.

19–20 *Posteā … famulus catēnās āmīsit, iūtus ā nullō*: Because Bacchus represents a freedom from societal confines, he resists being bound in chains.

24 *Hīc māter prīma illum, cernentem sacra oculīs profānīs, vīdit*: The word *cernentem* agrees with *illum*. Pentheus accidentally sees the secret rituals of the followers of Bacchus.

Agāvē, Agāvēs f.: Agave, mother of Pentheus
āmissus, a, um: lost
aper, aprī m.: a wild boar
āra, ae f.: altar
Baccha, ae f.: a Bacchante, female follower of Bacchus
cantus, ūs m.: song, melody
catēna, ae f.: chain, bond
cernēns, cernentis: spying, looking upon
Cithaerōn, Cithaerōnis m.: Cithaeron, a mountain near Thebes
colō, colere, coluī, cultum: to cultivate, tend, worship, inhabit
cruciātus, ūs m.: torture, torment
crucio, cruciāre, cruciāvī, cruciātum: to torture
cruentātus, a, um: bloody, made bloody
dēmēns, dēmentis: out of one's mind, insane
etiam: (adv.) also, too
famulus, ī m.: servant, attendant
ferē: (adv.) almost, nearly

frequentō, frequentāre, frequentāvī, frequentātum: to crowd, flock to, attend
furēns, furentis: raging
instrūmentum, ī n.: tool, instrument
iō: (interj.) the cry of the Bacchantes
iūtus, a, um: helped, aided
locus, ī m.: place
nox, noctis f.: night
perstō, perstāre, perstitī, perstātum: to stand firm
profānus, a, um: not sacred, uninitiated, ordinary
pūrus, a, um: pure, clean, simple, bare
rapiō, rapere, rapuī, raptum: to seize, take, rape
sacra, sacrōrum n. pl.: sacred rites
scindō, scindere, scidī, scissum: to cut, tear asunder
spectābilis, e: visible, worth looking at
Thēbānus, a, um: of Thebes, Theban
vādō, vādere: to go, hasten

PERFECT INDICATIVE ACTIVE

First conjugation

	Singular	Plural
1st person	parāvī	parāvimus
2nd person	parāvistī	parāvistis
3rd person	parāvit	parāvērunt

Second conjugation

	Singular	Plural
1st person	inhibuī	inhibuimus
2nd person	inhibuistī	inhibuistis
3rd person	inhibuit	inhibuērunt

Third conjugation

	Singular	Plural
1st person	discessī	discessimus
2nd person	discessistī	discessistis
3rd person	discessit	discessērunt

Fourth conjugation

	Singular	Plural
1st person	audīvī	audīvimus
2nd person	audīvistī	audīvistis
3rd person	audīvit	audīvērunt

esse

	Singular	Plural
1st person	fuī	fuimus
2nd person	fuistī	fuistis
3rd person	fuit	fuērunt

In this story, the daughters of Cadmus run freely on the mountain, playing musical instruments and ululating. Pentheus is disturbed by their behavior, which is not at all in keeping with expectations for noble women. Bacchus is a god of intoxication and madness, and he embodies a freedom from the confines of societal rules. He often is attended by women and creatures such as satyrs, whose animalistic half resonates with the wild element of the god. When filled with his essence, his followers experience *ekstasis*, which is a Greek word meaning "a standing outside of oneself." Cult activity for Bacchus included both *sparagmos* of animals and *omophagia*, which is the consumption of raw flesh.

13 Mars and Venus

(*Met.* 4.167–89)

When Venus has an affair with Mars, her husband Vulcan fashions a trap for the couple out of chains which are as fine as spiderwebs.

1 Sōl prīmus adulterium Veneris et Martis vīdit. Hic deus prīmus omnia videt. Ubi
2 Venerem cum Marte vīdit, factō indoluit. Sōl furta torī et locum furtī marītō
3 Veneris, Vulcānō Iūnōnigenae, monstrāvit. Dīxit: "Vulcāne, uxōrem tuam cum
4 Marte vīdī. Herī, ubi utrōsque vīdī, in torō tuō multās hōrās consūmpserant." Cor
5 Vulcānī excidit. Mēns Vulcānī excidit. Deus opus tenēbat, et quoque illud opus dē
6 dextrā excidit.

7 Deus dē arte eius cōgitāvit. Extemplō catēnās ex aere, rēte, laqueum ēlīmāvit.
8 Hae catēnae gracilēs oculōs fallere poterant. Stāmina tenuissima illud opus
9 vincere nōn poterant, nec arānea pendentia dē summō tignō. Deus sibi dīxit: "Sī
10 Mars ad tecta et torum Veneris vēnerit, hae catēnae amantēs inlaqueābunt! Tactus
11 levis et mōmentum parvum meās insidiās efficient." Tunc catēnās lectō
12 circumdedit et laqueum collocāvit.

Commentary

1–2 *Ubi Venerem cum Marte vīdit, factō indoluit:* The verb *indolescere* takes an ablative of the thing causing pain to the subject. Translate: *He (Sōl) was pained by the deed.*

3 *Vulcānō Iūnōnigenae:* This is in apposition to *marītō*.

5 *Deus opus tenēbat:* Vulcan is a craftsman-god, so he is engaged in his work when the Sun tells him about his wife's affair with Mars.

8–9 *Stāmina tenuissima illud opus vincere nōn poterant ... tignō:* Ovid uses the verb *vincere* here to indicate that Vulcan's artistry is more delicate than the finest woven works and even spiderwebs.

11–12 *Tunc catēnās lectō circumdedit:* The verb *circumdare* takes an accusative of the thing placed and a dative of the thing around which it is placed.

adulterium, ī n.: adultery

arāneum, ī n.: spiderweb

cōgitō, cōgitāre, cōgitāvī, cōgitātum: to think, reflect, consider

collocō, collocāre, collocāvī, collocātum: to place, locate

circumdō, circumdare, circumdedī, circumdatum: to set around, surround

consūmō, consūmere, consumpsī, consumptum: to consume, spend

cor, cordis n.: heart

efficiō, efficere, effēcī, effectum: to bring about, cause to happen

ēlīmō, ēlīmāre, ēlīmāvī, ēlīmātum: to polish, elaborate, perfect

excidō, excidere, excidī: to fall out, fall from, slip

extemplō: (adv.) immediately, straightway

gracilis, e: thin, delicate

herī: (adv.) yesterday

indolescō, indolescere, indoluī: to be pained, grieve

inlaqueō, inlaqueāre, inlaqueāvī, inlaqueātum: to trap, ensnare

insidiae, ārum f.: ambush, treachery

Iūnōnigena, ae m.: son of Juno

laqueus, ī m.: noose, snare, trap

lectus, ī m.: couch, marriage bed

Mars, Martis m.: Mars, the god of springtime and war

mōmentum, ī n.: movement

nec: (adv.) and not

pendēns, pendentis: hanging

rēte, rētis n.: net

stāmen, stāminis n.: the vertical warp on a loom, woven web, wool threads

tactus, ūs m.: touch

tenuissimus, a, um: very fine, most delicate

tignum, ī n.: beam, ceiling beam

torus, ī m.: couch, bed, marriage bed

Venus, Veneris f.: Venus, the Roman goddess of love and sexuality

Vulcānus, ī m.: Vulcan, the god of craftsmen and fire

13   Ubi Venus et adulter Mars in ūnum torum vēnērunt, ambō multum mōvērunt.
14   Mōmentum laqueum effēcit, et Venus et Mārs, dēprēnsī arte marītī, in mediīs
15   amplexibus haesērunt. Extemplō Lemnius valvās eburnās patefēcit, et deōs
16   immīsit. Illī ligātī turpiter iacuērunt. Aliquis dē dīs (nōn tristibus) dixit: "Optō sīc
17   turpis esse! Sī Venus mē ad thalamum vocāverit, illūc laetus ruam." Superī
18   rīsērunt, et haec fābula nōtissima in tōtō caelō diū erat.

Commentary

14 *Mōmentum laqueum effēcit*: *Mōmentum* is the subject, and *laqueum* is the direct object.
14 *et Venus et Mārs, dēprēnsī arte marītī*: The ablative of means goes with the word *dēprēnsī*.
17–18 *Superī rīsērunt, et haec fābula nōtissima in tōtō caelō diū erat*: The word *superī* is used frequently to mean *the gods*. Ovid means that this story was very popular among the gods.

adulter, adulterī m.: adulterer

ambō, ambae, ambo: (adj. and pron.) both

amplexus, ūs m.: embrace

dēprensus, a, um: seized, caught up

eburnus, a, um: made of ivory

haereō, haerēre, haesī, haesum: to stick, get stuck

iaceō, iacēre, iacuī, iacitum: to lie

illūc: (adv.) to that place

immittō, immittere, immīsī, immissum: to send in

Lemnius, ī m.: of Lemnos, epithet of Vulcan

ligātus, a, um: tied up, caught up

nōtissimus, a, um: most known, best known

patefaciō, patefacere, patefēcī, patefactum: to throw open, open, reveal

superus, a, um: high, supreme, situated above

tōtus, a, um: whole

tristis, e: sad

turpis, e: ugly, foul, shameful

turpiter: (adv.) in shame

PLUPERFECT INDICATIVE ACTIVE

All conjugations

	Singular	Plural
1st person	consumpseram	consumpserāmus
2nd person	consumpserās	consumpserātis
3rd person	consumpserat	consumpserant

esse

	Singular	Plural
1st person	fueram	fuerāmus
2nd person	fuerās	fuerātis
3rd person	fuerat	fuerant

FUTURE PERFECT INDICATIVE ACTIVE

All conjugations

	Singular	Plural
1st person	consumpserō	consumpserimus
2nd person	consumpseris	consumpseritis
3rd person	consumpserit	consumpserint

esse

	Singular	Plural
1st person	fuerō	fuerimus
2nd person	fueris	fueritis
3rd person	fuerit	fuerint

The story of the adulterous affair of Mars and Venus first appears in Homer's *Odyssey*. There, the blind bard Demodokos entertains everyone with the story at the court of the Phaiakians, where Odysseus has washed up after years of struggling to return home from the Trojan War. Homer compares the delicate chains, which the craftsman-god Hephaestus (Vulcan's Greek counterpart) creates, to spiderwebs, a comparison which makes its way into Ovid's story. The comparison has particular significance in Homer's poem. Later, when Odysseus returns to his homeland, Homer suggests that the marriage bed of Odysseus and Penelope might be full of spiderwebs. So, Odysseus is likened to Hephaestus, and the story of Hephaestus' triumph over his wife's lover by means of his art rather than by might foreshadows Odysseus' own victory over the suitors who have been pursuing Penelope in his absence. Indeed, Odysseus and Hephaestus share the Greek epithet *polymetis*, which means "very resourceful."

14 Salmacis and Hermaphroditus

(*Met.* 4.274–388)

Ovid gives an account of how the spring of Salmacis gains the power to emasculate men who bathe in its waters.

1   Nāidēs puerum, nātum Mercuriō et dīvā Venere, sub antrīs Īdaeīs ēnūtrīvērunt. In
2   faciē puerī mātrem et patrem cognoscere poterat, et puer nōmen, Hermaphrodītum,
3   ab illīs trāxit. Ubi tria quinquennia fēcit, montēs patriōs dēseruit et in locīs ignōtīs
4   errāvit. Ad Lyciās urbēs et Cāriam vēnit. Hīc stāgnum lymphae lūcentis usque ad
5   īmum solum vīdit. Salmacis, nympha, stāgnum colēbat. Nec nympha apta vēnātuī
6   erat, nec arcum flectere solēbat. Hōc diē flōrēs legēbat ubi puerum vīdit vīsumque
7   habēre optāvit.

8   Antequam puerum appellāvit, sē composuit. Amictūs circumspexit, et vultum
9   fīnxit. Tunc dixit: "Ō dignissime puer, speciēs tua similis deō est. Sīve deus es,
10 Cupīdō esse potes. Sīve mortālis es, frāter et pater tuus sunt beātī, et soror, māter,
11 et nūtrix sunt fortūnātae. Tibi nūbere cupiō." Rubor ōra puerī notāvit. Cum nympha
12 oscula poposcit, Hermaphrodītus dixit: "Nisi dēsinēs, hunc locum et tē
13 relinquam!" Salmacis puerō respondit: "Hunc locum tibi trādō." Nympha discēdere
14 simulāvit, et sē in fruticibus silvae cēlāvit.

Commentary

1–2 *In faciē puerī mātrem et patrem cognoscere poterat*: The verb *poterat* is used impersonally here. Translate: *It was possible* ...

amictus, ūs m.: dress, garment
antequam: (conj.) before
aptus, a, um: fitted to, suited to (+ dat.)
Cāria, ae f.: Caria, a district in Asia Minor
circumspiciō, circumspicere, circumspexī, circumspectum: to look round, survey, consider
compōnō, compōnere, composuī, compositum: to compose, put together, arrange
dēsinō, dēsinere, dēsiī, dēsitum: to cease, desist, stop
dignissimus, a, um: most worthy
dīvus, a, um: divine
ēnūtriō, ēnūtrīre, ēnūtrīvī, ēnūtrītum: to nourish, bring up
fingō, fingere, finxī, fictum: to shape, fashion, form
fortūnātus, a, um: blessed, happy
frāter, frātris m.: brother
frutex, fruticis m.: shrub, bush
Hermaphrodītus, ī m.: Hermaphroditus, the son of Mercury and Venus
Īdaeus, a, um: of Mt. Ida, a mountain near Troy

īmus, a, um: lowest, deepest
lūcēns, lūcentis: shining, gleaning
Lycius, a, um: of Lycia, a region of Asia Minor
lympha, ae f.: water
Mercurius, ī m.: Mercury, the god of messengers, thieves, and merchants
nūbō, nūbere, nupsī, nuptum: to cover, veil, marry (+ dat.)
notō, notāre, notāvī, notātum: to mark
poscō, poscere, poposcī: to request, ask for, demand
quinquennium, ī n.: a period of five years
respondeō, respondēre, respondī, responsum: to answer to, reply
rubor, rubōris m.: redness
Salmacis, Salmacidis f.: Salmacis, a nymph in Caria
similis, e: like, similar to (+ dat.)
solum, ī n.: floor, bottom
speciēs, speciēī f.: view, sight, appearance
trahō, trahere, traxī, tractum: to draw, drag, take
usque: (adv.) as far as, all the way to, continuously

15   Puer, ut inobservātus, amictum dē corpore tenerō pōnit, et multum nymphae
16   placuit. Salmacis cupīdine formae nūdae exarsit. Vix moram tolerat. Iam amplexūs
17   cupit, iam sē male continet. Ille in laticēs dēsilit, et corpus in aquīs liquidīs
18   translūcet. Nympha clāmat: "Vīcī, et meus est!" Omnēs vestēs procul iactat, et sē
19   in aquam immergit. Nympha sē puerō circumfundit, ut serpēns. Hermaphrodītus
20   perstat, et gaudium spērātum nymphae dēnegat. Illa premit, et corporī puerī haeret.
21   Salmacis dīcit: "Improbe, nōn effugiēs! Dī, ōrō, sinite nullam diem sēparātiōnis
22   venīre!"

23   Deī vōta nymphae audīvērunt. Corpora iunxērunt, et ūnam faciem illīs dedērunt.
24   Membra in complexū tenācī coiērunt. Nec duo sunt, nec ūnus est. Nec fēmina est,
25   nec vir est. Neutrum et utrumque. Ubi membra mollia in undā videt,
26   Hermaphrodītus clāmat: "Mūnus nātō vestrō date, pater et māter. Sī quis in hunc
27   fontem vēnerit, facite virum sēmivirum!" Parentēs verba nātī biformis audīvērunt,
28   et fontem incestō medicāmine tinxit.

Commentary

16 *Salmacis cupīdine formae nūdae exarsit*: The word *cupīdine* is an ablative of cause, explaining the reason why the nymph becomes inflamed. *formae nūdae* is an example of an objective genitive. Translate: *Salmacis burned with desire for the nude body*.

19 *Nympha sē puerō circumfundit*: The verb *circumfundere* takes an accusative of what is poured round and a dative of what is surrounded.

20 *Illa premit, et corporī puerī haeret*: The verb *haerēre* takes the dative here.

21 *Dī, ōrō*: *Dī* = *Deī*.

21–2 *sinite nullam diem sēparātiōnis venīre*: The accusative and infinitive depend on the verb *sinere*. Translate: *allow no day of separation to come*.

26–7 *Sī quis in hunc fontem vēnerit*: *Sī quis* = *sī aliquis*. After *sī*, *nisi*, *num*, and *nē*, the first part of *aliquis, aliquid* does not appear.

biformis, e: of double form

coeō, coīre, coiī, coitum: come together, assemble

contineō, continēre, continuī, contentum: to hold together, restrain

dēnegō, dēnegāre, dēnegāvī, dēnegātum: to deny

dēsiliō, dēsilīre, dēsiluī, dēsultum: to leap down

effugiō, effugere, effūgī: to flee

exardescō, exardescere, exarsī, exarsum: to burn, become excited

gaudium, ī n.: joy, gladness

immergō, immergere, immersī, immersum: to dip, plunge, immerse

improbus, a, um: wicked

incestus, a, um: impure, defiled, sinful

inobservātus, a, um: unseen, unobserved

iungō, iungere, iunxī, iunctum: to join, unite

latex, laticis m.: liquid, fluid

liquidus, a, um: liquid, fluid

malē: (adv.) badly

medicāmen, medicāminis n.: drug, medicine, poison

mollis, e: soft, tender

neuter, neutra, neutrum: neither

parēns, parentis m. or f.: parent

placeō, placēre, placuī, placitum: to please, be agreeable to (+ dat.)

premō, premere, pressī, pressum: to press, pursue closely

sēmivir, sēmivirī m.: a half-man, effeminate man

sēparātiō, sēparātiōnis f.: severance, separation

sinō, sinere, sīvī, situs: to let alone, allow, permit

spērātus, a, um: hoped for

tenax, tenācis: holding fast, clinging

tener, tenera, tenerum: soft, delicate, youthful

tingō, tingere, tinxī, tinctum: to wet, moisten, dye, imbue

translūceō, translūcēre: to shine across, shine through

vix: (adv.) with difficulty, scarcely

FIFTH DECLENSION

	Singular	Plural
Nominative	diēs	diēs
Genitive	diēī	diērum
Dative	diēī	diēbus
Accusative	diem	diēs
Ablative	diē	diēbus

In this story, Ovid offers an aetiological myth for hermaphroditism. In general, Greek and Roman society considered women to be threatening to men's masculinity. Women were thought to be cold and wet by nature and to need constant replenishment of the fluids lost through menstruation to stay healthy. One way to replenish these lost fluids was through sexual intercourse with men. Men were considered to be warm and dry by nature, and it was thought that losing too much masculine fluid through sex with women could cause men's bodies to become soft, their voices to get higher, and, overall, their strength to weaken. Here, the fountain assumes the emasculating power of the nymph herself.

15 The transformation of Cadmus

(*Met.* 4.563–603)

As prophesied, after the misfortunes of his family in Thebes, Cadmus himself becomes a serpent.

1 Cadmus, quī conditor Thēbānus fuerat, victus luctū fortūnāque malā et territus
2 ostentīs quae plūrima vīderat, ex urbe suā relīquit. Errōrēs longī Cadmum ēgunt.
3 Dēnīque fuga conditōrem Thēbānum cum coniuge ad fīnēs Illyricōs agit. Hīc gravēs
4 malīs annīsque fāta domūs retractant, et suōs labōrēs relegunt. Cadmus dīcit:
5 "Num sacer ille serpēns, quem cuspide meā trāiēcī et cuius dentēs vīpereōs per
6 humum sparsī, erat? Sī serpēns sacer erat, dī iniūriam tam malam vindicābant. Ipse
7 igitur dēbeō esse serpēns, porrectus in alvum longam. Hoc dīs placēbit."

8 Haec dīxit, et subitō dī senem in alvum longam porrexērunt. Cadmus serpēns erat!
9 Squāmās dūrātās sēnsit. Guttae caeruleae corpus variāvērunt, et prōnus in pectus
10 cecidit. Crūra sē in ūnum commīsērunt, et paulātim in acūmen teres crēvērunt.
11 Bracchia restābant. Bracchia quae restant tendit et cum lacrimīs dīcit: "Accēde,
12 accēde, miserrima uxor, dum aliquid dē mē superest. Mē tange, et manum accipe,

Commentary

1–2 *territus ostentīs quae plūrima vīderat*: *plūrima* agrees with *quae* but is more easily construed with the antecedent *ostentīs*. Translate: *scared by the very many portents which he had seen*.

3–4 *gravēs malīs annīsque*: The ablatives *malīs* and *annīs* explain the adjective *gravēs* here. Translate: *burdened with evils and the years*.

accēdō, accēdere, accessī, accessum: to approach, come near

accipiō, accipere, accēpī, acceptum: to receive, take, hear

acūmen, acūminis n.: point, sharpness, cunning

alvus, ī f.: belly, womb

cadō, cadere, cecidī, cāsum: to fall, sink, plunge

committō, committere, commīsī, commissum: to join, combine

conditor, conditōris m.: founder

dūrātus, a, um: made hard, hard

error, errōris m.: a wandering about, mistake

fātum, ī n.: fate, destiny

fīnis, fīnis m. or f.: border, limit

gravis, e: heavy, burdened, weighed down

gutta, ae f.: drop, spot

humus, ī f.: ground

Illyricus, a, um: of Illyria, a region bordering the Adriatic Sea

luctus, ūs m.: lamentation, grief

malus, a, um: bad, evil

miserrimus, a, um: very unhappy, very miserable

num: (interrog.) introduces a question expecting a negative answer

ostentum, ī n.: marvel, portent

paulātim: (adv.) little by little, gradually

porrectus, a, um: stretched out

porrigō, porrigere, porrexī, porrectum: to lay low, stretch out, extend

prōnus, a, um: stooped forward, leaning forward

quī, quae, quod: (rel. pron.) who, which, what, that

relegō, relegere, relēgī, relectum: to gather again, go over again

restō, restāre, restitī: to remain, stand against, oppose (+ dat.)

retractō, retractāre, retractāvī, retractātum: to undertake again, recall

squāma, ae f.: scale

supersum, superesse, superfuī, superfutūrum: to be above, remain

tam: (adv.) so, to such degree

tendō, tendere, tetendī, tentum and tensum: to stretch out, extend

teres, teretis: rounded, polished, smooth

trāiciō, trāicere, trāiēcī, trāiectum: to throw, pierce, penetrate

variō, variāre, variāvī, variātum: to change, alter, diversify

vindicō, vindicāre, vindicāvī, vindicātum: to make a claim, avenge

13   dum manus est, dum anguis tōtum mē nōn occupat!" Ille quidem plūra dīcere
14   cupiēbat, sed repente lingua in duās partēs fissa est. Quotiēscumque aliquōs
15   questūs ēdere parat, sībilat. Haec vōx quam nātūra illī relīquit erat.

16   Coniunx feriēns pectora nūda manū exclāmat: "Ō Cadme, infēlīx, manē et formam
17   quam serpēns habēre dēbet exue! Cadme, quid hoc est? Ubi pedēs, ubi umerī
18   manūsque, ubi color et faciēs et omnia? Cūr nōn, superī, mē quoque in eandem
19   anguem vertitis?" Dīxerat et ille ōra uxōris lambēbat, amplexūs dabat, adsuētum
20   collum petēbat. Quisquis adest (comitēs aderant) vīsū territus est. Illa collum
21   lūbricum dracōnis cristātī permulcet, et subitō duo dracōnēs serpunt. Quī tunc in
22   latebrās subeunt. Nunc dracōnēs placidī meminērunt vītae quam prius habēbant,
23   nec hominēs fugiunt nec hominēs vulnere laedunt.

Commentary

21–2 *Quī tunc in latebrās subeunt*: The relative pronoun *quī* introduces this sentence. Its antecedunt is *dracōnēs* in the previous sentence. It is not uncommon in Latin for sentences to begin with relative pronouns which refer to nouns and pronouns appearing earlier in the text.
22 *meminērunt vītae*: Verbs of remembering and forgetting often take a genitive object.
23 *hominēs vulnere laedunt*: Take *hominēs* as the object of *laedunt*.

adsuētus, a, um: customary, usual, familiar

color, colōris m.: color, hue

cūr: (interrog. adv.) why

cristātus, a, um: crested, plumed

draco, dracōnis m.: snake

ēdō, ēdere, ēdidī, ēditum: to put forth, give out, make known

exclamō, exclamāre, exclamāvī, exclamātum: to cry aloud, call out

exuō, exuere, exuī, exūtum: to take off, lay aside

feriēns, ferientis: beating, striking

fissus, a, um: split, divided

infēlix, infēlīcis: unhappy

laedō, laedere, laesī, laesum: to strike, injure

latebra, ae f.: retreat, hiding place

lūbricus, a, um: slippery, smooth

meminī, meminisse: (defect. verb) to remember (+ gen.)

permulceō, permulcēre, permulsī, permulsum: to stroke, soften

placidus, a, um: quiet, gentle

plūs, plūris: more

prior, ius: former, previous

questus, ūs m.: complaining, complaint

quidem: (adv.) surely, in fact, indeed

quisquis, quaequae, quidquid: whoever, whichever, whatever

quotiēscumque: (conj.) however often

repente: (adv.) suddenly

serpō, serpere, serpsī, serptum: to crawl, creep

sībilō, sībilāre, sībilāvī, sībilātum: to hiss

subeō, subīre, subiī or subīvī, subitum: to go under, pass under

vīta, ae f.: life

RELATIVE CLAUSES

Relative clauses appear with great frequency in Latin, so it is important to understand how they work. Relative clauses allow one sentence to be subordinated to another. In the sentence *Cadmus, quī conditor Thēbānus fuerat, victus luctū fortūnāque malā et territus ostentīs quae plūrima vīderat, ex urbe suā relīquit*, the sentence *Cadmus conditor Thēbānus fuerat* has been subordinated to and embedded within the sentence *Cadmus victus luctū fortūnāque malā et territus ostentīs quae plūrima vīderat ex urbe suā relīquit*. The first sentence thus becomes a relative clause within the second sentence. Relative clauses are introduced by relative pronouns, which, like any pronouns, stand for nouns. A relative pronoun takes its gender and number from its antecedent, but its grammatical function in the relative clause determines its case. In the sentence *Num sacer ille serpēns, quem cuspide meā trāiēcī et cuius dentēs vīpereōs per humum sparsī, erat?*, the relative pronoun *quem* is masculine and singular because its antecedent is *serpēns*, and it is in the accusative case because it functions as the direct object of *trāiēcī* within the relative clause. The relative pronoun *cuius* is masculine and singular because it also refers to *serpēns*, but it is in the genitive case because it indicates possession within the relative clause. Translate: *That was not a sacred serpent **which** I pierced with my spear and **whose** snaky teeth I scattered on the ground, was it?*

Relative pronoun

	Singular			*Plural*		
	Masculine	*Feminine*	*Neuter*	*Masculine*	*Feminine*	*Neuter*
Nominative	quī	quae	quod	quī	quae	quae
Genitive	cuius	cuius	cuius	quōrum	quārum	quōrum
Dative	cui	cui	cui	quibus	quibus	quibus
Accusative	quem	quam	quod	quōs	quās	quae
Ablative	quō	quā	quō	quibus	quibus	quibus

The story of Cadmus turning into a snake occurs in Book 4 of Ovid's poem, but it refers back to the story about the foundation of Thebes in Book 3. There, Cadmus slays a serpent and, when instructed to do so by Minerva, sows the teeth of the serpent in the ground, from which armed men grow. In general, snakes are chthonic symbols and signify a close connection to the earth. Athens, like Thebes, had myths about its foundation which involved snakes. Cecrops, an early king of Athens, was thought to be sprung from the earth and to have a snake's form on the lower half of his body, and Erichthonius, another early figure, also was part serpent. The Athenians, like the Thebans, considered themselves to be *autochthonous*.

16 Perseus and Atlas

(*Met.* 4.604–62)

When Atlas refuses to extend hospitality to Perseus, a son of Jupiter by Danaë, Perseus turns the giant into a mountain using the freshly severed head of Medusa.

1   Postquam Medūsa ā Perseō, quem Danaē ā pluviō aurō concēperat, necāta erat,
2   spolium monstrī vīpereī ā victōre portābātur. Perseus āera tenerum ālīs strīdentibus
3   carpsit. Cum victor super harēnās Libycās pendēbat, guttae cruentae capitis
4   Gorgoneī cecidērunt, quās terra excēpit et in angues variōs animāvit, unde illa terra
5   est infesta serpentibus. Inde Perseus per immēnsum spatium caelī ventīs
6   discordibus actus est, nunc hūc, nunc illūc, ut nūbēs aquōsae. Terrās despectat, et
7   tōtum orbem supervolat. Ter Arctōs gelidās, ter bracchia Cancrī vīdit. Iamque diēs
8   cadēbat, et, veritus sē noctī crēdere, in Hesperiā, regnō Atlantis, constitit. Hīc
9   requiēs ā victōre petīta est.

Commentary

1 *quem Danaē ā pluviō aurō concēperat*: In myth, when Danaë is locked away in a bronze chamber, Zeus visits and impregnates her in the form of a golden shower. Perseus is the product of the encounter.

2–3 *Perseus āera tenerum ... carpsit*: *āera* is accusative singular.

8 *veritus sē noctī crēdere*: The word *veritus*, meaning *fearful, fearing*, takes an explanatory infinitive here. Translate: *fearing to trust himself to the night*.

āēr, āeris m.: air

āla, ae f.: wing

animō, animāre, animāvī, animātum: to endow with life

aquōsus, a, um: watery

Arctos, ī f.: the constellations known as Great and Little Bear, the north

Atlās, Atlantis m.: Atlas, the god who holds up the sky

carpō, carpere, carpsī, carptum: to pluck, choose, seize

concipiō, concipere, concēpī, conceptum: to receive, take completely, conceive

crēdō, crēdere, crēdidī, crēditum: to trust, believe (+ dat.)

Danaē, ēs f.: Danaë, daughter of Acrisius and mother of Perseus

despectō, despectāre, despectāvī, despectātum: to look down

discors, discordis: disagreeing, opposed, not harmonious

excipiō, excipere, excēpī, exceptum: to take out, except, receive

Gorgoneus, a, um: of a Gorgon, belonging to a Gorgon

harēna, ae f.: sand

Hesperia, ae f.: Hesperia, a western land

iamque: (adv.) now, already

infestus, a, um: unsafe, dangerous, infested

Libycus, a, um: of Libya

Medūsa, ae f.: Medusa, a mortal Gorgon whose gaze causes petrification

necātus, a, um: having been killed

pendeō, pendēre, pependī: to hang suspended, suspend

Perseus, ī m.: Perseus, a son of Jupiter

postquam: (conj.) after

regnum, ī n.: rule, kingship, kingdom

requiēs, requiētis f.: rest

spolium, ī n.: spoil, booty

strīdēns, strīdentis: hissing, vibrating

super: (prep. + acc.) over, above

supervolō, supervolāre, supervolāvī, supervolātum: to fly above

ter: (adv.) three times

unde: (adv.) from where

veritus, a, um: fearful, fearing

10   Hīc Atlās, fīlius Īapetī, praestāns cunctīs hominibus corpore ingentī fuit. Mille
11   gregēs illī totidemque armenta per herbās errābant. Atlās arborem, cuius rāmī
12   radiantēs aurō erant et cuius pōma aurea erant, habēbat. "Hospes," Perseus illī
13   dixit, "Sī glōria magnī generis tē tangit (auctor generis mihi est Iuppiter),
14   hospitium requiemque petō." Sed ille memor sortis vetustae erat, quam Themis
15   dederat: "Tempus, Atlās, veniet quō tua arbor aurō spoliābitur, et nātus Iove hunc
16   titulum praedae habēbit." Atlās territus pōmārium moenibus clauserat, et omnēs
17   externōs ā suīs fīnibus serpente vastō arcēbat. Atlās Perseō dixit: "Vāde procul!
18   Hospitium tibi nōn dabō!"

19   Perseus, īrātus, Atlantī dixit: "Accipe mūnus, quoniam mea grātia parvī tibi est!"
20   Victor, versus retrō, faciem Medūsae porrexit. Subitō Atlās mōns factus est! Barba
21   et comae in silvās mūtātae sunt, et umerī manūsque iuga erant. Quod caput ante fuit,
22   nunc cacūmen in summō monte est. Ossa lapidēs facta sunt. Tum in immēnsum
23   crēvit, et caelum cum tot sīderibus in illō requiēvit.

Commentary

10 *praestāns cūnctīs hominibus corpore ingentī fuit*: The ablative explains in which capacity Atlas excels.

19 *quoniam mea grātia parvī tibi est*: The word *parvī* is a genitive of value, indicating what something is worth. Translate: *since my favor is worth little to you*.

22–3 *Tum in immēnsum crēvit*: The adjective *immēnsum* is used as a substantive here.

arceō, arcēre, arcuī, arctum: to enclose, shut in, keep at a distance

auctor, auctōris m.: author, progenitor, founder

barba, ae f.: beard

cacūmen, cacūminis n.: top, point, summit

claudō, claudere, clausī, clausum: to close, make inaccessible

coma, ae f.: hair

cunctus, a, um: all, collectively, the whole

externus, a, um: foreign, strange

genus, generis n.: birth, origin, class, type

glōria, ae f.: glory, fame

grātia, ae f.: favor, indulgence, service

grex, gregis m.: herd, flock

hospes, hospitis m.: host, guest, stranger

hospitium, ī n.: hospitality

iugum, ī n.: yoke, team of draft animals, mountain ridge

Īapetus, ī m.: Iapetus, the father of Atlas

memor, memoris: mindful, remembering

pōmārium, ī n.: orchard, garden for fruit

pōmum, ī n.: fruit

praeda, ae f.: spoil, plunder

praestāns, praestantis: standing before, excelling (+ dat.)

radiāns, radiantis: shining, gleaming

sīdus, sīderis n.: star, constellation

spoliō, spoliāre, spoliāvī, spoliātum: strip, despoil, rob

titulus, ī m.: glory, title, honor

tot: (adv.) so many

totidem: (indecl. adj.) just as many

vastus, a, um: empty, desolate, enormous

vetustus, a, um: old

PASSIVE VERB FORMS

Present indicative passive

	Singular	*Plural*
1st person	animor	animāmur
2nd person	animāris	animāminī
3rd person	animātur	animantur

Imperfect indicative passive

	Singular	*Plural*
1st person	praestābar	praestābāmur
2nd person	praestābāris	praestābāminī
3rd person	praestābātur	praestābantur

Future indicative passive

	Singular	*Plural*
1st person	claudar	claudēmur
2nd person	clauderis	claudēminī
3rd person	claudētur	claudentur

Perfect indicative passive

	Singular	*Plural*
1st person	requiētus sum	requiētī sumus
2nd person	requiētus es	requiētī estis
3rd person	requiētus est	requiētī sunt

Pluperfect indicative passive

	Singular	*Plural*
1st person	requiēta eram	requiētae erāmus
2nd person	requiēta erās	requiētae erātis
3rd person	requiēta erat	requiētae erant

Future perfect indicative passive

	Singular	Plural
1st person	requiētum erō	requiēta erimus
2nd person	requiētum eris	requiēta eritis
3rd person	requiētum erit	requiēta erunt

In this story, Perseus turns Atlas into a mountain by holding out Medusa's severed head. The three Gorgons were called Sthenno, Euryale, and Medusa. They are often represented as hideous women with snakes for hair, large round eyes, protruding tongues, and wings. Their apotropaic, mask-like gaze has the power to turn men to stone, and thus their land features many statues of humans who made the mistake of looking at them. Medusa was the only mortal Gorgon, and, in myth, Perseus manages to avoid her lethal stare by using his shield to look at her reflection rather than directly at her. When Perseus kills Medusa, the hero Chrysaor and the winged horse Pegasus are born from her body.

17 Perseus and Andromeda

(*Met.* 4.663–803)

Perseus rescues the princess Andromeda from a sea-monster and tells guests at their wedding the story of how he conquered the Gorgon and how Medusa came to have snakes in her hair.

1   Ubi Perseus spolium memorābile monstrī vīpereī portābat et āera tenerum
2   carpēbat, populōs Aethiopicōs et arva Cēphēa conspexit. Ibi Andromeda immerita
3   poenās mātris, quae deōs violāverat, dabat. Perseus vincula fēminam bellam ad
4   cautēs dūrās religāre vīdit. Tunc bēluam magnam ex undā venīre vīdit. Fīlius Iovis
5   parentibus fēminae dīxit sē Andromedam servātūrum esse. Dixit: "Sī mea nūpta
6   erit, Andromedam ē dentibus bēluae ēripiam!" Cassiopē et Cēpheus lēgem
7   accipiunt, et fīliō Iovis regnum dōtāle prōmittunt. Tunc Perseus bēluam necat, et
8   Andromedam ā vinculīs līberat.

9   Cassiopē et Cēpheus gaudent, et generum salūtant. Dīcunt Perseum servātōrem
10   domūs esse. Prōtinus Perseus Andromedam praemium factī magnī rapit. Hymēn
11   Amorque taedās praecutiunt. Odōrēs ignēs satiant, serta dē tectīs pendunt, et
12   ubīque lyra, tībia, et cantus sonant. Valvae reserātae sunt, et ātria aurea patent.
13   Procerēs Cēphēni rēgiam intrant, et convīvium magnum est.

Commentary

2–3 *Ibi Andromeda immerita ... dabat*: Cassiopea, Andromeda's mother, had offended the gods by boasting that she was more beautiful than the Nereids.

Aethiopicus, a, um: Ethiopian

Andromeda, ae: Andromeda, an Ethiopian princess

ātrium, ī n.: hall

bēlua, ae f.: beast, monster

Cassiopē, ēs f.: Cassiopea, mother of Andromeda

cautēs, cautis f.: crag, cliff

Cēphēnus, a, um: of Cepheus, ruled by Cepheus

Cēphēus, a, um: of Cepheus, a king of Ethiopia

Cēpheus, ī m.: Cepheus, father of Andromeda

conspiciō, conspicere, conspexī, conspectum: to look at, observe

convīvium, ī n.: banquet, feast

dōtālis, e: given as part of a dowry

gener, generī m.: son-in-law

Hymēn, Hymenis m.: Hymen, a god of marriage

immeritus, a, um: undeserving

lex, lēgis f.: a law, formal agreement

līberō, līberāre, līberāvī, līberātus: to free

lyra, ae f.: lyre

memorābilis, e: memorable, remarkable

nūpta, ae f.: married woman, wife

odor, odōris m.: smell

pateō, patēre, patuī: to lie open, be accessible

praecutiō, praecutere, praecussī, praecussum: to shake in front

praemium, ī n.: profit, reward

procer, proceris m.: a chief, prince, noble

prōmittō, prōmittere, prōmīsī, prōmissum: to promise

religō, religāre, religāvī, religātum: to tie

reserātus, a, um: unbarred, opened

salūtō, salūtāre, salūtāvī, salūtātum: to greet, say goodbye to

satiō, satiāre, satiāvī, satiātum: to satisfy, fill

servātor, servātōris m.: savior

taeda, ae f.: torch

ubīque: (adv.) everywhere

vinculum, ī n.: chain, bond

14   Postquam procerēs famem epulīs et sitim mūnere Bacchī satiāvērunt, Perseus
15   mōrēs animumque virōrum Cēphēnōrum quaesīvit. Quī ēdocuit dixit: "Nunc, ō
16   fortissime, dīc fābulam Gorgonis. Quantā virtūte et quibus artibus caput Medūsae,
17   crīnītum dracōnibus, superāvistī?" Perseus narrāvit sē per agrōs simulācra
18   hominum et ferārum conversa in silicem vīdisse, et sē tamen imāginem Medūsae in
19   clipeō aereō adspexisse. Somnum gravem dracōnēs et ipsam tenuisse, et sē caput ē
20   collō ēripuisse. Tunc fīlius Iovis dīxit Pēgasum et frātrem dē sanguine Gorgonis
21   nātōs esse.

22   Ūnus ex numerō procerum quaesīvit: "Cūr Medūsa sōla capillōs mixtōs anguibus
23   habet?" Hospes dīxit prīmam formam Medūsae esse clārissimam et capillōs esse
24   bellissimam partem tōtīus corporis. "Dīcunt rēctōrem pontī hanc fēminam bellam
25   in templō Minervae vitiāvisse. Minerva vultum castum aegide cēlāvit, et tunc
26   crīnem Gorgoneum in hydrōs turpēs mūtāvit. Nunc quoque dea anguēs quōs fēcit
27   in aegide suā sustinet."

Commentary

14 *sitim mūnere Bacchī satiāvērunt*: *sitim* is accusative singular.

15 *Quī ēdocuit dixit*: The relative clause *quī ēdocuit* serves as the subject of the verb *dixit*. The person who asks Perseus to share the story about his conquest of the Gorgon is the man who answers Perseus' questions about local customs and mentality.

17–18 *Perseus narrāvit ... in silicem*: *conversa* agrees with *simulācra*.

19–20 *Somnum gravem ... ēripuisse*: The indirect statement is dependent on the verb *narrāvit* in the previous sentence.

24 *rēctōrem pontī*: This descriptive phrase refers to Neptune, the god governing salty waters and the sea.

adspiciō, adspicere, adspexī, adspectum: to look at, notice

aegis, aegidis f.: aegis, special chest-armor embellished with a Gorgon-head

aereus, a, um: of bronze

bellissimus, a, um: most beautiful

clārissimus, a, um: brightest, clearest, most famous

clipeus, ī m.: shield

conversus, a, um: turned

crīnis, crīnis m.: hair

crīnītus, a, um: hairy

ēdoceō, ēdocēre, ēdocuī, ēdoctum: to explain, inform fully

epulae, ārum f. pl.: food, feast

famēs, famis f.: hunger

fortissimus, a, um: strongest, bravest

Gorgō, Gorgonis f.: Gorgon, a mythical monster

hydrus, ī m.: water-snake

mixtus, a, um: mixed

mōs, mōris m.: custom, habit

numerus, ī m.: a number

Pēgasus, ī m.: Pegasus, flying horse born from Medusa

rēctor, rēctōris m.: ruler

silex, silicis m.: stone

sitis, sitis f.: thirst

somnus, ī n.: sleep

sustineō, sustinēre, sustenuī, sustentum: to hold up, carry, sustain

virtūs, virtūtis f.: manliness, excellence, virtue

vitiō, vitiāre, vitiāvī, vitiātum: to injure, damage, rape

INFINITIVES

Active

Present	tenēre	to hold
Perfect	tenuisse	to have held
Future	tentūrus, a, um esse	to be about to hold

Passive

Present	tenērī	to be held
Perfect	tentus, a, um esse	to have been held
Future	tentum īrī	to be about to be held

INDIRECT STATEMENT

Indirect speech occurs when direct speech is reported by someone, as in the sentence *He said that the sailor was large*. The direct statement here would be *the sailor is large*, but it has been subordinated to the statement *he said*, thus turning it into indirect speech. Indirect statement occurs after verbs of speaking, thinking, perceiving, etc. and is constructed with an accusative subject plus an infinitive. In Latin, the sentence above would be *Dīxit nautam ingentem esse*. Thus, the sentence *Dīcunt Perseum servātōrem domūs esse* should be translated *They say that Perseus is the savior of the household*.

The overall structure of the *Metamorphoses* is complicated, and Ovid frequently embeds stories within other stories, thus creating multiple levels of narration. Here, Ovid has embedded the story about Perseus slaying Medusa within the story of Perseus and Andromeda. In the Western tradition, the epic convention of embedded narration dates back to Homer, who has Odysseus himself narrate several books of the *Odyssey*. In a poetic performance of his own, Odysseus describes to the Phaiakians his adventures since the Trojan War. Interestingly, Odysseus has a reputation for lying and thus may not be an entirely reliable narrator of his own exploits.

18 The rape of Proserpina
(*Met.* 5.346–571)

Proserpina is captured by Pluto, the god of the Underworld, and taken to his dark realm to be his wife.

1   Haud procul Hennaeīs moenibus lacus aquae altae est. Silva cingēns aquās corōnat,
2   et suīs frondibus ictūs Phoebēōs summovet. Rāmī frīgus dant, et humus ūmida
3   flōrēs Tyriōs dat. Vēr est perpetuum. Quō in locō Prōserpina lūdēns violās aut
4   candida līlia carpēbat. Dum studiō puellārī calathum implēns cum puellīs legere
5   multōs flōrēs certat, ā Plūtōne vīsa, amāta, et rapta est. Puella territa mātrem et
6   comitēs, sed mātrem saepius, clāmāvit. Raptor Prōserpinae incitāns equōs currum
7   ēgit.

8   Est aequor quod inclūsum cornibus angustīs coit. Hīc Cyanē erat, celeberrima inter
9   nymphās Sīcelidēs, ā cuius nōmine stāgnum dictum est. Quae mediā alvō exstāns
10   currum Dītis vīdit et deam agnōvit. "Nōn longius ībis! Nōn potes esse gener
11   Cereris invītae. Dēbēs rogāre nec rapere!" Dīxit, et tendēns bracchia in partēs
12   dīversās obstitit. Haud ultrā Dīs īram tenuit equōsque terribilēs hortātus sceptrum
13   rēgāle in īma gurgitis condidit. Tellūs icta viam in Tartara fēcit, et currum prōnum
14   in mediō crātēre recēpit. Cyanē, maerēns deam raptam et iūra contempta suī fontis,
15   vulnus inconsōlabile in mente gessit. Lacrimīs absumpta est, et ipsa in suās aquās
16   licuit.

Commentary

1 *Haud procul Hennaeīs moenibus*: The ablative follows the adverb *procul*. Translate: *Scarcely far from Henna's walls.*

8 *quod inclūsum cornibus angustīs coit*: The sea is formed by the points of land which enclose it.

12 *equōsque terribilēs hortātus*: The participle *hortātus* takes *equosque terribilēs* as its object.

absūmō, absumere, absumpsī, absumptum: to reduce, consume

aequor, aequoris n.: flat surface, plain, sea

agnoscō, agnoscere agnōvī, agnītum: to recognize, know

angustus, a, um: narrow, confined

aut: (conj.) or

calathus, ī m.: wicker basket

candidus, a, um: shining, bright, white

celeberrimus, a, um: very famous, most celebrated

Cerēs, Cereris f.: Ceres, goddess of grain and agriculture

cingō, cingere, cinxī, cinctum: to gird, surround

condō, condere, condidī, condītum: to found, hide, bury

contemnō, contemnere, contempsī, contemptum: to despise, think badly of

coronō, coronāre, coronāvī, coronātum: to wreathe, crown

crātēr, crātēris m.: mixing bowl, fissure in the earth

currus, ūs m.: chariot

Cyanē, ēs f.: Cyane, a Sicilian nymph

Dīs, Dītis m.: Dis, another name for Pluto

exstō, exstāre: to stand out, show oneself

frīgus, frīgoris n.: cold, coolness

gurges, gurgitis m.: whirlpool, pool

haud: (adv.) not at all, by no means

Hennaeus, a, um: of Henna, a Sicilian city

hortātus, a, um: having urged

īciō, īcere, īcī, ictum: to strike, hit

incitō, incitāre, incitāvī, incitātum: to urge, motivate, excite

inclūdō, inclūdere, inclūsī, inclūsum: to close in, enclose

inconsōlābilis, e: incurable, inconsolable

invītus, a, um: unwilling

iūs, iūris n.: right, law

lacus, ūs m.: hollow, lake

līlium, ī n.: lily

liquescō, liquescere, licuī: to become liquid, dissolve, melt

longius: (adv.) farther

maereō, maerēre: to mourn, grieve

perpetuus, a, um: continuous, unending

Phoebeus, a, um: of Phoebus, of Apollo

Plūto, Plūtōnis m.: Pluto, god of the Underworld

Prōserpina, ae f.: Proserpina, goddess of springtime

puellāris, e: girlish

raptor, raptōris m.: robber, kidnapper, rapist

recipiō, recipere, recēpī, receptum: to take back, recover

rēgālis, e: royal

saepius: (adv.) more often

Sīcelis, Sīcelidis: of Sicily

summoveō, summovēre, summōvī, summōtum: to move up from below, drive off, remove

Tartara, ōrum n. pl.: Tartarus, the infernal regions

tellūs, tellūris f.: earth, ground

terreō, terrēre, terruī, territum: to terrify, alarm

terribilis, e: dreadful, frightful

ultrā: (adv.) beyond, further

viola, ae f.: a violet

17   Intereā Cerēs, petēns filiam, per multās terrās ad Cyanēn vēnit. Nympha deae
18   omnia quae vīderat dīcere nōn poterat, sed signa tamen manifesta dedit. Zōnam
19   Persephonēs in undīs ostendit, quam dea agnōvit. Nunc Cerēs filiam raptam esse
20   scīvit. Dīva capillōs inordinātōs laniāvit et pectus percussit. Arātra glaebās
21   vertentia frēgit, et īrāta agricolās bovēsque lētō dedit. Fertilitās terrae dēficere
22   incēpit. Deinde Arethūsa, nympha fontis Sīcelidis, deae dixit Prōserpinam nunc
23   rēgīnam tyrannī infernī esse. Māter stupuit.

24   Mox invidiōsa ante Iovem stat. Dea dīcit: "Supplex tibi vēnī, Iuppiter. Sī nulla
25   grātia mātris est, fātum filiae movēre patrem dēbet. Tua filia digna marītō quī eam
26   rapuit nōn est." Rēx deōrum respondet: "Hoc factum nōn est iniūria, sed amor. Dīs,
27   frāter meus, gener nōbīs pudendus nōn erit. Sed sī illīc nullōs cibōs contigit,
28   Prōserpina caelum repetet." Puella autem septem grāna pōmī pūniceī ēderat. At
29   Iuppiter, medius frātris sorōrisque maestae, annum volventem aequē dīvidit. Nunc
30   dea, nūmen commūne duōrum regnōrum, cum mātre totidem mensēs, cum coniuge
31   totidem mensēs est.

Commentary

21 *īrāta agricolās bovēsque lētō dedit*: Translated literally, this sentence means *angry, she gave farmers and cows to ruin*. In other words, Ceres causes the earth and its creatures to become infertile.

24–5 *Sī nulla grātia mātris est, fātum filiae movēre patrem dēbet*: Ceres means that if her own indignation about her daughter's rape does not move Jupiter, his own concern should move him. Proserpina is Jupiter's daughter by Ceres.

25–6 *Tua filia digna marītō quī eam rapuit nōn est*: Approach this sentence as if it reads *Tua filia nōn est digna marītō quī eam rapuit*.

30–1 *totidem mensēs ... totidem mensēs est*: The accusatives indicate extent of time.

aequē: (adv.) equally

arātrum, ī n.: plow

Arethūsa, ae f.: Arethusa, a Sicilian nymph

cibus, ī m.: food

commūnis, e: that which is shared, common

contingō, contingere, contigī, contactum: to touch, affect

dēficiō, dēficere, dēfēcī, dēfectum: to fail, run short, become weak

dīversus, a, um: separate, different, opposed

dīvidō, dīvidere, dīvīsī, divīsum: to divide

ēdō, ēdere, ēdī, ēsum: to eat

fertilitās, fertilitātis f.: fruitfulness, fertility

frangō, frangere, frēgī, fractum: to break, break into pieces

grānum, ī n.: grain, seed

illīc: (adv.) there, in that place

infernus, a, um: lower, from below

invidiōsus, a, um: envious, hateful, hostile

laniō, laniāre, laniāvī, laniātum: to tear to pieces

lētum, ī n.: death, ruin

maestus, a, um: sad, dejected

manifestus, a, um: clear, visible

ostendō, ostendere, ostendī, ostentum: to show, hold out, display

pudendus, a, um: deserving of shame, shameful

pūniceus, a, um: red, purple

volvō, volvere, volvī, volūtum: to roll, twist, turn round

PARTICIPLES

Participles are adjectives which derive from verbs, so they possess both verbal and adjectival elements. Like any adjectives, they have masculine, feminine, and neuter forms. While they function grammatically as adjectives within a sentence, their verbal essence can govern objects, introduce indirect statement, and introduce subjunctive clauses, for example. There are four participles in Latin. The present active participle is declined as a third declension adjective while the other participles are declined as first-second declension adjectives.

Present active

	Singular			Plural		
	Masculine	*Feminine*	*Neuter*	*Masculine*	*Feminine*	*Neuter*
Nominative	obstāns	obstāns	obstāns	obstantēs	obstantēs	obstantia
Genitive	obstantis	obstantis	obstantis	obstantium	obstantium	obstantium
Dative	obstantī	obstantī	obstantī	obstantibus	obstantibus	obstantibus
Accusative	obstantem	obstantem	obstāns	obstantēs	obstantēs	obstantia
Ablative	obstantī/e	obstantī/e	obstantī/e	obstantibus	obstantibus	obstantibus

Perfect passive

	Singular			Plural		
	Masculine	*Feminine*	*Neuter*	*Masculine*	*Feminine*	*Neuter*
Nominative	lūsus	lūsa	lūsum	lūsī	lūsae	lūsa
Genitive	lūsī	lūsae	lūsī	lūsōrum	lūsārum	lūsōrum
Dative	lūsō	lūsae	lūsō	lūsīs	lūsīs	lūsīs
Accusative	lūsum	lūsam	lūsum	lūsōs	lūsās	lūsa
Ablative	lūsō	lūsā	lūsō	lūsīs	lūsīs	lūsīs

Future active

	Singular			Plural		
	Masculine	*Feminine*	*Neuter*	*Masculine*	*Feminine*	*Neuter*
Nominative	fractūrus	fractūra	fractūrum	fractūrī	fractūrae	fractūra
Genitive	fractūrī	fractūrae	fractūrī	fractūrōrum	fractūrārum	fractūrōrum
Dative	fractūrō	fractūrae	fractūrō	fractūrīs	fractūrīs	fractūrīs
Accusative	fractūrum	fractūram	fractūrum	fractūrōs	fractūrās	fractūra
Ablative	fractūrō	fractūrā	fractūrō	fractūrīs	fractūrīs	fractūrīs

Future passive (gerundive)

	Singular			Plural		
	Masculine	Feminine	Neuter	Masculine	Feminine	Neuter
Nominative	cingendus	cingenda	cingendum	cingendī	cingendae	cingenda
Genitive	cingendī	cingendae	cingendī	cingendōrum	cingendārum	cingendōrum
Dative	cingendō	cingendae	cingendō	cingendīs	cingendīs	cingendīs
Accusative	cingendum	cingendam	cingendum	cingendōs	cingendās	cingenda
Ablative	cingendō	cingendā	cingendō	cingendīs	cingendīs	cingendīs

Translations

Present active	obstāns	standing against
Perfect passive	lūsa	having been played
Future active	fractūrum	about to break
Future passive (gerundive)	cingendus	to be surrounded

Ovid's account of the rape of Proserpina is actually narrated by Calliope, the Muse of epic poetry, as part of a musical contest. With her excellent tale sung on behalf of the Muses, Calliope wins the competition against the Pierides, who are punished by being turned into magpies for foolishly thinking that they could sing better than the Muses. Minerva listens to the account of the contest in Book 5 and is inspired by the Muses' victory. At the beginning of the next book, the goddess of weaving turns her mind to Arachne, a famous weaver who has refused in her artistry to yield to Minerva. Minerva and Arachne then engage in their own competition. The connection between the two narratives further demonstrates the complexity of the structure of Ovid's poem.

19 Arachne and Minerva

(*Met.* 6.1–145)

When Arachne does not properly acknowledge Minerva's preeminence as an artist, the goddess contends with the mortal weaver.

1   Fābulā dē Prōserpinā narrātā, Minerva carmina Mūsārum probāvit. Tum sēcum
2   dixit: "laudāre est parum; dēbeō laudārī et nōn sinere meum nūmen spernī sine
3   poenā." Animum fātīs Maeoniae Arachnēs intendit, quam sibi nōn cēdere
4   laudibus artis lānificae audīverat. Nōn sōlum vestēs factās, sed quoque illam
5   labōrantem spectāre multīs iuvābat, sīve rudem lānam in prīmōs orbēs glomerābat,
6   seu opus digitīs subigēbat, seu vellera aequantia nebulās repetītaque longō tractū
7   molliēbat, sīve fūsum teretem levī pollice versābat. Omnēs Arachnēn doctam esse
8   ā Minervā putābant, sed illa tamen negābat. Saepe Arachnē dīcēbat: "Minerva
9   mēcum certāre dēbet!"

10   Pallas anum simulat, et cānōs falsōs in tempora artūsque īnfirmōs, quōs baculō
11   sustinet, addit. Tum puellae Maeoniae dixit: "Nōn grandior aetās omnia quae
12   fugimus habet: ūsus ā sērīs annīs venit. Nē sperne meum consilium. Cēde deae et
13   rogā veniam tuīs dictīs. Illa veniam tibi rogantī dabit." Arachnē īrāta respondit:
14   "Inops mentis et confecta longā senectā venīs! Nimium diū vixisse nocet! Cūr dea

Commentary

1 *Fābulā dē Prōserpinā ... probāvit*: The story of Arachne and Minerva at the beginning of Book 6 of the poem follows an account of a singing contest between the Muses and the Pierides in Book 5. Calliope, the Muse of epic poetry, tells Minerva about the singing contest, in which she had sung the story of the rape of Proserpina.

2–3 *laudāre est parum ... spernī sine poenā*: *laudāre* is the subject of *est*, and *spernī* is a passive infinitive.

4–5 *vestēs factās ... illam labōrantem spectāre multīs iuvābat*: The infinitive *spectāre* is the subject of *iuvābat*. *vestēs factās* and *illam labōrantem* are objects of *spectāre*.

5–7 *sīve rudem lānam in prīmōs orbēs glomerābat ... levī pollice versābat*: Ovid vividly describes the process of turning raw wool into thread and rolling it up on a spindle in preparation for weaving.

11–12 *Nōn grandior aetās omnia quae fugimus habet*: Approach this as if it reads *Nōn grandior aetās habet omnia quae fugimus*.

14 *Nimium diū vixisse nocet*: The infinitive is the subject of *nocet*.

aetās, aetātis f.: age, period of life

aequō, aequāre, aequāvī, aequātum: to equal, make equal

Arachnē, ēs f.: Arachne, a Maeonian weaver

carmen, carminis n.: song, poem

cēdō, cēdere, cessī, cessum: to depart, yield (+ dat.)

conficiō, conficere, confēcī, confectum: to accomplish, wear out

consilium, ī n.: deliberation, counsel, plan, advice

fūsus, ī m.: spindle

glomerō, glomerāre, glomerāvī, glomerātum: to gather into a ball

grandior, grandius: bigger, greater

īnfirmus, a, um: feeble, weak

inops, inopis: lacking in (+ gen.)

intendō, intendere, intendī, intentum: to direct, stretch

lāna, ae f.: wool

lānificus, a, um: having to do with wool-working

laus, laudis f.: praise

Maeonius, a, um: of Maeonia, the eastern part of Lydia in Asia Minor

molliō, mollīre, mollīvī, mollītum: to soften

Mūsa, ae f.: a Muse

nē: (adv.) not

nebula, ae f.: cloud

noceō, nocēre, nocuī, nocitum: to be harmful (often with dat.)

parum: (adv.) too little, not enough

pollex, pollicis m.: thumb

rudis, e: unworked, crude

saepe: (adv.) often

senecta, ae f.: old age

sērus, a, um: late, advanced

subigō, subigere, subēgī, subāctum: to work up, work into a smooth thread

tractus, ūs m.: a pulling

ūsus, ūs m.: practical experience, use

venia, ae f.: pardon

vīvō, vīvere, vixī, victum: to live

15   ipsa nōn venit? Cūr haec certāmina vītat?" Tum Minerva dixit: "Vēnit!" Hōc
16   dictō formam anīlem remōvit, et suam formam vēram exhibuit. Arachnē territa nōn
17   est, sed tamen ērubuit.

18   Nāta Iovis nōn recūsat nec ulterius monet. Sine morā tēlās in dīversīs partibus
19   constituunt, et geminās tēlās stāmine gracilī intendunt. Illīc purpura quae aēnum
20   Tyrium sēnsit texitur. Illīc etiam aurum lentum fīlīs immittitur. In tēlā vetus
21   argūmentum dēdūcitur. Pallas scopulum Māvortis in arce Cecropiā et lītem
22   antīquam dē nōmine terrae pingit. Bis sex caelestēs in sēdibus altīs augustā
23   gravitāte sedent. Imāgō Iovis est rēgālis. Minerva imāginī suae clipeum, hastam, et
24   galeam dat. Pectus aegide dēfenditur. Dea terram suā cuspide percussam ēdere
25   fētum cum bācīs cānentis olīvae simulat. Arachnē Eurōpam ēlūsam imāgine taurī
26   dēsignat. Facit Lēdam recubāre sub ālīs olōrīnīs. Addit Iovem cēlātum imāgine
27   satyrī Antiopam geminō fētū implentem. Illīc Neptūnum, ut torvum iuvencum,
28   cum virgine in Aeoliā pōnit. Phoebus imāgō agrestis, imāgō accipitris, imāgō
29   leōnis est. Ut pastor Issēn lūdit. Ultima pars tēlae flōrēs intertextōs hederīs
30   nexilibus habet.

31   Nōn Pallas, nōn Līvor carpere illud opus poterat. Flāva dea successū doluit, et rūpit
32   vestēs pictās, crīmina deōrum. Minerva radium tenēbat, et ter, quater frontem
33   Arachnēs percussit. Īnfēlīx puella nōn tolerāre poterat et guttur suum laqueō
34   ligāvit. Pallas pendentem levāvit et dixit: "Vīve quidem, improba, tamen pendē."
35   Hīs dictīs Minerva sūcīs herbae Hecatēiae sparsit. Subitō comae medicāmine tāctae
36   dēflūxērunt, et nāsus et aurēs. Caput est minimum; parva quoque in tōtō corpore
37   est. Digitī in latere prō crūribus haerent. Venter cētera habet, dē quō tamen illa
38   remittit stāmen et arānea antīquās tēlās exercet.

Commentary

19–20 *Illīc purpura quae aēnum Tyrium sēnsit texitur*: The imagery here is of threads being
dyed purple in bronze cauldrons.
21–2 *Pallas scopulum Māvortis in arce Cecropiā et lītem antīquam dē nōmine terrae pingit*:
Minerva depicts the battle between herself and Neptune for preeminence in the city of Athens.
In the myth, Minerva gives the Athenians the olive tree while Neptune produces a salty spring
for them. The Athenians choose the olive tree, and thus Athens becomes Minerva's special city.
22–3 *Bis sex caelestēs in sēdibus altīs augustā gravitāte sedent*: *augustā gravitāte* is an
ablative of manner. Translate: *Twelve heavenly ones sit on high seats with majestic seriousness.*
25–9 *Arachnē Eurōpam ēlūsam imāgine taurī dēsignat ... lūdit*: With bold irreverence,
Arachne depicts the male gods in disguise raping both goddesses and mortal women.
31 *Nōn Pallas, nōn Līvor carpere illud opus poterat*: The word *carpere* here means *to carp at,
find a flaw with*.

accipiter, accipitris m.: hawk

aēnum, ī n.: something made of bronze, bronze cauldron

Aeolia, ae f.: Aeolia, a region on the northwest coast of Asia Minor

agrestis, agrestis m.: rural person

Antiopa, ae f.: Antiope, mother of Amphion and Zethus

argūmentum, ī n.: tale, proof

arx, arcis f.: citadel, stronghold

augustus, a, um: august, majestic

bāca, ae f.: fruit

caelestis, e: heavenly, celestial

cāneō, cānēre, cānuī: to be gray

Cecropius, a, um: of Cecrops, a legendary king of Athens

crīmen, crīminis n.: accusation, crime

dēdūcō, dēdūcere, dēdūxī, dēdūctum: to draw out, spin

dēfendō, dēfendere, dēfendī, dēfensum: to defend

dēfluō, dēfluere, dēfluxī, dēfluxum: to fall down, drop off, disappear

dēsignō, dēsignāre, dēsignāvī, dēsignātum: to signify, indicate, mark out

ēlūdō, ēlūdere, ēlūsī, ēlūsum: to fool

ērubēscō, ērubēscere, ērubuī: to blush, grow red

exerceō, exercēre, exercuī, exercitum: to bother, work

exhibeō, exhibēre, exhibuī, exhibitum: to bring out, reveal, show

fētus, ūs m.: offspring, sapling, fruit

fīlum, ī n.: thread

frons, frontis f.: forehead, brow

geminus, a, um: double, twin, two

gravitās, gravitātis f.: seriousness, solemnity, weight

guttur, gutturis n.: throat

hasta, ae f.: a spear

Hecatēius, a, um: of Hecate, goddess of witchcraft

hedera, ae f.: ivy

intertexō, intertexere, intertexuī, intertextum: to interweave

Issē, ēs f.: Isse, a princess of Lesbos

iuvencus, ī m.: young bull

Lēda, ae f.: Leda, mother of Helen of Troy

lentus, a, um: supple, malleable, slow

ligō, ligāre, ligāvī, ligātum: to tie

Līvor, Līvōris f.: Envy, the goddess of jealousy

Māvors, Māvortis m.: archaic name for the god Mars

minimus, a, um: smallest, least

nāsus, ī m.: a nose

nexilis, e: tied together

olīva, ae f.: olive

olōrīnus, a, um: belonging to a swan

pastor, pastōris m.: shepherd, herdsman

pingō, pingere, pinxī, pictum: to paint, depict

purpura, ae f.: purple

quater: (adv.) four times

recūsō, recūsāre, recūsāvī, recūsātum: to reject, refuse

remittō, remittere, remīsī, remissum: to send back, let go back

rumpō, rumpere, rūpī, ruptum: to break, shatter, burst

satyrus, ī m.: a satyr, goat-man

scopulus, ī m.: boulder

sēdēs, sēdis f.: seat

successus, ūs m.: outcome, success

sūcus, ī m.: juice

tēla, ae f.: that which is woven, web, warp, loom

texō, texere, texuī, textum: to weave

torvus, a, um: fierce

ulterius: (adv.) further, for a longer time

venter, ventris m.: belly

ABLATIVE ABSOLUTE

This construction consists of a noun or pronoun plus a participle in the ablative case. Although ablative absolutes provide relevant information about attendant circumstances, they are grammatically independent from the rest of the sentence. Any type of participle can be used in an ablative absolute. In the sentence *Fābulā dē Prōserpinā narrātā, Minerva carmina Mūsārum probāvit, Fābulā dē Prōserpinā narrātā* is an ablative absolute consisting of the noun *fābula* and the perfect passive participle *narrātus, a, um*. The sentence should be translated *With the story about Proserpina having been narrated, Minerva approved the songs of the Muses*. In the sentence *Mūsā fābulam narrante, Minerva carmina probāvit, Mūsā fābulam narrante* is an ablative absolute which uses a present active participle. The sentence should be translated *With the Muse narrating the story, Minerva approved the songs*. In the sentence *Mūsā fābulam narrātūrā, Minerva carmina probāvit, Mūsā fābulam narrātūrā* is an ablative absolute which uses a future active participle. The sentence should be translated *With the Muse about to narrate the story, Minerva approved the songs*.

In the ancient epic tradition, poetry and weaving are seen as parallel activities. While men weave words and thoughts together to express themselves verbally, epic women tend to express themselves visually by weaving textiles. In this story, Minerva depicts herself and the other gods as she wants to be seen, but Arachne's tapestry shows the gods as they actually behave. Some scholars think that Ovid identifies with Arachne and that her woven tapestry stands for the *Metamorphoses* itself. Indeed, there are some striking similarities between the images on Arachne's tapestry and Ovid's narration of the same stories in the poem proper.

20 Niobe

(*Met.* 6.146–312)

The Theban queen Niobe offends the goddess Latona and loses everything because of her hubristic attitude.

1   Lȳdia tōta fremit, et rūmor de certāmine Arachnēs per oppida Phrygiae it. Niobē
2   Arachnēn cognōverat, nec tamen poenā Arachnēs admonita est. Multa animōs
3   rēgīnae dabant, sed enim nihil illī placuit ut sua prōgeniēs.

4   Nunc Mantō, fīlia Tīresiae, praescia ventūrōrum, per mediās viās Thēbārum
5   currēbat et clāmābat: "Ismēnides, īte et date Lātōnae tūra cum precibus, et innectite
6   crīnem laurō. Lātōna ōre meō vōs iubet." Omnēs pārent, et omnēs Thēbāides sua
7   tempora iussīs frondibus ōrnant tūraque et precēs in sanctis flammīs dant.

8   Ecce Niobē venit cum turbā comitum, spectābilis vestibus Phrygiīs intextō aurō et
9   formōsa—quantum īra sinit. Niobē superba dīcit: "Quī furor est praepōnere
10   auditōs caelestēs vīsīs? Aut cūr Lātōna per ārās colitur; cūr meum nūmen sine tūre
11   est? Tantalus est auctor, cui sōlī tangere mensās superōrum licuit. Mea māter est
12   soror Plēiadum. Atlās quī aetherium axem fert avus est. Iuppiter est alter avus.
13   Domina rēgiae Cadmī sum. Faciēs mea est digna deā. Habeō septem nātās et
14   totidem iuvenēs, et mox generōs nurūsque! Lātōna sōlum est parēns duōrum. Sum
15   fēlix (quis enim potest negāre hoc?) fēlixque manēbō (quis hoc quoque dubitāre
16   potest?). Laurum capillīs dēpōnite. Mē, nōn Lātōnam, colite. Ego vōbīs colenda
17   sum!" Thēbāides laurōs dēpōnunt et sacra infecta relinquunt, sed Lātōnam tacitō
18   murmure adhūc colunt.

Commentary

4 *praescia ventūrōrum*: The future participle *ventūrōrum* is used as a substantive in the neuter plural. The word *praescius, a, um* takes a genitive of what is known.

6 *Lātōna ōre meō vōs iubet*: *ōre meō* is an ablative of means.

9–10 *Quis furor est praepōnere audītōs caelestēs vīsīs*: The verb *praepōnere* takes an accusative object of what is preferred and a dative of what that object is preferred to. There is an understood *caelestīs* with the participle *vīsīs*.

16–17 *Ego vōbīs colenda sum*: A passive periphrastic construction consists of a future passive participle (gerundive) used with a form of the verb *esse*. It conveys an idea of necessity and takes a dative of agent rather than an ablative of agent. Translate: *I ought to be worshipped by you.*

admoneō, admonēre, admonuī, admoni-tum: to warn

aetherius, a, um: heavenly

avus, ī m.: grandfather

axis, axis m.: axle, axis

dēpōnō, dēpōnere, dēposuī, dēpositum: to put down

domina, ae f.: royal lady, wife

ecce: (interj.) behold! look!

fēlix, fēlīcis: fortunate, happy

formōsus, a, um: beautiful

infectus, a, um: (infaciō) undone, unfinished

innectō, innectere, innexuī, innexum: to entwine

intexō, intexere, intexuī, intextum: to weave in

Ismēnis, Ismēnidis f.: a Theban woman

Lātōna, ae f.: Latona, mother of Apollo and Diana

laurus, ī f.: the laurel tree, laurels

Lȳdia, ae f.: Lydia, a region of Asia Minor

Mantō, Mantūs f.: Manto, a Theban prophetess

mensa, ae f.: table

murmur, mumuris n.: murmur, rumbling

Niobē, ēs f.: Niobe, a queen of Thebes born in Lydia

nurus, ūs f.: daughter-in-law

oppidum, ī n.: town

ōrnō, ōrnāre, ōrnāvī, ōrnātum: to decorate

Phrygia, ae f.: Phrygia, a region of Asia Minor

Phrygius, a, um: of Phrygia

Plēias, Plēiadis f.: one of the Pleiades

praepōnō, praepōnere, praeposuī, praepositum: to put before

praescius, a, um: having foreknowledge, prescient

prex, precis f.: prayer, plea

prōgeniēs, ēī f.: offspring

rūmor, rūmōris m.: a rumor, report

sanctus, a, um: holy, sacred

superbus, a, um: arrogant

tacitus, a, um: silent

Tantalus, ī: Tantalus, a king of Lydia

Thēbāis, Thēbāidis f.: a Theban woman

tūs, tūris n.: frankincense

19   Dea Lātōna indignāns est, et filiō et filiae dīcit: "Ego rēgīnam Thēbārum nōn
20   crēdere mē esse deam sentiō. Dīcit mē esse orbam: verba eius in ipsam reccidant."
21   Phoebus dīcit: "Rēgīna superba orba sit!" Apollō et Diāna volant per nūbēs,
22   et Thēbānam arcem contingunt. Ibi septem filiī rēgīnae Thēbārum in equōs
23   conscendunt, et premunt terga rubentia Tyriō sūcō. Iuvenēs habēnās gravēs aurō
24   regunt. Ē quibus Ismēnus quī prīmus filius mātrī fuerat suum currum in certum
25   orbem flectit, et conclāmat. Tēlum fixum in mediō pectore gerit, et frēnīs remissīs
26   paulātim in latus ā dextrō armō equī dēfluit. Tum Apollō cēterōs filiōs necāvit.

27   Niobē corporibus gelidīs incumbit, et oscula per omnēs nātōs dispēnsat. Tollēns
28   bracchia ad caelum dīcit: "Crūdēlis Lātōna, per fūnera septem filiōrum efferor:
29   exsultā victrixque inimīca triumphā! Cūr autem victrix? Post tot fūnera quoque
30   vincō. Septem filiās adhūc habeō!" Dīxerat, et nervus ab arcū sonuit, quī omnēs
31   praeter Niobēn terruit. Illa audāx erat; illa erat stulta. Deinde cūnctae sorōrēs ā filiō
32   Lātōnae subitō necātae sunt.

33   Tum Niobē orba residet inter exanimēs nātōs nātāsque, et dērigēscit. Aura nullōs
34   capillōs movet, in vultū color est sine sanguine, lūmina stant immōta. Nihil est
35   vīvum in imāgine. Lingua ipsa interius cum dūrō palātō congelat, et vēnae
36   dēsistunt posse movērī. Intrā viscera quoque saxum est. Flet tamen, et circumdata
37   turbine in patriam rapta est. Ibi fīxa in cacūmine montis flet, et etiam nunc marmor
38   lacrimās mānat. Hūmānī cum dīs nē certent!

Commentary

20 *verba eius in ipsam reccidant*: *ipsam* refers to Niobe. Latona will punish Niobe according to how Niobe has verbally insulted the goddess.

23 *premunt terga rubentia Tyriō sūcō*: The ablatives *Tyriō sūcō* are ablatives of means which explain *rubentia*.

25–6 *frēnīs remissīs paulātim in latus ā dextrō armō equī dēfluit*: *frēnīs remissīs* is an ablative absolute. When hit with Apollo's arrow, the youth drops the reins and slowly slides down the horse.

29 *Cūr autem victrix?*: Niobe questions what she herself has just said, thus revealing that she does not yet believe that Latona has won. Foolishly, she goes on to point out how she still surpasses the goddess.

33–4 *Aura nullōs capillōs movet ... lūmina stant immōta*: Ovid describes Niobe's transformation into a statue. *lūmina* means *eyes* here.

36–7 *et circumdata turbine in patriam rapta est*: A whirlwind scoops up the petrified Niobe and carries her back to her own country.

armus, ī m.: shoulder

audāx, audācis: bold

conclāmō, conclāmāre, conclāmāvī, conclāmātum: to cry out loudly

congelō, congelāre, congelāvī, congelātum: to freeze thoroughly

crūdēlis, e: cruel

dērigēscō, dērigēscere, dēriguī: to stiffen

dēsistō, dēsistere, dēstitī, dēstitum: to cease

dispēnsō, dispēnsāre, dispēnsāvī, dispēnsātum: to distribute

efferō, efferre, extulī, ēlātum: to carry off, carry away, bury, destroy

exanimis, e: lifeless

exsultō, exsultāre, exsultāvī, exsultātum: to jump up, leap up, exult

frēnum, ī n.: bridle, reins

fūnus, fūneris n.: funeral, burial

immōtus, a, um: unmoved

incumbō, incumbere, incubuī, incubitum: to lie down on, lean on

indignāns, indignantis: offended, impatient

inimīcus, a, um: hostile, unkind

interius: (adv.) inside

intrā: (prep. + acc.) inside, within

Ismēnus, ī m.: Ismenus, one of Niobe's sons

mānō, mānāre, mānāvī, mānātum: to pour, shed

nervus, ī m.: sinew, bowstring

orbus, a, um: orphaned, childless

palātum, ī n.: palate, roof of mouth

patria, ae f.: fatherland, native country

praeter: (prep.+ acc.) besides, except

recidō, recidere, reccidī, recāsūrum: to fall back

regō, regere, rexī, rēctum: to rule, control

resideō, residēre, resēdī, resessum: to sit back

tollō, tollere, sustulī, sublatum: to raise, lift up, remove, destroy

triumphō, triumphāre, triumphāvī, triumphātum: to celebrate a triumph, gain victory

turbō, turbinis m.: whirlwind

vēna, ae f.: blood vessel, vein

victrix, victrīcis f.: female victor

viscera, viscerum n. pl.: the flesh, inner organs, entrails

PRESENT SUBJUNCTIVE

The present subjunctive is formed by a vowel change in the present system forms. First conjugation uses "ē" for the present subjunctive; second conjugation uses "eā;" third conjugation uses "ā;" third -*io* and fourth conjugations use "iā." The present subjunctive of *mānō, mānāre, mānāvī, mānātum* is shown in the tables.

Active

	Singular	Plural
1st person	mānem	mānēmus
2nd person	mānēs	mānētis
3rd person	mānet	mānent

Passive

	Singular	Plural
1st person	māner	mānēmur
2nd person	mānēris	mānēminī
3rd person	mānētur	mānentur

Present subjunctive of *sum, esse, fuī, futūrum*

	Singular	Plural
1st person	sim	sīmus
2nd person	sīs	sītis
3rd person	sit	sint

JUSSIVE SUBJUNCTIVE

The subjunctive mood is used in many constructions in Latin, and it is necessary to know how it is being used in order to translate it correctly. There are both independent and dependent uses of the subjunctive. The jussive subjunctive is an independent use of the subjunctive mood which conveys a mild or indirect sense of command. It is translated with the word "let' or "may" before the verb. For example, the sentence *Verba eius in ipsam reccidant* should be translated *Let her words fall back onto her.*

The story of Niobe directly follows the story of Arachne's weaving contest with Minerva in Book 6, and both stories involve humans who challenge goddesses. In general, the *Metamorphoses* includes many stories in which humans are punished for attempting to step into divine roles. At the very end of the poem, Ovid offers an account of the apotheosis of Julius Caesar in which Caesar's soul is taken by Venus up to the stars. It is interesting to consider how Ovid's audience might interpret his account of Caesar's divine transformation after so many stories in which humans suffer miserable fates for trying to rival gods.

21 Tereus, Procne, and Philomela

(*Met.* 6.401–674)

The Thracian king Tereus is overcome with desire when he sees his sister-in-law for the first time and is driven by lust to rape and mutilate her.

1   Pandīōn, rēx Athēnaeus, Thrēicium Tēreum sibi cōnūbiō Procnēs iunxit. Nōn Iūnō,
2   nōn Hymenaeus aderat. Eumenidēs facēs raptās dē fūnere tenuērunt et torum
3   strāvērunt. Būbō tectō incubuit thalamīque in culmine sēdit. Procnē Tēreusque hāc
4   ave coniunctī sunt, et parentēs hāc ave factī sunt.

5   Post quīnque autumnōs, Procnē cum blanditiā virō dīcit: "Cupiō vīsitāre meam
6   sorōrem, Philomēlam. Sī ulla grātia mea est, mitte mē Athēnās vel hūc Philomēlam
7   invītā." Tēreus carīnās in freta dēdūcī iubet, et vēlō rēmigiōque portum Cecropium
8   intrat. Dexteram socerō dat, et Tēreus coepit referre mandāta coniugis. Ecce
9   Philomēla dīves parātū venit, dīvitior fōrmā. Cōnspectā virgine Tēreus subitō
10   exardet nōn secus quam sī quis suppōnit ignem aristīs cānīs. Faciēs quidem digna,
11   sed etiam innāta libīdō rēgem exstimulat.

12   Impetus illī erat vel corrumpere nūtrīcem vel sollicitāre Philomēlam ipsam
13   mūneribus datīs vel rapere et dēfendere raptam bellō. Nihil est quod nōn audēbit.
14   Iam Tēreus morās male ferēbat, et amor fācundum faciēbat. Philomēla, quae
15   multum vidēre sorōrem cupiēbat, rogābat patrem suum sinere sē cum Tēreō
16   nāvigāre. Tēreus spectābat eam quae dīcēbat blanda et circumdābat bracchia in
17   collō patris, et rēx Thrāciae cupiēbat eadem blanda et bracchia. Pandīōn timēbat ut
18   Philomēla tūta esset, sed precēs rēgis et fīliae patrem vīcērunt. Philomēla gaudēbat.

Commentary

1 *Pandīōn … sibi cōnūbiō Procnēs iunxit*: *cōnūbiō* is an ablative of means and governs the genitive *Procnēs*.

7–8 *et vēlō rēmigiōque portum Cecropium intrat*: *vēlō* and *rēmigiō* are ablatives of means.

9 *dīves parātū venit, dīvitior fōrmā*: The ablatives are ablatives of specification with *dīves* and *dīvitior*. Translate: *rich in her apparel, richer in beauty.*

9–10 *Tēreus subitō exardet nōn secus quam sī quis suppōnit ignem aristīs cānīs*: Ovid uses the imagery of someone setting fire to dried ears of grain to illustrate how inflamed with lust Tereus becomes. Ovid uses similar imagery to describe Apollo's desire in the story of Apollo and Daphne.

arista, ae f.: stalk of grain
Athēnae, ārum f. pl.: Athens
Athēnaeus, a, um: of Athens
audeō, audēre, ausus sum: to dare
avis, avis f.: bird, omen
blanditia, ae f.: gentleness, coaxing,
  flattery
blandus, a, um: flattering, coaxing
būbō, būbōnis m.: owl
carīna, ae f.: keel, ship
coepiō, coepere, coepī, coeptum: to begin,
  commence
**coniungō, coniungere, coniunxī,
  coniunctum:** to join together, marry
**corrumpō, corrumpere, corrūpī,
  corruptum:** to corrupt, destroy, spoil
culmen, culminis n.: summit, rooftop
dīves, dīvitis: rich
dīvitior, ius: richer
Eumenidēs, um f. pl.: Furies, goddesses of
  vengeance
**exstimulō, exstimulāre, exstimulāvī,
  exstimulātum:** to spur on
fācundus, a, um: eloquent
fretum, ī n.: strait
Hymenaeus, ī m.: Hymenaeus, a god of
  marriage
impetus, ūs m.: impulse

innātus, a, um: inborn
invītō, invītāre, invītāvī, invītātum: to invite
libīdō, libīdinis f.: lust
mandātum, ī n.: instruction, demand
Pandīōn, Pandīonis m.: Pandion, father of
  Procne and Philomela
parātus, ūs m.: preparation, apparel
Philomēla, ae f.: Philomela, daughter of
  Pandion
portus, ūs m.: port
Procnē, ēs f.: Procne, daughter of Pandion
referō, referre, rettulī, relātum: to bring
  back, carry back, return, report
rēmigium, ī n.: rowing, the oars, oarsmen
secus: (adv.) otherwise
socer, socerī m.: father-in-law
sollicitō, sollicitāre, sollicitāvī, sollicitātum:
  to move violently, incite, seek to obtain
  by bribery
sternō, sternere, strāvī, strātum: to spread,
  make (a bed)
Tēreus, ī m.: Tereus, husband of Procne
Thrācia, ae f.: Thrace
Thrēicius, a, um: of Thrace, a region north
  of Greece
ullus, a, um: any, anyone
vīsitō, vīsitāre, vīsitāvī, vīsitātum: to see,
  visit

19   Ut semel Philomēla in carīnā pictā posita est, Tēreus exclāmat: "Vīcī!" Iter factum
20   est, et carīna in portum Thrēicium nāvigat. Rēx Philomēlam in stabulum in silvīs
21   trahit. Tēreus Philomēlam, timentem nē quid malum accidat, spectat, et puellae
22   territae dīcit: "Tē rapiam!" Tum malus rēx Philomēlam, clāmantem parentem,
23   sorōrem, et dīvōs, rapit. Ubi mēns redit, Philomēla laniat capillōs et clāmat: "Ō
24   barbare, crūdēlis! Nec mandāta parentis cum lacrimīs piīs nec cūra sorōris nec mea
25   virginitās nec coniugiālia iūra tē mōvent? Pudōre prōiecto omnibus tē rapuisse mē
26   dīcam!" Tālibus verbīs īra et nōn minus hāc metus tyrannī crēscit. Tēreus metuit nē
27   Procnē sē Philomēlam rapuisse cognoscat. Ensem ā vāgīnā līberat. Philomēla
28   iugulum parat, sed rēx malus linguam forcipe comprehendit et ense abstulit. Rādix
29   micat, et ipsa lingua in terrā tremēns iacet.

30   Sōl bis sex signa annō actō lustrāverat: quid Philomēla faciet? Custōdia fugam
31   claudit, et moenia stabulī solidō saxō rigent. Ōs mūtum indice factī caret. Ingenium
32   dolōris est grande, et sollertia in miserīs rēbus venit. Stāmen dē barbaricā tēlā
33   suspendit, purpureāsque notās fīlīs albīs intexuit, indicium sceleris. Perfectum
34   servae trādidit, et gestū eam ferre ad Procnēn iussit. Serva ad Procnēn pertulit.
35   Mātrōna ēvolvit vestēs, fātum miserābile suae germānae lēgit, et siluit. Illā nocte
36   Procnē ad stabulum vēnit, portās refrēgit, et germānam līberāvit.

37   Dum Procnē īrā ardet, Itys, fīlius suus, ad mātrem venit. Vidēns puerum Procnē
38   putat lētum Ityos pūnītūrum esse Tēreum. Procnē Ityn trahit, et ēnse puerum,
39   clāmantem et tendentem manūs, ferit. Sorōrēs dīlaniant membra. Inde pars in aēnīs
40   cavīs exsultat, pars in veribus strīdit. Itys est nunc cibus, et Tēreus sua vīscera
41   edit. Tum sorōrēs tyrannō facinus patefaciunt. Flēns Thrācius necāre fēminās
42   temptat. Currentēs sorōrēs videntur pendere pennīs; sunt avēs! Tēreus vēlōx in
43   volucrem vertitur; est epops!

Commentary

19 *Ut semel Philomēla in carīnā pictā posita est*: *Ut semel* means *as soon as*.

26 *īra et nōn minus hāc metus tyrannī crēscit*: *hāc* is an ablative of comparison and refers to *īra*. Translate: *anger and, not less than this, fear . . .*

30 *Sōl bis sex signa annō āctō lustrāverat*: Ovid refers to the zodiac signs appearing through the year to indicate that a year has gone by. *annō āctō* is an ablative absolute.

38–9 *Procnē Ityn trahit . . . ferit*: *Ityn* is accusative singular. Note that Procne's anger drives her to mutilate her son as Tereus had mutilated her sister, something which Ovid emphasizes by having both Philomela and Itys call out to a parent as they are attacked.

accidō, accidere, accidī: to fall upon, happen, occur

auferō, auferre, abstulī, ablātum: to carry away, remove

barbaricus, a, um: barbarian

barbarus, ī m.: barbarian

careō, carēre, caruī, caritum: to lack (+ abl.)

cavus, a, um: hollow, concave

comprehendō, comprehendere, comprehendī, comprehēnsum: to grab, understand

coniugiālis, e: marital

cūra, ae f.: care, attention

custōdia, ae f.: watch, guard, protection

dīlaniō, dīlaniāre, dīlaniāvī, dīlaniātum: to tear to pieces

dolor, dolōris m.: pain, sorrow, distress

ensis, ensis m.: sword

epops, epopis m.: hoopoe, a bird with a crown of feathers and a long beak

ēvolvō, ēvolvere, ēvolvī, ēvolūtum: to unroll

facinus, facinoris n.: deed, evil deed, crime

forceps, forcipis f.: pair of tongs, pincers

germāna, ae f.: sister

gestus, ūs m.: gesture

incidium, ī n.: sign, evidence

index, indicis m.: informer, that which informs, sign

iter, itineris n.: journey, way

Itys, Ityos m.: Itys, the son of Tereus and Procne

mātrōna, ae f.: married woman, matron

metuō, metuere, metuī, metūtum: to fear, be afraid of

metus, ūs m.: fear, dread

minus: (adv.) less

miserābilis, e: pitiable, miserable, wretched

mūtus, a, um: mute, quiet, silent

nota, ae f.: mark

penna, ae f.: feather, wing

perferō, perferre, pertulī, perlātum: to carry all the way

perficiō, perficere, perfēcī, perfectum: to complete, perfect

prōiciō, prōicere, prōiēcī, prōiectum: to throw forward, fling away

pudor, pudōris m.: modesty, shame

pūniō, pūnīre, pūnīvī, pūnītum: to punish

rādix, rādīcis f.: root

redeō, redīre, rediī, reditum: to come back

refringō, refringere, refrēgī, refrāctum: to break open

rēs, reī f.: a thing, affair, matter

rigeō, rigēre: to be stiff, be hard

scelus, sceleris n.: crime, wicked deed, evil

semel: (adv.) once

serva, ae f.: slave

sileō, silēre, siluī: to be silent

sollertia, ae f.: cleverness

stabulum, ī n.: quarters, stable, brothel

strīdō, strīdere, strīdī: to make a harsh noise, creak, hiss

suspendō, suspendere, suspendī, suspensum: to hang, hang up, suspend

Thrācius, a, um: of Thrace

tremō, tremere, tremuī: to shake, quiver, tremble

vāgīna, ae f.: sheath

vēlox, vēlōcis: swift, quick

veru, ūs n.: a spit

virginitās, virginitātis f.: virginity

volucris, volucris f.: a bird, flying thing

IMPERFECT SUBJUNCTIVE

The imperfect subjunctive is formed by adding personal endings to the present infinitive. The imperfect subjunctive of *pūniō, pūnīre, pūnīvī, pūnītum* is:

Active

	Singular	Plural
1st person	pūnīrem	pūnīrēmus
2nd person	pūnīrēs	pūnīrētis
3rd person	pūnīret	pūnīrent

Passive

	Singular	Plural
1st person	pūnīrer	pūnīrēmur
2nd person	pūnīrēris	pūnīrēminī
3rd person	pūnīrētur	pūnīrentur

Imperfect subjunctive of *sum, esse, fuī, futūrum*

	Singular	Plural
1st person	essem	essēmus
2nd person	essēs	essētis
3rd person	esset	essent

FEAR CLAUSES

Fear clauses are used after verbs of fearing to indicate what is feared, although sometimes an implied idea of fear can precede them. They are introduced by the words *nē* and *ut*, but, unlike most clauses which are introduced by *ut*, positive clauses are introduced by *nē* and negative clauses are introduced by *ut*. The sentence *Tēreus Philomēlam, timentem nē quid malum accidat, spectat* contains a positive fear clause introduced by the present participle *timentem*. It should be translated *Tereus looks at Philomela, who fears that something bad will happen*. The sentence *Pandīon timēbat ut Philomēla tūta esset* contains a negative fear clause introduced by the finite verb *timēbat*. It should be translated *Pandion feared that Philomela would not be safe*.

The rape-narrative about Tereus, Procne, and Philomela is one of the most violent stories in the *Metamorphoses*, and Ovid relates it in graphic detail. At the beginning of the account, Ovid tells his audience that Tereus is descended from Mars Gradivus. Augustus restored many temples and took special interest in traditional Roman cults, including the cult of Mars Gradivus. The Salii, twelve priests who performed ritual processions and dances throughout the city, were championed by the princeps and probably held feasts in the Forum of Augustus. Augustus' name was actually inserted into the *Salian Hymn* circa 28 BCE. It is possible that Ovid is using the story to make a political statement about the silencing of speech under tyranny, especially when one considers it along with the story of Arachne and Minerva, where a woven tapestry also reveals the truth.

22 Boreas and Orithyia

(*Met.* 6.675–721)

Boreas, the north wind, takes Orithyia to be his wife by force when her father rejects him.

1   Dolor Philomēlae et Procnēs Pandīonem ad Tartareās umbrās mīsit. Erechtheus,
2   potēns armīs et iūstitiā, sceptrum locī moderāmenque rērum cēpit. Quattuor
3   iuvenēs ab illō nātī sunt et totidem fēminae. Forma duārum, Ōrīthyiae et Procris,
4   pār erat. Ē quibus Procris coniunx Cephalī erat. Athēniēnsēs Tēreum Thrācesque
5   ōdērunt, et odium Boreae nocēbat, quia Boreas etiam terrās glaciālēs colēbat. Deus
6   sīc Ōrīthyiā dīlēctā caruit. Boreās Erechtheum cōnūbium Ōrīthyiae rogābat, et
7   ūtēbatur precibus magis quam vīribus.

8   Ubi nihil blanditiīs agitur, horridus īrā, quae illī ventō solita est, rogat: "Quid enim
9   mea tēla relīquī, saevitiam et vīrēs īramque animōsque minācēs, et precibus ūsus
10   sum, quārum ūsus mē dēdecet? Vīs apta mihi est. Vī tristia nūbila pellō; vī freta
11   concutiō; vī nōdōsa rōbora vertō indūrōque nivēs; vī terrās grandine pulsō. Īdem
12   ego, cum frātrēs in caelō apertō nanciscor (nam caelum est campus mihi), luctor
13   magnō mōlīmine: medius aether nostrīs concursibus insonat et ignēs ēlīsī nūbibus
14   cavīs exsiliunt. Īdem ego, cum subiī convexa forāmina terrae supposuīque ferox
15   mea terga cavernīs īmīs, sollicitō mānēs tōtumque orbem terrārum tremōribus

Commentary

4–5 *Athēniēnsēs Tēreum Thrācesque ōdērunt ... colēbat*: The Athenians hated the Thracians because of Tereus' outrages against Procne and Philomela. Because Boreas inhabited a land near Thrace, he too was hated by the Athenians.

6 *Boreās Erechtheum cōnūbium Ōrīthyiae rogābat*: The verb *rogāre* takes an accusative both of the person asked and the thing requested.

8 *quae illī ventō solita est*: The antecedent of *quae* is *īra*.

9 *saevitiam et vīrēs īramque animōsque minācēs*: The accusatives explain Boreas' *tēla*.

10 *quārum ūsus mē dēdecet*: The impersonal verb *dēdecet* takes an accusative of the person or thing not fitted. The relative pronoun *quarum* refers to *precibus*. Translate: *The use of which things is not fitting for me.*

11–14 *Īdem ... Īdem*: These demonstratives have an adverbial force here. Translate: *Likewise ...*

aperiō, aperīre, aperuī, apertum: to open, uncover, lay bare

Athēniēnsis, e: of Athens

caverna, ae f.: cavern, cave

Cephalus, ī m.: Cephalus, son of Pandion

concursus, ūs m.: collision, attack

concutiō, concutere, concussī, concussum: to beat, strike, shake violently

convexus, a, um: arched, vaulted

dēdecet, dēdecēre, dēdecuit: (impers. verb) it is unfitting, not suitable

dīligō, dīligere, dīlēxī, dīlēctum: to have affection for, choose

ēlīdō, ēlīdere, ēlīsī, ēlīsum: to squeeze out, strike

Erechtheus, ī m.: Erechtheus, an early king of Athens

exsiliō, exsilīre, exsiluī, exsultum: to jump out

ferox, ferōcis: courageous, wild, warlike

forāmen, forāminis n.: an opening, hole

glaciālis, e: icy, frozen

grandō, grandinis f.: hail, hailstorm

indūrō, indūrāre, indūrāvī, indūrātum: to harden, make hard

insonō, insonāre, insonuī: to resound

luctor, luctārī, luctātus sum: to wrestle, struggle, contend

iūstitia, ae f.: justice

magis: (adv.) more, rather

mānēs, mānium m. pl.: ghosts, souls of the departed

minax, minācis: threatening

moderāmen, moderāminis n.: a means of guiding, government

mōlīmen, mōlīminis n.: great effort, exertion

nanciscor, nancisci, nactus sum: to meet, light upon

nōdōsus, a, um: knotty

nix, nivis f.: snow

nūbilum, ī n.: cloud mass

ōdī, ōdisse: (defect. verb) to hate

odium, ī n.: hatred

Ōrīthyia, ae f.: Orithyia, a daughter of Erechtheus

pār, paris: equal, like

pellō, pellere, pepulī, pulsum: to beat, strike, drive away

Procris, Procris f.: Procris, a daughter of Erechtheus

pulsō, pulsāre, pulsāvī, pulsātum: to beat

quia: (conj.) because

rōbur, rōboris n.: oak

saevitia, ae f.: ferocity, savagery

Tartareus, a, um: of Tartarus, a region of the Underworld

Thrax, Thrācis: of Thrace

umbra, ae f.: shade, shadow, dead spirit

ūtor, ūtī, ūsus sum: to use (+ abl.)

16   meīs. Hīs vīribus uxōrem petīvisse dēbuī. Erechtheus socer mihi nōn ōrandus erat,
17   sed faciendus erat!

18   Locūtus haec verba et alia verba nōn inferiōra, Boreās pennās excussit, quārum
19   iactātibus omnis tellūs adflāta est et lātum aequor perhorruit. Trahēns pulveream
20   pallam per summa cacūmina humum verrit. Tectus cālīgine Boreās fulvīs ālīs
21   Ōrīthyiam amplectitur. Dum volat, ignēs amōris fortius ardent. Nec raptor prius
22   cursūs supprimit, quam populōs et moenia Ciconum tenet.

23   Illīc Ōrīthyia coniunx gelidī tyrannī facta est, et illīc ēnīxa partūs gemellōs genetrix
24   facta est. Quī cētera mātris, sed pennās genitōris habuērunt. Memorant hās pennās
25   ūnā cum corporibus nōn nātās esse. Prīmum Calais et Zētēs implūmēs erant, sed
26   puerīs adolescentibus pennae crēvērunt. Posteā Calais et Zētēs vellus aureum cum
27   Minyīs per mare in prīmā carīnā petīvērunt.

Commentary

16–17 *Erechtheus socer mihi nōn ōrandus erat, sed faciendus erat*: Understand *esse* before *socer* and *mihi*, a dative of agent, with both passive periphrastic constructions.

18–19 *quārum iactātibus*: *iactātibus* is an ablative of means. Translate: *by the flutterings of which*

21–2 *prius … quam*: The conjunction *priusquam* (separated here) means *before*.

24 *Quī cētera mātris, sed pennās genitōris habuērunt*: The antecedent of *quī* is *partūs gemellōs*. Relative pronouns often begin sentences in Latin.

adflō, adflāre, adflāvī, adflātum: to blow on

adolescō, adolescere, adolēvī: to grow up

amplector, amplectī, amplexus sum: to embrace, wrap around

Calais, is m.: Calais, a son of Boreas and Orithyia

cālīgō, cālīginis f.: darkness, mist

Cicones, um m. pl.: Ciconians, a people in Thrace

cursus, ūs m.: course, path, journey

ēnītor, ēnītī, ēnīxus sum: to struggle, exert oneself, give birth to

excutiō, excutere, excussī, excussum: to shake out

fortior, ius: stronger, more powerful

gemellus, a, um: twin

genetrix, genetrīcis f.: mother

genitor, genitōris m.: father

iactātus, ūs m.: a shaking, fluttering, moving quickly up and down

implūmis, e: featherless

inferior, ius: lower

lātus, a, um: wide, broad

loquor, loquī, locūtus sum: to speak

mare, maris n.: the sea

memorō, memorāre, memorāvī, memorātum: to recall, relate

Minyae, ārum m. pl.: Minyans, the Argonauts

partus, ūs m.: offspring, birth

perhorrēscō, perhorrēscere, perhorruī: to shudder, be terrified at

pulvereus, a, um: dusty

supprimō, supprimere, suppressī, suppressum: to block, check, push down

ūnā: (adv.) together

verrō, verrere, verrī, versum: to sweep

Zētēs, ae m.: Zetes, a son of Boreas and Orithyia

DEPONENT VERBS

Deponent verbs have passive forms but are translated actively. So, *ūtor* is translated *I use*, even though it looks like a passive verb, and *ūtī* is translated *to use* rather than *to be used*. Deponent verbs only have three principal parts, and all of these have active meanings. The participles of deponent verbs are translated just like the participles of regular verbs, with the exception of the perfect participle, which for deponent verbs is translated actively (see table). Some deponent verbs, including *ūtor* (*to use*), *fungor* (*to occupy oneself with something*), *potior* (*to possess*), and *fruor* (*to enjoy*), take an ablative object.

PARTICIPLES OF DEPONENT VERBS

Present active participle	ūtēns	using
Perfect participle	ūsus, a, um	having used
Future active participle	ūtūrus, a, um	about to use
Future passive participle	ūtendus, a, um	to be used, needing to be used

The story of Boreas and Orithyia ends Book 6 of the *Metamorphoses*, and the final lines of the book are about the sons born to the north wind and his new bride, Calais and Zetes. Ovid describes how the boys later went with Jason and the Argonauts to fetch the golden fleece. The story of the quest for the golden fleece and Jason's love affair with Medea begins the very next book. Ovid's account of the story of Boreas and Orithyia is quite short, and one wonders why he did not just save it for the beginning of Book 7. This organization is another example of how stories in the poem frequently bleed from one book to the next, and there often do not seem to be clear divisions between books, thus making Ovid's poem seem even more like a complex tapestry of overlapping images.

23 Medea's rejuvenation of Aeson

(*Met.* 7.159–293)

Medea, the daughter of King Aeëtes of Colchis and a woman skilled in witchcraft, restores youthfulness to Jason's father.

1   Calais et Zētēs, fīliī Boreae, cum Iāsone ut vellere aureō potīrentur nāvigāvērunt.
2   Mēdēa, fīlia Aeētae, quī vellus habēbat, capta amōre Iāsonem herbīs et verbīs cantātīs
3   iūvit, et Iāsōn vellus cēpit. Fīlius Aesonis, superbus spoliō et portāns sēcum
4   Mēdēam coniugem, portum Iolcī tetigit. Haemoniae mātrēs grandaevīque patrēs
5   dōna prō nātīs receptīs tulērunt, et tūra in flammīs liquefēcērunt. Victimae cecidērunt.
6   Omnēs Iāsonī grātābantur. Aesōn autem abfuit, iam fessus senīlibus annīs.

7   Iāsōn dīcit: "Ō coniunx, cui confiteor mē dēbēre salūtem meam, quamquam cuncta mihi
8   dedistī, sī tua carmina facere hoc possunt (quid enim nōn possunt?), dēme meōs annōs et
9   adde annōs meōs demptōs patrī." Nec lacrimās tenet, et Mēdēa pietāte rogantis mōta est.
10   Mēdēa respondet: "Quod scelus ē tuō ōre excidit, coniunx? Videorne posse transcrībere
11   cuiquam spatium tuae vītae? Hecatē hoc nōn sinet. Sed experiar dare maius mūnus istō
12   quod petis, Iāsōn. Meā arte, nōn tuīs annīs, longum aevum patris revocāre temptābō."

Commentary

7 *cui confiteor mē dēbēre salūtem meam*: Ovid begins with a relative pronoun and then moves into indirect statement after *confiteor*. Translate: *to whom I confess that I owe my welfare*.
11–12 *maius mūnus istō quod petis*: *istō* is an ablative of comparison after *maius* and also the antecedent of *quod*.

absum, abesse, abfuī, abfutūrum: to be away from, be absent

Aeētēs, Aeētae m.: Aeētes, king of Colchis

Aesōn, Aesonis m.: Aeson, father of Jason

cantō, cantāre, cantāvī, cantātum: to sing

confiteor, confitērī, confessus sum: to acknowledge, confess

dōnum, ī n.: gift

grandaevus, a, um: aged, old

grātor, grātārī, grātātus sum: to congratulate, wish joy to

Haemonius, a, um: of Haemonia, of Thessaly

Hecatē, ēs f.: Hecate, goddess of witchcraft

Iāsōn, Iāsonis m.: Jason, leader of the Argonauts

Iolcus, ī f.: Iolcus, a city in Thessaly and Jason's home

liquefaciō, liquefacere, liquefēcī, liquefactum: to melt, liquefy

Mēdēa, ae f.: Medea, a princess of Colchis and a sorceress

pietās, pietātis f.: sense of duty, piety

potior, potīrī, potītus sum: to obtain, possess (+ acc. or abl.)

salus, salūtis f.: health, welfare, safety

senīlis, e: aged, old

transcrībō, transcrībere, transcrīpsī, transcrīptum: to write over, transfer, convey

13 Iam nōna diēs et nōna nox Mēdēam lustrantem terrās in currū pennīsque dracōnum ut
14 aptās herbās et ūtilēs sūcōs invenīret vīdit. Statuit bīnās ārās dē caespite: dextera āra
15 Hecatēs est, et in laevā parte āra Iuventae est. Duās scrobēs ut sacra faciat effodit.
16 Cultrum in guttur bidentis ātrī cōnicit, et sanguine patulās fossās perfundit. Tum
17 invergēns carchēsia liquidī mellis et carchēsia tepidī lactis, simul verba fundit.
18 Nūminibus precibus plācātīs, Mēdēa corpus fessum Aesonis prōferrī ad ārās iubet.
19 Carmine Aesonem in somnum resolvit, et corpus simile exanimī in herbīs strātīs porrigit.

20 Mēdēa, passīs capillīs, rītū Bacchantium flagrantēs ārās circumit. Ter flammā, ter aquā,
21 ter sulfure lustrat. Intereā medicāmen in aēnō fervet; medicāmen exsultat et spūmīs
22 tumentibus albet. Mēdēa addit herbās, et immiscet. Quācumque ignis spūmās ex
23 cavō aēnō ēicit et guttae calentēs in terram cadunt, humus vernat flōrēsque et mollia
24 pābula surgunt. Quae simul atque vīdet, ēnse strictō Mēdēa iugulum senis reclūdit, et
25 Mēdēa, passa veterum cruōrem exīre, corpus sūcīs suīs replet. Postquam Aesōn
26 medicāmen combibit, barba et coma colōrem nigrum rapit, maciēs fugit, pallor situsque
27 abeunt, et membra luxuriant. Aesōn mīrātur et hunc esse sē ante quater dēnōs annōs
28 reminiscitur.

Commentary

13–14 *Iam nōna diēs et nōna nox ... vīdit*: Ovid personifies the day and night here, making them the subjects of the sentence. *pennīs* is an ablative of means. The singular verb *vīdit* emphasizes the subjects as individual elements.

18 *Nūminibus precibus plācātīs*: *precibus* is an ablative of means. The other ablatives are used as an ablative absolute.

24 *Quae simul atque vīdet*: The antecedents of *quae*, which is neuter plural, are all of the things which have just been described.

27 *ante quater dēnōs annōs*: Literally, *before four-tens of years*. Translate: *forty years before*.

albeō, albēre: to be white

āter, ātra, ātrum: black, dark

Bacchantēs, Bacchantium f. pl.: followers of Bacchus

bidens, bidentis: with two teeth (often used for sheep)

bīnī, bīnae, bīna: two, double, a pair

caespis, caespitis m.: turf, sod, earthen mound

caleō, calēre, caluī: to be hot

carchēsium, ī n.: drinking cup

circumeō, circumīre, circumiī or circumīvī, circumitum: to go around

combibō, combibere, combibī: to drink

conicio, conicere, coniēcī, coniectum: to throw, bring together, drive, force

culter, cultrī m.: knife

dēnī, dēnae, dēna: by tens

effodiō, effodere, effodī, effossum: to dig out

ēiciō, ēicere, ēiēcī, ēiectum: to throw out, expel

experior, experīrī, expertus sum: to try, test, attempt

ferveō, fervēre, ferbuī: to boil, burn

flagrō, flagrāre, flagrāvī, flagrātum: to blaze

fossa, ae f.: ditch, trench

immisceō, immiscēre, immiscuī, immixtum: to mix in, blend, intermingle

inveniō, invenīre, invēnī, inventum: to find, discover

invergō, invergere: to pour upon

Iuventa, ae f.: Juventa, the goddess of youth

luxuriō, luxuriāre, luxuriāvī, luxuriātum: to be abundant, enlarge, grow rapidly

maciēs, maciēī f.: leanness

mīror, mīrārī, mīrātus sum: to admire, wonder at

nōnus, a, um: ninth

pallor, pallōris m.: paleness

pandō, pandere, pandī, passum: to spread out, extend

patior, patī, passus sum: to suffer, allow, experience, tolerate

patulus, a, um: open, wide, broad

plācātus, a, um: quiet, peaceful, calm

prōferō, prōferre, prōtulī, prōlātum: to carry forward, bring forth, offer

quācumque: (adv.) wherever

reclūdō, reclūdere, reclūsī, reclūsum: to open, reveal, disclose

reminiscor, reminiscī: to recollect, remember

repleō, replēre, replēvī, replētum: to refill, fill up

resolvō, resolvere, resolvī, resolūtum: to untie, release, open

rītus, ūs m.: religious ceremony, rite

scrobis, scrobis m.: ditch, trench

simul: (adv.) at the same time

situs, ūs m.: decay, neglect

spūma, ae f.: foam

statuō, statuere, statuī, statūtum: to set up, fix upright

stringō, stringere, strixī, strictum: to pull out (a weapon), tighten

sulfur, sulfuris n.: brimstone, sulfur

ūtilis, e: useful, beneficial, profitable

vernō, vernāre, vernāvī, vernātum: to flourish, bloom

PURPOSE CLAUSES

Purpose clauses are subjunctive clauses which indicate why something is done. They are introduced by *ut* or, in the case of a negative purpose clause, *nē*. In the sentence *Calais et Zētēs, filiī Boreae, cum Iāsone ut vellere aureō potīrentur nāvigāvērunt*, the purpose clause is *ut vellere aureō potīrentur*. The sentence should be translated *Calais and Zetes, sons of Boreas, sailed with Jason in order to obtain the golden fleece*. Purpose clauses are common, but there also are other types of subjunctive clauses introduced by *ut*. Frequently, you must use context to determine which kind of clause is at work.

Medea is the granddaughter of the Sun-god Helios, and she is a niece of Circe, the sorceress who turns Odysseus' men into pigs in the *Odyssey*. Like her aunt, Medea is skilled in magic and in concocting powerful potions, and Jason very much is dependent on her talents for his success in bringing the golden fleece back from Colchis to Iolcus. When they return to Iolcus with the fleece, Pelias refuses to turn the throne over to Jason, who is the rightful heir, and Medea avenges the offense in a manner so gruesome that the two are driven out of Iolcus. They end up in Corinth, where Jason casts Medea aside for the princess Glauke. To punish Jason, Medea sends the princess a poisoned robe and then kills her own children. She then escapes to Athens, where King Aegeus accepts her as his wife. Later, Medea attempts to kill Aegeus' son Theseus.

24 Medea's punishment of Pelias

(*Met.* 7.294–349)

When the daughters of Pelias learn of Medea's rejuvenation of Aeson, they ask Medea to restore their father's vigor. Medea uses the opportunity to avenge Pelias' ill treatment of her husband.

1   Iuventūte Aesonis redditā Mēdēa falsum odium cum coniuge adsimulat, et supplex
2   ad līmina Peliae confugit. Quoniam Peliās ipse gravis senectūte est, nātae Mēdēam
3   excipiunt. Tempore parvō, callida fēmina imāgine falsā amīcitiae fidem virginum
4   capit, et, dum dīcit situm Aesonis demptum esse (in hāc parte fābulae morātur),
5   spēs est virginibus arte Mēdēae suum parentem posse revirēscere. Nātae artem
6   similem petunt. Illa brevī spatiō silet, et dubitāre vidētur. Animōs rogantium fictā
7   gravitāte suspendit. Ubi mox pollicētur, dīcit: "Ut fidūcia maior huius mūneris
8   sit, dux gregis quī maximus aevō est inter ovēs agnus medicāmine meō fīet."

9   Prōtinus lāniger, fessus innumerīs annīs, attrahēbātur, cornibus flexīs circum cava
10   tempora. Mēdēa cultrō marcens guttur fōdit, et ferrum exiguō sanguine maculāvit;
11   membra sūcōsque tantōs venēficōs in aēnō cavō mersit ut cornua exūrerent et
12   corpus minuerent. Tener bālātus in mediō aēnō audītus est. Sine morā, virginibus
13   bālātum mīrantibus, agnus exsiluit et lactāns ūber quaesīvit.

14   Fīliae Peliae obstipuērunt. Postquam prōmissa fidem exhibērunt, tum vērō fīliae
15   artem Mēdēae cupiēbant. Post trēs noctēs, sīdera radiantia micābant, cum fallax

Commentary

3 *Tempore parvō*: This is an example of an ablative of time within which. Translate: *within a short time.*

5 *spēs est virginibus arte Mēdēae suum parentem posse revirēscere*: The idea that there is hope (*spēs est*) introduces the indirect statement.

6–7 *Animōs rogantum fictā gravitāte suspendit*: In other words, Medea holds the daughters in suspense with feigned seriousness.

8 *quī maximus aevō est*: *aevō* is an ablative of specification which explains *maximus*. Translate: *greatest in age.*

9 *cornibus flexīs*: an ablative absolute.

10 *ferrum exiguō sanguine maculāvit*: The ram is so old that it has very little blood.

14 *Postquam prōmissa fidem exhibērunt*: The substantive *prōmissa* is the subject of *exhibērunt.*

adsimulō, adsimulāre, adsimulāvī, adsimulātum: to make like, imitate
amīcitia, ae f.: friendship
bālātus, ūs m.: a bleating
callidus, a, um: skillful, crafty, cunning
confugiō, confugere, confūgī: to flee to, take refuge with
exiguus, a, um: scant, few, small
exūrō, exūrere, exussī, exustum: to burn out, burn up
fallax, fallācis: deceitful, deceptive
fīctus, a, um: formed, fashioned, feigned
fidēs, fideī f.: trust, belief, faith
fīdūcia, ae f.: trust, confidence, security
fīō, fierī, factus sum: to become, occur, be done
fodiō, fodere, fōdī, fossum: to dig, pierce, stab
innumerus, a, um: innumerable, countless
iuventus, iuventūtis f.: youth, prime of life
lactō, lactāre, lactāvī, lactātum: to give milk, contain milk

lāniger, lānigerī m.: ram
līmen, līminis n.: threshold
maculō, maculāre, maculāvī, maculātum: to stain, pollute
marceō, marcēre: to wither, be faint, be weak
minuō, minuere, minuī, minūtum: to lessen, diminish
moror, morārī, morātus sum: to delay, linger
obstipescō, obstipescere, obstipuī: to be amazed
ovis, ovis f.: sheep
Peliās, Peliae m.: Pelias, king of Thessaly
polliceor, pollicērī, pollicitus sum: to promise, offer
revirescō, revirescere, revirescuī: to grow strong again
senectus, senectūtis f.: old age
spēs, speī f.: hope
ūber, ūberis n.: udder
venēficus, a, um: magical, poisonous
vērō: (adv.) truly

16   fēmina pūrum laticem et herbās sine vīribus in rapidō igne impōsuit. Iam somnus
17   similis necī rēgem (et, cum rēge, custōdēs eius) habēbat, quem cantus et potentia
18   magicōrum verbōrum dederant. Nātae in līmina cum Mēdēā intrāvērunt et
19   circumiērunt torum.

20   "Quid, inertēs, nunc dubitātis?" Mēdēa dīcit. "Stringite gladiōs et haurīte veterum
21   crurorem ut vacuās vēnās iuvenālī sanguine repleam! In manibus vestrīs vīta
22   aetāsque parentis sunt. Sī pietās ulla est nec spēs inānēs agitātis, senectūtem tēlīs
23   exigite. Ferrō coniectō saniem ēmittite!"

24   Ut quaeque pia est, quaeque impia est. Nē scelerāta sit, quaeque scelus facit. Haud
25   tamen ulla ictūs suōs spectāre potest, oculōsque reflectunt, dantēs caeca vulnera
26   saevīs dextrīs. Peliās, fluēns cruōre, tamen sē in cubitō adlevat, et sēmilacer ex torō
27   consurgere temptat. Inter tot gladiōs tendēns bracchia ille clāmat: "Quid facitis,
28   nātae? Vōs ictūs tantōs saevōs pellitis ut mē necētis!"

29   Animī manūsque illīs cecidērunt. Virginibus dubitantibus, Mēdēa guttur senis
30   locūtūrī plūra fōdit, et corpus laniātum in calidīs undīs mersit. Statim Mēdēa
31   serpentibus pennātīs in aurās īvit, et fūgit certās poenās. Pennīs vīpereīs Corinthiās
32   terrās contigit. Postquam nova nūpta venēnīs Colchicīs arsit, impius ēnsis Mēdēae
33   sanguine nātōrum suōrum perfūsus est. Quis huic fābulae crēdiderit?

Commentary

17–18 *quem cantus et potentia magicōrum verbōrum dederant*: The word *somnus* is the antecedent of *quem*. Medea had caused the king and his guards to sleep by means of her spells.

24 *Ut quaeque pia est*: Translate *ut* here as *as*. *quaeque* refers to each of Pelias' daughters. In other words, in acting to help their father, the daughters actually commit an impious act.

24 *Nē scelerāta sit*: This is a negative purpose clause.

31 *serpentibus pennātīs* and *Pennīs vīpereīs*: Both constructions are ablatives of means.

32–3 *Postquam nova nūpta ... perfūsus est*: In Corinth, Jason rejects Medea for the princess of that city. Medea sends a poisoned robe to the girl which causes her to burn up and then kills her own children to punish Jason.

33 *Quis huic fābulae crēdiderit*: The subjunctive is used in questions implying doubt, indignation, or impossibility. Here, a perfect subjunctive is used. Translate: *Who could believe this story?*

adlevō, adlevāre, adlevāvī, adlevātum: to lift up, erect

agitō, agitāre, agitāvī, agitātum: to drive about, keep in movement, agitate

caecus, a, um: blind

calidus, a, um: warm, hot

Colchicus, a, um: of Colchis, a region on the Black Sea

consurgō, consurgere, consurrexī, consurrectum: to raise oneself, rise, stand up

Corinthius, a, um: of Corinth, a city in southern Greece

cubitum, ī n.: elbow

ēmittō, ēmittere, ēmīsī, ēmissum: to send out, send away

exigō, exigere, exēgī, exactum: to drive out

hauriō, haurīre, hausī, haustum: to draw out, drink

impius, a, um: impious, disrespectful

impōnō, impōnere, imposuī, impositum: to lay or place upon, impose on

inānis, e: empty, void

iners, inertis: inactive, idle

iuvenālis, e: youthful

nex, necis f.: death

pennātus, a, um: winged, feathered

potentia, ae f.: power, ability

quisque, quaeque, quidque: (pron.) each, every

rapidus, a, um: swift, hurrying

reflectō, reflectere, reflexī, reflectum: to turn back, reflect

saniēs, saniēī f.: diseased blood, poison

sēmilacer, sēmilacera, sēmilacerum: half-mangled

vacuus, a, um: empty, void

PERFECT SUBJUNCTIVE

The perfect subjunctive active is almost identical to the future perfect indicative. When translating, it sometimes can be difficult to determine whether a verb is future perfect indicative or perfect subjunctive, and one must use context to decide which form is at work. The perfect subjunctive passive is formed by a combination of the perfect passive participle and the present subjunctive of *esse*.

crēdō, crēdere, crēdidī, crēditum: active

	Singular	Plural
1st person	crēdiderim	crēdiderimus
2nd person	crēdideris	crēdideritis
3rd person	crēdiderit	crēdiderint

crēdō, crēdere, crēdidī, crēditum: passive

	Singular	Plural
1st person	crēditum sim	crēdita sīmus
2nd person	crēditum sīs	crēdita sītis
3rd person	crēditum sit	crēdita sint

sum, esse, fuī, futūrum

	Singular	Plural
1st person	fuerim	fuerimus
2nd person	fueris	fueritis
3rd person	fuerit	fuerint

RESULT CLAUSES

Like purpose clauses, result clauses are subjunctive clauses introduced by *ut*, although negative result clauses use words other than *nē*, such as *nōn*; *numquam*; *nihil*; or *nullus, a, um*. Result clauses show the outcome of an action. It sometimes can be difficult to distinguish between result clauses and purpose clauses, but words in the main clause such as *ita* (*thus*); *tantus, a, um* (*so much, so great*); *sīc* (*thus*); and *tam* (*so, to such a degree*) often signal that an *ut* clause which follows is a result clause. For example, in the sentence *Membra sūcōsque tantōs venēficōs in aēnō cavō mersit ut cornua exūrerent et corpus minuerent*, the adjective *tantōs* indicates that *ut cornua exūrerent et corpus minuerent* is a result clause. The sentence should be translated

She plunged the limbs and juices so magical in the hollow bronze that they burned off the horns and reduced the body in size. That the juices burned off the horns and reduced the animal in size is the outcome of the power of the magical juices. A purpose clause would indicate why Medea used the magical juices rather than the result of their use.

Medea's use of potions and magical drugs is in keeping with ancient ideas about the exotic nature of such compounds. In Homer's *Odyssey*, for example, Helen drops a *pharmakon*, which is a Greek word for drug, into the wine when Telemachus visits Sparta. The situation is uncomfortable because Telemachus is looking for his father, who went to war for Helen's sake, and Helen aims to ease the tension. Homer tells his audience that Helen got her drug from Egypt, where she met a woman skilled in such arts. Helen's source for the drug is exotic, just as Medea herself is exotic in that she is from Colchis on the Black Sea. Interestingly, poetry itself is frequently described by ancient authors as having an effect on its audience which is similar to the effect of powerful drugs.

25 Scylla and Nisus

(*Met.* 8.1–151)

When the daughter of King Nisus falls in love with Minos, who wages war against her kingdom, she offers the enemy-king her father's famous purple lock of hair.

1 Rēx Mīnōs lītora Megarae vastābat et vīrēs suās in urbe temptābat, quam Nīsus
2 habēbat. Cui crīnis purpureus inter honōrātōs cānōs in mediō vertice haerēbat. Crīnis
3 splendidus fīdūcia magnī regnī erat. Sex novae lūnae resurrexērant, et adhūc fortūna
4 bellī pendēbat, diūque Victōria inter utrumque rēgem dubiīs pennīs volābat.

5 In urbe, turris addita erat vōcālibus mūrīs in quibus prōlēs Lātōnae fertur auream
6 lyram dēposuisse: sonus eius in saxō haesit. In pace, Scylla, fīlia Nīsī, illūc
7 ascendere solēbat, et, iactāns lapillum, resonantia saxa petere solēbat. Nunc in
8 bellō, dē turre spectāre certāmina Martis solēbat. Iam nōmina procerum armaque
9 equōsque habitūsque pharetrāsque cognōvit.

10 Ante omnēs aliōs faciem Mīnōis nōverat—plūs etiam quam satis nōvisse est.
11 Mīnōs, rēx Crētum, seu caput casside cristātā abdiderat, in galeā formōsus erat; seu
12 clipeum fulgentem sumpserat, clipeum sūmpsisse decēbat; seu hastīlia torserat,
13 virgō artem et vīrēs laudābat. Cum vērō faciem casside demptā nūdāverat
14 purpureusque tergum albī equī insigne strātīs pictīs premēbat, vix virgō compos
15 mentis sānae erat. Impetus illī erat ferre virgineōs gradūs per agmen hostīle;
16 impetus illī erat mittere corpus ē summīs in Cnōsia castra.

Commentary

2 *Cui crīnis purpureus*: The antecedent of *cui* is *Nīsus*.

2–3 *Crīnis splendidus fīdūcia magnī regnī erat*: Nisus' purple lock of hair was his source of strength, so the security of his kingdom was dependent on it.

5–6 *turris addita erat vōcālibus mūrīs ... dēposuisse:* The walls of rock themselves produced musical sounds, perhaps from the wind blowing through them. *fertur* is used here to mean *it is said* and introduces the indirect statement. Latona is Apollo's mother.

10 *plūs etiam quam satis nōvisse est*: Translate: *even more than it is sufficient to know*. The infinitive is used with *satis est*. Ovid's language reveals Scylla's powerful attraction to the Cretan king.

14 *purpureusque tergum ... premēbat*: Minos is wearing the regal color purple. *insigne* describes *tergum*, and *strātīs pictīs* is an ablative qualifying *insigne*.

15 *impetus illī erat*: *illī* refers to Scylla. In other words, she wants to walk or jump off the tower into the Cretan camp.

abdō, abdere, abdidī, abditum: to hide, conceal

agmen, agminis n.: army, battle line

ascendō, ascendere, ascendī, ascensum: to ascend, climb

cassis, cassidis f.: helmet

castra, ōrum n. pl.: military encampment

Cnōsius, a, um: of Knossos, a city on Crete

compos, compotis: having mastery of, possessed of (+ gen.)

Crēs, Crētis m.: a Cretan

dubius, a, um: doubtful, uncertain

fulgeō, fulgēre, fulsī: to flash, shine

gradus, ūs m.: step, pace

habitus, ūs m.: condition, attire, dress, bearing

hastīle, hastīlis n.: shaft of a spear, spear

honōrātus, a, um: honored, respected

hostīlis, e: hostile, unfriendly

insignis, insigne: distinguished, remarkable

lapillus, ī m.: little stone, pebble

lītus, lītoris n.: the shore

Megara, ae f.: Megara, a city in Greece

Mīnōs, Mīnōis m.: Minos, king of Crete

mūrus, ī m.: city wall

Nīsus, ī m.: Nisus, king of Megara

nūdō, nūdāre, nūdāvī, nūdātum: to strip, lay bare

pax, pācis f.: peace, tranquility

resonō, resonāre, resonāvī, resonātum: to resound, echo

resurgō, resurgere, resurrexī, resurrectum: to rise again, appear again

sānus, a, um: healthy, rational

Scylla, ae f.: Scylla, daughter of Nisus

sonus, ī m.: a sound, noise

splendidus, a, um: splendid, bright, distinguished

sūmō, sūmere, sumpsī, sumptum: to take up, assume, select

strātum, ī n.: coverlet, horsecloth

turris, turris f.: a tower, citadel

vastō, vastāre, vastāvī, vastātum: to devastate, ravage, make empty

vertex, verticis m.: whirlpool, crown of head, summit

vōcālis, e: uttering sounds, singing, vocal, sonorous

17   Ut spectāns candida tentōria rēgis Crētum sedēbat, dixit: "Doleō, quod Mīnōs
18   hostis mihi amantī est. Sī fēmina quae tē peperit tālis erat, pulcherrime rēgum,
19   quālis es ipse, meritō rēx deōrum amore illīus arsit. Ō ego ter fēlix erō, sī, lāpsa per
20   aurās pennīs in Cnōsiaca castra, poterō fatērī meum amōrem rēgī. Custos aditūs
21   servat, et pater claustra portārum tenet. Patrem sōlum timeō; sōlus mea vōta
22   morātur. Amor mē hortātur ut perdam quod obstat meō amōrī. Opus est mihi crīne
23   paternō. Ille mihi est pretiōsior aurō; ille purpureus crīnis mē beātam faciet."

24   Tālibus dictīs, nox intervēnit, et audācia in tenebrīs crēvit. Taciturna fīlia
25   thalamum paternum intrat et (heu facinus!) parentem crīne spoliat. Portāns
26   praedam nefandam per mediōs hostēs pervenit ad rēgem. Scylla illī dīcit: "Amor
27   facinus suāsit: ego Scylla, fīlia Nīsī, patriam Penātēsque meōs tibi trādō. Petō ā tē
28   ut mē amēs. Cape purpureum crīnem pignus amōris." Mīnōs, turbātus imāgine factī
29   novī, mūnus refugit, et respondet: "Dī tē summoveant ē suō orbe, ō īnfamia nostrī
30   saeculī. Tellūs pontusque tibi negentur! Certē ego nōn patiar tantum monstrum
31   contingere Crētam, incūnābula Iovis."

32   Lēgibus captīs hostibus impositīs, Mīnōs imperāvit ut classis solverētur et puppēs
33   rēmige impellerentur. Scylla clāmat: "Mē miseram! Mīnōs virōs eius properāre
34   iubet, et cīvēs patriae mē ōdērunt. Sequar tē invītum, rēx Cnōsiace, et amplexa
35   puppim per freta longa trahar!" Vix dīxerat, insiluit in undās, et secūta est ratēs
36   cupīdine faciente vīrēs. Invidiōsa comes Cnōsiacae carīnae haesit. Pater, quī (modo
37   factus haliaeetus) iam pendēbat in aurā, ībat ut illam rōstrō aduncō lacerāret. Illa
38   metū puppim dīmīsit, et levis aura cadentem sustinēre vīsa est. Plūma palmīs subit:
39   mūtāta in avem Cīris vocātur, et hoc nōmen ā tonsō capillō adepta est.

Commentary

18 *Sī fēmina quae tē peperit*: Minos' mother was Europa, whom Jupiter impregnated.

19 *amore illīus*: The genitive *illīus* is an objective genitive. Translate: *love for that woman*.

22–3 *Opus est mihi crīne paternō*: *Opus est* (*there is need*) is a common construction in Latin. Here, the person in need is in the dative, and the thing needed is in the ablative.

23 *pretiōsior aurō*: *aurō* is an ablative of comparison. Translate: *more precious than gold*.

25 *et (heu facinus!) parentem crīne spoliat*: The verb *spoliāre* here takes an accusative of the person robbed and an ablative of the thing taken.

32 *Lēgibus captīs hostibus impositīs*: *Lēgibus impositīs* is an ablative absolute, and *captīs hostibus* is dative after *impositīs*.

36 *cupīdine faciente vīrēs*: *cupīdine faciente* is an ablative absolute. *vīrēs* is the object of *faciente*.

37–8 *Illa metū puppim dīmīsit*: *metū* is an ablative of cause. Translate: *That one let go of the ship out of fear*.

adipiscor, adipiscī, adeptus sum: to arrive at, obtain, acquire

aditus, ūs m.: approach, entrance, access

aduncus, a, um: hooked

audācia, ae f.: boldness, courage

Cīris, Cīris f.: a colorful bird

cīvis, cīvis m. or f.: citizen

classis, classis f.: fleet

claustra, ōrum n. pl.: bar, bolt

Cnōsiacus, a, um: of Knossos

custos, custōdis m.: guard

dīmittō, dīmittere, dīmīsī, dīmissum: to send away, let go

fateor, fatērī, fassus sum: to confess, acknowledge

haliaeetus, ī m.: osprey, sea-eagle

heu: (interj.) oh! alas!

hortor, hortārī, hortātus sum: to encourage, urge on

impellō, impellere, impulī, impulsum: to push, drive, set in motion

imperō, imperāre, imperāvī, imperātum: to command, order

incūnābula, ōrum n. pl.: cradle, birthplace

insiliō, insilīre, insiluī: to leap on, leap into

interveniō, intervenīre, intervēnī, interventum: to come between, intervene, interrupt

lābor, lābī, lapsus sum: to glide down, fall, slip

lacerō, lacerāre, lacerāvī, lacerātum: to tear, lacerate

meritō: (adv.) deservedly, justly

modo: (adv.) only, just now, lately

nefandus, a, um: impious, heinous

palma, ae f.: palm of the hand

pariō, parere, peperī, partum: to bring forth, produce

Penātēs, Penātium m. pl.: household gods

perveniō, pervenīre, pervēnī, perventum: to come to, reach

plūma, ae f.: feather, plumage

pretiōsior, ius: more precious, more valuable

properō, properāre, properāvī, properātum: to hasten

pulcherrimus, a, um: most beautiful

puppis, puppis f.: stern of a ship

quod: (conj.) because

refugiō, refugere, refūgī: to flee, escape

rēmex, rēmigis m.: bench of oarsmen, rower

sequor, sequī, secūtus sum: to follow, pursue

suādeō, suādēre, suāsī, suāsum: to advise, recommend, persuade

tentōrium, ī n.: tent

tondeō, tondēre, totondī, tonsum: to shear, clip, shave

turbātus, a, um: troubled, disturbed, agitated

JUSSIVE NOUN CLAUSES

Jussive noun clauses are another type of subjunctive clause introduced by *ut* or *nē*, so they are easy to confuse with result clauses and, especially, with purpose clauses. As the name suggests, a jussive noun clause is an indirect command. These clauses are often introduced by verbs of seeking, asking, urging, or ordering, and they essentially function as objects of the verbs which introduce them. In the sentence *Amor mē hortātur ut perdam quod obstat meō amōrī*, the *ut* clause is a jussive noun clause, and the sentence should be translated *Love urges me to destroy that which stands against my love*. Essentially, a jussive noun clause is just another way of expressing indirect speech, like accusative-infinitive constructions. Literally, the sentence above reads *Love urges me that I destroy that which stands against my love*. Here, the *ut* clause serves as the object of the verb *hortātur*. To some degree, jussive noun clauses are interchangeable with accusative-infinitive constructions, although certain verbs consistently govern one or the other.

In this story, Ovid presents Scylla as a girl so overcome by passion for Minos that she commits an act of incredible treachery, something which she probably would not do under normal circumstances. In Greek and Roman literature, erotic love is associated with madness, and this association is especially true for women. In Vergil's *Aeneid*, for example, when Dido discovers that Aeneas is secretly preparing to leave Carthage, she loses her mind and rages through the city in the manner of a female follower of Bacchus who has been intoxicated with the power of the god, and ultimately she kills herself. Erotic love causes one to lose control of oneself just like wine, drugs, and Bacchus himself.

26 Pomona and Vertumnus

(*Met.* 14.623–771)

Vertumnus attempts to win over the wood nymph Pomona by disguise and persuasion.

1   Pōmōna sub rēge Procā vixit, quā nulla inter Latīnās hamadryadēs hortōs sollertius
2   coluit, et nulla studiōsior arboreī fētūs fuit. Illa nōn silvās nec amnēs, sed rūs et
3   rāmōs ferentēs pōma amābat, unde nōmen tenēbat. Nec dextera iaculum habēbat,
4   sed habēbat aduncam falcem quā luxuriem premēbat et bracchia spatiantia
5   compescēbat. Nec arborēs sentīre sitim passa est, sed recurvās fibrās bibulārum
6   rādīcum irrigāvit. Hic amor Pōmōnae, hoc studium erat. Nulla cupīdō Veneris erat.
7   Metuēns vim agrestium, sē in pōmāriō clausit, et prohibuit refūgitque accessūs
8   virīlēs.

9   In amōre nymphae deus Vertumnus omnēs superābat, sed nōn fēlix erat. Ō
10   quotiens in habitū dūrī messōris—et imāgō vērī messōris fuit—aristās in corbe
11   Pōmōnae tulit! Sī stimulum manū portet, iūrēs deum modo iuvencōs fessōs
12   disiunxisse. Falce datā frondātor erat putātorque. Sī scālās portet, putēs
13   Vertumnum lectūrum esse pōma. Mīles erat gladiō datō, piscātor erat harundine
14   datā. Per multās figūrās poterat spectāre Pōmōnam.

15   Ille etiam positīs per tempora cānīs, anum adsimulāvit, et, innītēns baculō, in
16   hortōs intrāvit. Deus pōma mīrātus est. Pauca oscula Pōmōnae dedit, quālia anus
17   vēra numquam dedisset. In glaebā anus resēdit. Contrā erat ulmus speciōsa vīte
18   ūvārum. Quam postquam pariter cum sociā vīte probāverat, anus falsa dixit: "Sī

Commentary

1–2 *quā nulla ... sollertius coluit*: The antecedent of the relative pronoun is Pōmōna. It is in the ablative because it functions as an ablative of comparison after *sollertius*. Translate: *than whom no one of the wood nymphs of Latium cultivated gardens more skillfully.*

6 *Nulla cupīdō Veneris erat*: *Veneris* is an objective genitive and stands for romantic love rather than the goddess herself. In other words, Pomona is not interested in romance.

14 *Per multās figūrās poterat spectāre Pomonam*: Vertumnus uses his many disguises to create opportunities to see Pomona.

16–17 *quālia ... dedisset*: The word *quālia* refers to *oscula*.

18 *Quam postquam*: The antecedent of *quam* is *ulmus*. Disguised as the old woman, Vertumnus praises the elm with its companion-vine to allow him to bring up the subject of love and coupling.

accessus, ūs m.: approach, entrance, access

amnis, amnis m.: river

arboreus, a, um: of a tree

bibulus, a, um: drinking freely, absorbing

compescō, compescere, compescuī: to confine, check, restrain

contrā: (adv.) on the opposite side

corbis, corbis m.: basket

disiungō, disiungere, disiunxī, disiunctum: to disjoin, separate, unyoke

falx, falcis f.: pruning-hook, scythe

fibra, ae f.: fiber

frondātor, frondātoris m.: one who prunes

hamadryas, hamadryadis f.: a wood nymph

harundo, harundinis f.: fishing rod

hortus, ī m.: garden

iaculum, ī n.: dart, javelin

innītor, innītī, innixus sum: to lean upon, rest on

irrigō, irrigāre, irrigāvī, irrigātum: to water, irrigate

Latīnus, a, um: of Latium, the region which includes Rome

luxuriēs, luxuriēī f.: extravagance, excess

messor, messōris m.: reaper, mower

pariter: (adv.) equally

paucus, a, um: few, small in number

piscātor, piscātoris m.: fisherman

Pōmōna, ae f.: Pomona, goddess of fruit-trees

Proca, ae m.: Proca, a king of the Italian city of Alba

prohibeō, prohibēre, prohibuī, prohibitum: to hold back, restrain, prevent

putātor, putātoris m.: pruner of trees

quotiens: (adv.) how often

recurvus, a, um: turned back, bent

rūs, rūris n.: country, land

scāla, ae f.: ladder, flight of stairs

socius, a, um: sharing, companion

sollertius: (adv.) more skillfully

spatior, spatiārī, spatiātus sum: to spread out, expand

speciōsus, a, um: beautiful, splendid

stimulus, ī m.: spur, cattle prod

studiōsior, ius: more diligent about, more eager for (+ gen.)

ulmus, ī f.: elm

Vertumnus, ī m.: Vertumnus, god of the cycle of the seasons

vērus, a, um: true

vītis, vītis f.: vine

19   trunca stāret caelebs sine vīte, nihil praeter frondēs habēret. Nisi haec vītis, quae in
20   ulmō requiēscit, cum arbore nupta foret, acclīnāta in terram iacēret. Tū tamen
21   exemplō huius arboris nōn tangeris, et amantēs fugis. Cupiās amāre, sint tibi plūrēs
22   amantēs quam Helenae vel coniugī Ulixis. Sed sī audīveris hanc anum, quae tē
23   plūs omnibus illīs amō, et cupīveris iungere tē bene, sēligēs tibi Vertumnum
24   socium torī. Deus iuvenis et pulcher est. Decus habet, et potest fingī in omnēs
25   formās. Miseresce Vertumnī, quī tē sōlam amat. Habē in memoriā Īphin et
26   Anaxaretēn. Īphis Anaxaretēn vīdit et amāvit, sed Anaxaretē, saevior fretō surgente
27   et dūrior ferrō, amantem spernēbat et inrīdēbat. Infēlix Īphis serta vincula laqueī
28   religāvit, et caput īnseruit, et dixit "Haec serta tibi placēbunt, crūdēlis et impia
29   Anaxaretē!" Mox infēlix corpus iuvenis fauce ēlīsā pependit. Sī Anaxaretē eum
30   amāvisset, Īphis nōn mortuus esset. Dēpōne fastūs, precor, nympha, et cēde
31   amantī!"

32   Ubi deus nēquīquam haec ēdiderat, in formam iuvenis rediit et anīlia īnstrūmenta
33   dempsit. Vim parābat, sed vī nōn opus est. Nympha figūrā deī capta est, et mūtua
34   vulnera amōris sēnsit.

Commentary

19–20 *Nisi* ... *foret:* *foret* is the third person singular imperfect subjunctive of *esse.*

22 *quam Helenae vel coniugī Ulixis:* Helen was the most beautiful woman in the world, and Ulysses' wife, Penelope, was pursued by over a hundred suitors while the hero was away at war.

22–3 *quae* ... *amō:* The relative pronoun *quae* refers to *anus*, but the verb is in the first person because Vertumnus is talking about himself in disguise.

25 *Miseresce Vertumnī:* The verb *miserescere* takes a genitive object of the person or thing pitied.

26–7 *saevior fretō surgente et dūrior ferrō:* The ablatives *fretō* and *ferrō* are ablatives of comparison.

acclīnātus, a, um: leaning on

Anaxaretē, ēs f.: Anaxarete, a young woman from Cyprus

caelebs, caelibis: unmarried, uncoupled, single

decus, decoris n.: honor, glory, charm

durior, ius: harder, tougher

fastus, ūs m.: haughtiness, arrogance, pride

faux, faucis f.: throat, narrow entrance

Helena, ae f.: Helen of Troy, queen of Sparta

inserō, inserere, inseruī, insertum: to put in, insert

Īphis, Īphis m.: Iphis, a young man from Cyprus

morior, morī, mortuus sum: to die

mūtuus, a, um: reciprocal, mutual

nēquīquam: (adv.) in vain, to no purpose

precor, precārī, precātus sum: to beg, entreat, pray

pulcher, pulchra, pulchrum: beautiful

saevior, ius: more savage

sēligō, sēligere, sēlēgī, sēlectum: to choose, select

serō, serere, seruī, sertum: to connect, bind together, weave

truncus, ī m.: trunk of a tree

Ulixes, Ulixis m.: Ulysses, the Greek hero Odysseus

PLUPERFECT SUBJUNCTIVE

The pluperfect subjunctive active is formed by adding personal endings to the perfect infinitive. The pluperfect subjunctive passive is formed by a combination of the perfect passive participle and the imperfect subjunctive of *esse*.

inserō, insere, inseruī, insertum: active

	Singular	Plural
1st person	inseruissem	inseruissēmus
2nd person	inseruissēs	inseruissētis
3rd person	inseruisset	inseruissent

inserō, insere, inseruī, insertum: passive

	Singular	Plural
1st person	insertum essem	inserta essēmus
2nd person	insertum essēs	inserta essētis
3rd person	insertum esset	inserta essent

sum, esse, fuī, futūrum

	Singular	Plural
1st person	fuissem	fuissēmus
2nd person	fuissēs	fuissētis
3rd person	fuisset	fuissent

CONDITIONS

There are six kinds of conditional sentences in Latin. Three use verbs in the indicative, and three use verbs in the subjunctive. Conditions are often introduced by *sī* or *nisi*. They have two elements: a protasis, which is the premise, and an apodosis, which is the outcome.

- **Simple Fact Present**: Uses present indicative verbs in both the protasis and the apodosis. *Sī puerum amat, puella beata est.* (*If she loves the boy, the girl is happy.*)
- **Simple Fact Past**: Uses imperfect or perfect indicative verbs in both the protasis and the apodosis. *Sī puerum amābat, puella beata erat.* (*If she loved the boy, the girl was happy.*)
- **Future More Vivid**: Uses future or future perfect indicative in both the protasis and the apodosis. *Sī puerum amābit, puella beata erit.* (*If she loves [will love] the boy, the girl will be happy.*)

- **Future Less Vivid**: Uses present subjunctive in both the protasis and the apodosis. *Sī puerum amet, puella beata sit.* (*If she should love the boy, the girl would be happy.*)
- **Present Contrary to Fact**: Uses imperfect subjunctive in both the protasis and the apodosis. *Sī puerum amāret, puella beata foret.* (*If she were loving the boy, the girl would be happy.*)
- **Past Contrary to Fact**: Uses pluperfect subjunctive in both the protasis and the apodosis. *Sī puerum amāvisset, puella beata fuisset.* (*If she had loved the boy, the girl would have been happy.*)

In order to translate conditions correctly, it is essential to recognize which type of condition is at work. In the sentence *Sī trunca stāret caelebs sine vīte, nihil praeter frondēs habēret*, both verbs are in the imperfect subjunctive, so the sentence is a present contrary to fact condition and should be translated *If the trunk were standing uncoupled, without the vine, it would have nothing besides leaves*. In the sentence *Cupiās amāre, sint tibi plūrēs amantēs quam Helenae vel coniugī Ulixis*, both verbs are in the present subjunctive, so the sentence is a future less vivid condition and should be translated *Should you desire to love, there would be more lovers for you than for Helen or for the wife of Ulysses*. Note that in this condition, the protasis is not introduced by *sī* or *nisi*.

The story of Pomona and Vertumnus is one of many stories in the *Metamorphoses* in which a god operates in disguise. In the story about the contest between Arachne and Minerva, for example, Minerva is disguised as an old woman when she first approaches Arachne. In that same story, Arachne's tapestry depicts the male gods disguising themselves in order to deceive and rape both mortal and divine women. Ovid tells his audience that the frustrated Vertumnus prepares to use force against Pomona but does not end up doing so when Pomona unexpectedly falls in love with him upon seeing his true form. Thus, unlike many of Ovid's stories which involve disguise and deception, this story ends happily.

27 Quirinus

(*Met.* 14.805–51)

After Romulus successfully establishes Rome, he is honored with deification. His wife Hersilia
follows him.

1 Rōmulus erat prīmus rēx Rōmānōrum, et Māvors erat pater Rōmulī. Rhēa Silvia, ā
2 Māvorte rapta, mater rēgis Rōmānī erat. Dum Rōmulus iūra populō dat, Māvors
3 casside positā tālibus verbīs parentem dīvōrumque hominumque adfātur: "Tempus
4 adest, genitor. Cum rēs Rōmāna valeat, solve praemia quae prōmissa sunt mihi
5 dignōque nepōtī tuō, et pōne Rōmulum in caelō. Quondam in conciliō deōrum
6 (nam pia verba in animō notāvī) tū mihi dīxistī: 'Erit ūnus quem tū in caelum
7 tollēs.' Summa tuōrum verbōrum sit rata!"

8 Omnipotēns pater adnuit, et āera nūbibus caecīs occuluit. Tonitrū et fulgure orbem
9 terrārum terruit. Cum Grādīvus signa prōmissa sentīret, innīxus hastā currum,
10 ductum equīs tēmōne cruentō pressīs, cōnscendit, et ictū verberis increpuit. Lapsus
11 prōnus per āera in summō colle nemorōsī Palātīnī cōnstitit. Rōmulum reddentem
12 iam iūra Rōmānīs abstulit. Corpus mortāle per aurās tenuēs dīlāpsum est, ut glāns
13 plumbea missa lātā fundā solet intābēscere in mediō caelō. Rōmulus faciem
14 digniōrem pulvīnāribus altīs habuit. Quālis est fōrma Quirīnī. Rōmulus est
15 Quirīnus, novus deus!

Commentary

4 *Cum rēs Rōmāna valeat*: *rēs Rōmāna* means *the Roman state*.

7 *Summa … sit rata*: Jussive subjunctive. The participle *rata* is used here in a passive sense to mean *ratified*, *fixed*, or *settled*, even though it is from a deponent verb. Translate: *May the sum of your words be ratified*.

10 *ductum equīs tēmōne cruentō pressīs*: Ovid describes the yoke of the chariot as bloody to illustrate the ferocity of the horses.

12–13 *ut glāns plumbea missa lātā fundā*: *lātā fundā* is an ablative of means.

14 *digniōrem pulvīnāribus altīs*: *dignior, ius* (the comparative of *dignus, a, um*) can be followed by an ablative or a genitive. Romulus is undergoing a transformation from human to god and is thus worthy of divine couches.

adfor, adfārī, adfātus sum: to speak to, address

adnuō, adnuere, adnuī, adnūtum: to nod, give assent

collis, collis m.: hill

dignior, ius: more worthy

dīlābor, dīlābī, dīlapsus sum: to fall down, fall apart, perish

dūcō, dūcere, duxī, ductum: to lead

fulgur, fulguris n.: lightning

funda, ae f.: sling

glāns, glandis f.: ball of lead, bullet

Gradīvus, ī m.: Gradivus, epithet of Mars meaning "He who walks in battle"

increpō, increpere, increpuī, increpitum: to make a noise, resound

intābescō, intābescere, intābuī: to melt away, dissolve

nemorōsus, a, um: wooded

Palātīnus, a, um: of the Palatine, one of the seven hills of Rome

pulvīnar, pulvīnāris n.: cushioned seat, seat of honor

Quirīnus, ī m.: Quirinus, a god with whom the deified Romulus was identified

quondam: (adv.) once, formerly

reddō, reddere, reddidī, redditum: to give back, restore, return to

reor, rērī, ratus sum: to calculate, judge, reckon

rēs Rōmāna, reī Rōmānae f.: Roman state

Rhēa Silvia, Rhēae Silviae f.: Rhea Silvia, the mother of Romulus and Remus

Rōmānus, a, um: of Rome

Rōmulus, ī m.: Romulus, the first king of Rome

summa, ae f.: a summary, most important point, sum total

tēmō, tēmōnis m.: beam, yoke

tenuis, e: thin, fine

tonitrus, ūs m.: thunder

valeō, valēre, valuī, valitum: to be strong, be healthy

verber, verberis n.: lash, whip

16   Coniunx Rōmulī, Hersilia, virum ut āmissum flet, cum Iūnō Īrin dēscendere ad
17   Hersiliam et referre sīc sua mandāta imperat. Īris pāret, et dēlapsa per arcūs pictōs
18   in terram Hersiliam iussīs verbīs compellat. "Ō mātrōna, dignissima fuisse ante
19   coniunx tantī virī, nunc esse coniunx Quirīnī, siste tuōs flētūs. Sī vidēre coniugem
20   cupis, mēcum lūcum in colle Quirīnī pete quī viret et templum rēgis Rōmānī
21   obumbrat." Hersilia vix tollēns lūmina dīcit: "Ō dea (nam certa dīva es), dūc, ō
22   dūc, et offer ōra coniugis mihi! Cum mē terreās, cupiō tamen vidēre virum. Sī fāta
23   dederint mē posse vidēre semel ōra coniugis, mē accēpisse caelum fatēbor!"

24   Sine morā, ingreditur collem Rōmuleum cum deā. Ibi sīdus lapsum ab aethere
25   dēcidit in terrās. Crīnibus ā lūmine sīderis flagrantibus, Hersilia cum sīdere in
26   aurās cessit. Conditor urbis Rōmānae hanc manibus nōtīs excēpit, et priscum
27   nōmen pariter cum corpore mūtāvit. Hora vocātur, quae nunc dea Quirīnō iuncta
28   est.

Commentary

16 *cum Iūnō Īrin dēscendere*: *Īrin* is accusative singular.
18–19 *Ō mātrōna, dignissima fuisse ante coniunx tantī virī, nunc esse coniunx Quirīnī*: Understand *dignissima* with both infinitive constructions.
21 *Hersilia vix tollēns lūmina*: *lūmina* means *eyes* here.
23 *dederint mē posse vidēre*: Understand *dederint* to mean *grant* here. Translate: *If the fates will have granted* ...
23 *mē accēpisse caelum fatēbor*: Hersilia means that she will be very happy, but Ovid's language also foreshadows her transformation into a star.
25–26 *Crīnibus ā lūmine sīderis flagrantibus* ... *cessit*: *Crīnibus flagrantibus* is an ablative absolute. After her hair bursts into flames, Hersilia rises up into the air with the star.

compellō, compellāre, compellāvī, compellātum: to address, accost

dēcidō, dēcidere, dēcidī: to fall down, fall away

dēlābor, dēlābī, dēlapsus sum: to glide down, fall down, sink

flētus, ūs m.: tears, weeping

Hersilia, ae f.: Hersilia, wife of Romulus

Hora, ae f.: Hora, the name of deified Hersilia

ingredior, ingredī, ingressus sum: to step in, enter, walk

Īris, Īris f.: Iris, goddess of the rainbow and messenger of the gods

obumbrō, obumbrāre, obumbrāvī, obumbrātum: to overshadow, cover

priscus, a, um: old, ancient

Rōmuleus, a, um: of Romulus

sistō, sistere, stitī: to stand, cause to stand still, stop

vireō, virēre, viruī: to be green

CUM CLAUSES

Cum clauses feature verbs in either the indicative or the subjunctive mood. When the verb is in the indicative, the cum clause is a temporal clause and *cum* should be translated *when*. When the verb is in the subjunctive, the *cum* clause is one of three types. In a circumstantial *cum* clause, *cum* should be translated *when*, and the clause describes the circumstances under which something happens rather than the time at which it happens (which would be the case with a verb in the indicative). In a causal *cum* clause, *cum* should be translated *since*. In a concessive *cum* clause, *cum* should be translated *although*. When you encounter a *cum* clause which features a verb in the subjunctive, you have to decide which type of clause is represented. In the sentence *Cum rēs Rōmāna valeat, solve praemia quae prōmissa sunt mihi dignōque nepōtī tuō, et pōne Rōmulum in caelō*, the *cum* clause is best interpreted as a causal clause and the *cum* should be translated *since*. In the sentence *Cum mē terreās, cupiō tamen vidēre virum*, the *tamen* indicates that the *cum* clause is concessive. Thus, *cum* should be translated *although*.

Roman history traditionally is divided into three main periods, and the earliest of these is a period in which Rome is ruled by seven kings. The period starts in 753 BCE when Rome is founded by Romulus, and runs until the last king is expelled in 510–509 BCE. Romulus' name simply means "man of Rome," and the king is mythical rather than historical. According to myth, Rhea Silvia is impregnated by the god Mars and subsequently gives birth to both Romulus and his twin brother Remus. When their birth is discovered, the twins are placed into a basket and set afloat on the Tiber River. The basket washes up on a shore, and the twins are nursed by a she-wolf until they are found. Eventually, they restore their ousted grandfather to the throne of Alba Longa and set out to establish a new city. Because of rivalry between the brothers, Romulus kills Remus and becomes the first king of Rome. The deification in this story anticipates the apotheosis of Julius Caesar at the end of the *Metamorphoses*.

28 Cipus

(Met. 15.547–621)

When Cipus realizes that horns have grown from his head and that he stands to become king of Rome, he exiles himself from the city to avoid the office.

1 Cīpus Rōmānus cui tȳrannis odiōsa foret erat. Sīc nēmō stupuit magis quam Cīpus
2 cum sē vīdit in undā flūmineā. Ille in undā sua cornua vīdit, et, crēdēns imāginem
3 esse falsam, saepe digitōs ad frontem referēbat. Quae vīdit, tetigit. Nec monstrō
4 restitit, sed, ut victor ab hoste domitō remeābat, tollēns oculōs et bracchia ad
5 caelum dixit: "Superī, quidquid istō monstrō portenditur, seu laetum est, laetum
6 patriae populōque Quirīnī sit, seu mināx, mināx mihi sit."

7 Āram herbōsam ē caespite viridī facit, et deōs ignibus odōrātīs plācat. Vīnum in
8 paterīs dat, et trepidantia exta bidentium mactātārum consulit. Quae simul haruspex
9 Tyrrhēnus adspicit, magna mōlīmina rērum in illīs videt, nōn tamen manifesta.
10 Cum vērō oculōs ad cornua Cīpī tollit, dīcit: "Ō rēx! Haec cornua sunt quae
11 virum rēgem faciant! Tibi enim, tibi, Cīpe, tuīsque cornibus hic locus et arcēs
12 Latiae pārēbunt. Tū modo morās rumpe, et approperā intrāre portās patentēs! Sīc
13 fāta iubent. Nam, receptus in urbe, rēx eris, et tūtus sceptrō potiēris."

14 Ille pedem refert, et, āvertēns faciem torvam ā moenibus urbis, dīcit: "Procul! Dī
15 procul rēgēs pellant! Iustius multō ego exsul aevum agam. Rōma mē rēgem nē

Commentary

1 *cui tȳrannis odiōsus foret*: *foret* is the same as *esset*, the imperfect subjunctive of *esse*.
3 *Quae vīdit, tetigit*: The antecedent of *quae* is *cornua*.
8–9 *Quae simul haruspex Tyrrhēnus adspicit*: The antecedent of *quae* is *exta*. Cipus has consulted a haruspex to determine what is indicated by his new horns.
14 *Ille pedem refert*: Cipus takes a step backwards.
15 *Iustius multō*: *multō* is an ablative of degree of difference with the comparative adverb *iustius*. Translate: *more justly by much*.

appropero, approperare, approperavi, approperatum: to hasten

averto, avertere, averti, aversum: to turn away, remove, avert

Cipus, i m.: Cipus, an early Roman praetor

domo, domare, domui, domitum: to tame, subdue

exsul, exsulis m. or f.: an exile, banished person

exta, extorum n. pl.: the entrails of an animal

flumineus, a, um: of a river

haruspex, haruspicis m.: a soothsayer who prophesies by looking at entrails

herbosus, a, um: grassy

iustius: (adv.) more justly

Latius, a, um: of Latium

macto, mactare, mactavi, mactatum: to slay, sacrifice

nemo, neminis m. or f.: no one, nobody

odiosus, a, um: hateful, despised

odoro, odorare, odoravi, odoratum: to make odorous, make sweet-smelling

patera, ae f.: a shallow dish, saucer

placo, placare, placavi, placatum: to soothe, calm

porta, ae f.: a gate, door

portendo, portendere, portendi, portentum: to indicate, predict

remeo, remeare, remeavi, remeatum: to return, go back

Roma, ae f.: Rome

trepido, trepidare, trepidavi, trepidatum: to be agitated

tyrannis, tyrannidis f.: tyranny, despotic rule

Tyrrhenus, a, um: of Etruria, Etruscan

vinum, i n.: wine

16   videat!" Verbīs dictīs extemplō populumque senātumque convocat; ante tamen
17   cornua laurō pācālī vēlat. Priscōs deōs precātur, et dīcit: "Ūnus est hīc, quī, nisi
18   vōs hunc ex urbe pepuleritis, rēx erit. Hunc dīcam nōn nōmine sed signō. Cornua
19   in fronte gerit! Augur indicat vōbīs, sī Rōmam intrāverit, famulāria iūra datūrum
20   esse. Ille quidem irrumpere portās apertās potuit, sed ego obstitī, quamvīs nēmō est
21   coniunctior mihi illō. Prohibēte virum ab urbe, Rōmānī, vel, sī dignus erit, aut
22   vincīte catēnīs gravibus, aut fīnīte metum morte tyrannī fātālis!"

23   Per confūsa verba vulgī ūna vōx ēminet: "Quis ille est?" Cīvēs frontēs spectant, et
24   cornua praedicta quaerunt. Cīpus dīcit: "Quem poscitis, habētis," et, corōnā laurī
25   demptā, tempora praesignia cornibus exhibet. Omnēs oculōs dēmittunt, et gemitum
26   dant. Nec patientēs illum ulterius carēre honōre, impōnunt corōnam laurī. At
27   procerēs, quoniam intrāre mūrōs vetārīs, Cīpe, rūs magnum tibi honōrātō dant.
28   Cornua in aerātīs postibus portārum insculpunt, mansūra per longum aevum. Cīpus
29   vir quem Rōmānī ament est.

Commentary

19–20 *sī Rōmam intrāverit . . . datūrum esse*: This is a future more vivid condition in indirect statement after *indicat*.

21 *coniunctior mihi illō*: *illō* is ablative of comparison after the comparative *coniunctior*. Translate: *more connected to me than that man*.

22 *aut fīnīte metum morte tyrannī fātālis*: *morte* is an ablative of means.

26–7 *At procerēs . . . rūs magnum tibi honōrātō dant*: Ovid addresses Cipus directly here, making the story more vivid for his audience. *rūs* refers to an estate in the country rather than the country itself.

aerātus, a, um: made of bronze

augur, auguris m. or f.: augur, soothsayer

confundō, confundere, confūdī, confūsum: to pour together, mix up

coniunctior, ius: more connected, more joined

convocō, convocāre, convocāvī, convocātum: to call together, assemble

ēmineō, ēminēre, ēminuī: to project, stand out

famulāris, e: relating to slaves

fātālis, e: fated, destined

fīniō, fīnīre, fīnīvī, fīnītum: to put an end to, limit

gemitus, ūs m.: groan

indicō, indicāre, indicāvī, indicātum: to make known, show

insculpō, insculpere, insculpsī, insculptum: to cut into, engrave

irrumpō, irrumpere, irrūpī, irruptum: to break in, rush in

pācālis, e: peaceful

postis, postis m.: a door post

praedīcō, praedīcere, praedixī, praedictum: to prophesy, foretell

senātus, ūs m.: the senate

vetō, vetāre, vetuī, vetitum: to forbid, prohibit

RELATIVE CLAUSES OF CHARACTERISTIC

Relative clauses of characteristic are subjunctive clauses introduced by relative pronouns. Whereas a relative clause which contains a verb in the indicative mood offers actual information about the antecedent of the relative pronoun, a relative clauses of characteristic offers less concrete information about its antecedent. For example, in the sentence *Cīpus Rōmānus cui tȳrannis odiōsa foret erat*, the relative clause *cui tȳrannis odiōsa foret* contains a verb in the imperfect subjunctive and is a relative clause of characteristic. The sentence should be translated *Cipus was **the type of** Roman man for whom tyranny was hateful*, as opposed to *Cipus was a Roman man for whom tyranny was hateful*. The information provided by the clause is more general than that provided by a relative clause which uses a verb in the indicative. Similarly, the sentence *Cīpus vir quem Rōmānī ament est* should be translated *Cipus is **the sort of** man whom the Romans love*.

> The story of Cipus, who is honored for refusing to become a Roman king even though he is given the opportunity, captures the Romans' negative attitude towards monarchy. Although early Roman kings such as Romulus and Numa Pompilius were regarded with reverence, in general Romans celebrated their republican government and opposed the idea of absolute rule. Julius Caesar was assassinated by men who feared his status as dictator. Thus, when establishing himself as the first emperor, Augustus was careful to construct an image of himself which did not suggest kingship.

29 Aesculapius

(*Met.* 15.622–744)

When a deadly plague strikes the city, the Romans invite the god of medicine to come to Rome from Epidaurus.

1   Quondam dīra luēs aurās Rōmānās vitiāverat, et corpora pallida morbō squālēbant.
2   Virī, fessī fūneribus, mortālia temptāmenta esse nihil cernunt et artēs medentium
3   nōn posse. Rōmānī sē quid luem fēcerit rogant, sed nōn sciunt quae causa fuerit vel
4   quid iuvet vel quōs consulere dēbeant. Auxilium caeleste petunt, et Delphōs,
5   tenentēs mediam humum orbis, adeunt. Ōrāculum Phoebī petunt. Ōrant ut deus
6   mala urbis fīniat. Et locus et laurus et pharetra, quam deus ipse habet, intremiscunt.
7   Cortīna ex adytō hanc vōcem reddit, et pectora pavefacta movet: "Quod hinc
8   petitis, Rōmānī, petite nunc in aliō locō. Nec opus est Phoebō, sed Phoebēiō nātō.
9   Īte cum bonīs avibus prōlemque meam arcessite."

Commentary

1 *Quondam dīra … squālēbant*: Ovid begins his account with a vivid description of poisoned air and pale bodies wasted by the disease. Ancient Greek medical texts discuss the importance of the quality of air for health.

2–3 *et artēs medentium nōn posse*: This accusative-infinitive construction is still in indirect statement after *cernunt*, and *posse* is used here to mean *to be effective*.

5 *tenentēs mediam humum orbis*: The sanctuary of Delphi was thought to be located at the center of the earth.

6 *Et locus et laurus et pharetra, quam deus ipse habet, intremiscunt*: Ovid refers to the sanctuary's statue of the god and its adornments here.

7 *Cortīna ex adytō hanc vōcem reddit*: The priestess of Apollo sat on a large tripod when prophesying. The tripod stands for the priestess herself.

8 *Nec opus est Phoebō*: The construction *opus est* takes an ablative of the thing needed.

adeō, adīre, adiī, aditum: to go or come to, approach

adytum, ī n.: the innermost area of a temple

arcessō, arcessere, arcessīvī, arcessītum: to summon, call to a place

auxilium, ī n.: help, assistance

cernō, cernere, crēvī, crētum: to separate, distinguish, perceive

cortīna, ae f.: cauldron, tripod

Delphī, ōrum m. pl.: Delphi, a place famous for Apollo's oracle

dīrus, a, um: horrible, dire

intremiscō, intremiscere: to tremble

luēs, luis f.: disease, pestilence, plague

medēns, medentis m.: a physician

morbus, ī m.: disease, illness

pallidus, a, um: pale

pavefactus, a, um: terrified

Phoebēius, a, um: of Phoebus, of Apollo

squāleō, squālēre, squāluī: to be stiff, be dirty

temptāmentum, ī n.: a trial, attempt

10   Postquam senātus verba deī accipit, quam urbem fīlius Phoebī colat explōrat.
11   Virōs ad Epidauria lītora mittit. Cum virī missī Epidauria lītora tangunt, adeunt
12   concilium Graiōsque patrēs. Rōmānī ōrant ut Epidauriī patrēs deum Rōmam
13   mittant, quī fūnera Rōmānōrum fīniat. Sententiae patrum dissident et variant. Pars
14   putat auxilium nōn dēbēre negārī, sed dēbēre multī deum suum nōn ēmittere putant.

15   Dum dubitant, nox umbrās orbī terrārum indūcit. Rōmānī in cubiculō dormiunt. In
16   somniīs Rōmānōrum deus opifer consistere ante torum vidētur. Deus vidētur
17   ēmittere tālia verba: "Pōne metum! Epidaurum relinquam, et veniam Rōmam.
18   Perspice hunc serpentem, quī baculum nexibus ambit. Vertar in hunc, sed maior
19   erō." Extemplō deus cum vōce somnōque abit.

20   Aurōra ignēs sīdereōs fugat, et procerēs, nōn scientēs quid agant, conveniunt ad
21   templum deī. Procerēs ōrant deum ut indicet signīs caelestibus in quā urbe ipse
22   esse cupiat. Vix verbīs dictīs, deus, in formā serpentis, sībila praenuntia mittit, et
23   adventū suō signumque ārāsque forēsque fastīgiaque aurea movet. Turba territa
24   pavet, sed sacerdōs nūmen cognōvit. Clāmat: "Deus est! Deus est! Ō pulcherrime
25   Aesculāpī, populōs colentēs tua sacra iuvā!" Omnēs nūmen venerantur. Rōmānī
26   deum auxilium rogant. Hīs deus adnuit. Tum deus gradibus dēlābitur, et adsuētum
27   templum salūtat. Inde ingēns serpēns tendit per mediam urbem ad portum, et
28   corpus in rate Rōmānā pōnit. Nāvis onus nūminis sentit, pressa gravitāte deī.
29   Rōmānī gaudent, et retinācula nāvis solvunt.

30   Nāvis ad portum Tiberīnum nāvigat, et hūc omnis turba populī (mātrēsque
31   patrēsque fēminaeque quae ignēs Vestae servant) ruit, et deum laetō clāmōre
32   salūtant. Ut cita nāvis per undās dūcitur, tūra in ārīs super rīpās factīs aurās
33   odōrant. Iam deus urbem Rōmānam intrat. Serpēns ērigitur et collum movet,
34   circumspiciēns sēdēs sibi aptās. Flūmen circumfluum in geminās partēs scinditur:
35   hīc insula Tiberīna est. Hūc anguis dīvus sē ā nāve confert, et speciē caelestī
36   resumptā fīnem lūctibus impōnit venitque salūtifer urbī.

Commentary

13 *quī fūnera Rōmānōrum fīniat*: This is a relative clause of purpose, a relative clause with a subjunctive verb which also indicates why something is done. Translate: *so that the god will put an end to the funerals of the Romans*.

19 *Extemplō deus cum vōce somnōque abit*: In other words, the vision of the god leaves along with his voice, and the Romans who were dreaming wake up.

21 *ut indicet signīs caelestibus*: *signīs caelestibus* is ablative of means.

22–3 *Vix verbīs dictīs, deus, in formā serpentis ... movet*: As the god approaches, his powerful presence causes everything to shake. *signum* refers to the sanctuary's statue.

25 *populōs colentēs tua sacra iuvā*: *tua sacra* is the direct object of *colentēs*.

adventus, ūs m.: an arrival

Aesculāpius, ī m.: Aesculapius, god of healing

ambiō, ambīre, ambīvī, ambītum: to go around, surround

circumfluus, a, um: flowing around

citus, a, um: quick, speedy

conferō, conferre, contulī, conlātum: to bring together, collect, bring to a place

consistō, consistere, constitī, constitum: to put oneself in a place, take a stand, be posted

conveniō, convenīre, convēnī, conventum: to meet, come together

cubiculum, ī n.: bedchamber

dissideō, dissidēre, dissēdī, dissessum: to be different, disagree

dormiō, dormīre, dormīvī, dormītum: to sleep

Epidaurius, a, um: of Epidaurus, a town in Greece

Epidaurus, ī f.: Epidaurus, a town famous for the sanctuary of Aesculapius

ērigō, ērigere, ērexī, ērēctum: to lift up, raise, excite

explōrō, explōrāre, explōrāvī, explōrātum: to search out, investigate

flūmen, flūminis n.: a flowing, river

Graius, a, um: of Greece

indūcō, indūcere, induxī, inductum: to bring in, introduce, draw over a surface (+ dat.)

insula, ae f.: island

nāvis, nāvis f.: ship

onus, oneris n.: burden, load

opifer, opifera, opiferum: bringing aid, helpful

perspiciō, perspicere, perspexī, perspectum: to see through, observe closely

praenuntius, a, um: foretelling

rēsūmō, rēsūmere, rēsumpsī, rēsumptum: to take again, resume

retinācula, ōrum n. pl.: rope, cable

sacerdōs, sacerdōtis m. or f.: priest, priestess

salūtifer, salūtiferī m.: bringer of health

sīdereus, a, um: belonging to the stars

somnium, ī n.: dream

Tiberīnus, a, um: of the Tiber River

veneror, venerārī, venerātus sum: to ask, entreat with reverence, worship

Vesta, ae f.: Vesta, goddess of the hearth

INDIRECT QUESTION

Like an indirect statement, an indirect question is a representation of indirect speech; however, an indirect question is formed as a subordinate clause with a verb in the subjunctive rather than as a construction which uses an accusative and infinitive. Indirect questions are introduced by interrogative words such as *quis* (*who*), *quid* (*what*), *cūr* (*why*), *ubi* (*where*), or *quandō* (*when*), for example, and they usually follow verbs of speaking, thinking, or sensing. In the sentence *Rōmānī sē quid luem fēcerit rogant, sed nōn sciunt quae causa fuerit vel quid iuvet vel quōs consulere dēbeant*, the clauses *quid luem fēcerit*, *quae causa fuerit*, *quid iuvet*, and *quōs consulere dēbeant* are all indirect questions. The sentence should be translated *The Romans ask themselves what caused the plague, but they do not know what the cause was, what would help, or whom they ought to consult.*

The panhellenic sanctuary at Epidaurus was famous as a place of healing. It was dedicated to the god Aesclepius, the Greek equivalent of Aesculapius, and the sanctuary included temples as well as a large hall for sleeping, a theater, and places for athletic activities. Those seeking cures would spend the night in the sanctuary hoping for some kind of dream-visitation from the god, an experience known as *incubation*. Snakes figured prominently in the cult, and several accounts exist of the god being taken from Epidaurus in the form of a snake to assist with epidemics in other places. Licks from sacred dogs living in the sanctuary also were important in the healing process. Inscriptions found at the sanctuary celebrate many miraculous cures.

30 The apotheosis of Caesar

(*Met.* 15.745–870)

When Julius Caesar is assassinated, Venus takes his soul in the form of a comet to join the gods in the vault of heaven.

1   Aesculāpius advena Rōmam nāvigandō aequora vēnit, sed Caesar est deus in urbe
2   suā. Quem praecipuum Marte togāque bella fīnīta triumphīs et rēs domī gestae in
3   stellam comantem nōn vertērunt magis quam sua prōgeniēs. Neque enim dē āctīs
4   Caesaris ullum maius opus est quam quod pater huius Augustī fuit. Domuisse
5   aequoreōs Britannōs, ēgisse navēs per septemflua flūmina Nīlī papȳriferī, meruisse
6   multōs sed ēgisse aliquōs triumphōs sunt nōn maiōra quam genuisse tantum virum.
7   Ille igitur deus faciendus erat, nē Augustus crētus e mortālī sēmine foret.

8   Cum Venus Caesarem faciendum esse deum vīdit, trīste lētum pontificī suō parārī
9   quoque vīdit. Dea metū palluit. Omnibus dīvīs dixit: "Adspice quantā mōle
10 insidiae parentur, quantāque fraude caput Caesaris petātur. Cernitis scelerātōs
11 ensēs acuī. Quōs prohibēte, precor! Repellite facinus! Nē exstinguite flammās

Commentary

2–3 *Quem praecipuum Marte togāque ... prōgeniēs*: The antecedent of *quem* is *Caesar.* *Marte* and *togā* are ablatives of specification after *praecipuum*, standing for war and peace. *bella*, *rēs*, and *prōgeniēs* are all subjects of *vertērunt*. *domī* is locative and should be translated *at home*. Ovid is saying that the fact Caesar was the father of Augustus was the primary reason for his deification.

3–4 *Neque enim dē āctīs Caesaris ... fuit*: *ullum maius opus est*, taken with *neque*, means *there is no greater work*. *quod* should be translated *the fact that* here.

4–6 *Domuisse aequoreōs Britannōs ... virum*: The infinitive phrases are the subjects of *sunt*.

7 *Ille igitur deus faciendus erat*: A passive periphrastic. Translate: *That man had to become (be made) a god*. Ovid praises Augustus by suggesting that he could not have been born from mortal seed.

8–9 *Cum Venus Caesarem faciendum esse deum vīdit ... vīdit*: Ovid refers to the assassination of Julius Caesar in 44 BCE. Among many other offices he held, Julius Caesar served as pontifex maximus.

10–11 *Cernitis scelerātōs ensēs acuī*: *acuī* is a present passive infinitive.

11 *Quōs prohibēte*: The antecedent of *quōs* is *ensēs*.

acuō, acuere, acuī, acūtum: to sharpen

aequoreus, a, um: surrounded by sea

Augustus, ī m.: Augustus, the first Roman emperor

Britannī, ōrum m. pl.: the Britons

Caesar, Caesaris m.: Julius Caesar, Roman general and dictator

gignō, gignere, genuī, genitum: to produce, give birth to

mereō, merēre, meruī, meritum: to deserve, earn

mōles, mōlis f.: weight, bulk

palleō, pallere, palluī: to be pale, grow pale

papȳrifer, papȳrifera, papȳriferum: papyrus-bearing

pontifex, pontificis m.: a priest

praecipuus, a, um: peculiar, excellent, distinguished

stella comans, stellae comantis f.: a hairy star, a comet

toga, ae f.: toga, garment worn by Roman men

triumphus, ī m.: a triumphal procession, victory

12 Vestae caede sacerdōtis!" Anxia Venus tālia verba iēcit, et superōs mōvit,
13 quamquam superī nōn possunt rumpere ferrea dēcrēta veterum sorōrum. Nōn erat
14 spēs servandī virum.

15 Superī tamen signa haud incerta futūrī lūctūs dant. Ferunt arma crepitantia inter
16 nigrās nūbēs terribilēsque tubās cornuaque audīta in caelō praemonuisse nefās.
17 Saepe facēs in caelō ardēre vīsae sunt. Saepe guttae cruentae inter nimbōs
18 cecidērunt. In mīlle locīs Stygius būbō tristia ōmina dedit. Ferunt canēs in forō
19 ululāvisse et umbrās silentium errāvisse. Praemonitūs deōrum vincere īnsidiās
20 malās fātaque ventūra nōn potuērunt. Gladiī in cūriam Caesaris necandī causā
21 lātī sunt.

22 Tum vērō Cytherēa pectus percussit, et vēlāre Caesarem nūbe mōlīta est. Tālibus
23 verbīs Iuppiter Venerī dīxit: "Nāta, parāsne sōla movēre insuperābile fātum?
24 Nātus tuus, Cytherēa, sua tempora quae terrae dēbuit complēvit. Tū et nātus
25 Caesaris, Augustus, faciētis ut Caesar deus in caelum accēdat et in templīs colātur.
26 Pāce omnibus terrīs datā Augustus animum ad cīvīlia iūra vertet; iustissimus auctor
27 lēgēs feret. Exemplō suō mōrēs reget. Intereā fac hanc animam, raptam dē corpore
28 caesō Caesaris, stellam, ut semper dīvus Iūlius Capitōlium nostrum forumque dē
29 excelsō templō prospectet."

30 Vix pater dīxerat, cum Venus in mediā sēde senātūs cōnstitit, et, nōn passūra
31 animam Caesaris solvī in āera, animam ēripuit. In caelestia astra tulit. Ut tulit,
32 Venus animam ignēscere sēnsit. Ēmīsit sinū, et anima altius lūnā volāvit. Trahēns
33 crīnem flammiferum nunc micat stella.

Commentary

13 *quamquam superī . . . veterum sorōrum*: The *old sisters* are the Fates, who determine all that will happen.

15–16 *Ferunt . . . praemonuisse nefās*: *Ferunt* here means *they say* and introduces indirect statement.

24–5 *Tū et nātus Caesaris . . . colātur*: The *ut* clause follows *faciētis* and indicates what will be accomplished.

30–1 *nōn passūra animam Caesaris solvī in āera*: *passūra* describes Venus and is followed by the accusative-infinitive construction.

32 *et anima altius lūnā volāvit*: *lūnā* is an ablative of comparison after the comparative adverb *altius*.

altius: (adv.) higher

anxius, a, um: anxious, nervous

astrum, ī n.: star

caedō, caedere, cecīdī, caesum: to cut, strike, kill

Capitōlium, ī n.: the temple of Jupiter on the Tarpeian Rock

causā: (+ gen., always after its object) for the sake of

cīvīlis, e: civil, relating to a citizen

crepitō, crepitāre, crepitāvī, crepitātum: to rattle, crash, clatter

cūria, ae f.: the senate-house in Rome

Cythereūs, a, um: of Cythera, epithet of Venus

dēcrētum, ī m.: a decree

excelsus, a, um: lofty, high

exstinguō, exstinguere, exstinxī, exstinctum: to put out, extinguish

flammifer, flammifera, flammiferum: carrying flames

forum, ī n.: public space in Rome, center for business and politics

iaciō, iacere, iēcī, iactum: to throw

ignescō, ignescere: to catch fire

incertus, a, um: uncertain, doubtful

insuperābilis, e: insurmountable

Iūlius, ī m.: Julius Caesar

iustissimus, a, um: most just

mōlior, mōlīrī, mōlītus sum: to set in motion, work at

nefās n.: (indecl.) a crime, abomination

ōmen, ōminis n.: sign, omen

praemoneō, praemonēre, praemonuī, praemonitum: to warn beforehand

praemonitus, ūs m.: prediction, warning

prospectō, prospectāre, prospectāvī, prospectātum: to gaze out at, look out on

repellō, repellere, reppulī, repulsum: to drive back, drive away

sinus, ūs m.: a bending, fold, pocket, lap

GERUNDS AND GERUNDIVES

A gerund is a verbal noun which only has forms in the neuter singular. There is no nominative form for the gerund; instead, the infinitive is used as a subject. The gerundive is a verbal adjective which is equivalent to the future passive participle. Because it is an adjective, it has masculine, feminine, and neuter endings in the singular and plural. The declensions of the gerund and the gerundive for *necō, nēcāre, nēcāvī, nēcātum* follow.

Gerund

Nominative	XXX	XXX
Genitive	necandī	of killing
Dative	necandō	to/for killing
Accusative	necandum	killing
Ablative	necandō	by, with killing

Gerundive *(to be killed)*

	Singular			Plural		
	Masculine	*Feminine*	*Neuter*	*Masculine*	*Feminine*	*Neuter*
Nominative	necandus	necanda	necandum	necandī	necandae	necanda
Genitive	necandī	necandae	necandī	necandōrum	necandārum	necandōrum
Dative	necandō	necandae	necandō	necandīs	necandīs	necandīs
Accusative	necandum	necandam	necandum	necandōs	necandās	necanda
Ablative	necandō	necandā	necandō	necandīs	necandīs	necandīs

Latin uses both gerunds and gerundives, but there is a general preference for gerundives, even when an active meaning is sought. In the sentence *Aesculāpius advena Rōmam nāvigandō aequora vēnit, nāvigandō* is a gerund which takes as its object *aequora*. The sentence should be translated *Aesculapius came to Rome as a stranger by sailing the seas.* In the sentence *Gladiī in cūriam Caesaris necandī causā lātī sunt, necandī* is a gerundive modifying *Caesaris*. The gerundive phrase is used here with *causā (for the sake of)* to indicate purpose, and the sentence should be translated *Swords were carried into the curia for the sake of killing Caesar* (literally *for the sake of Caesar to be killed*). This use of the gerundive is idiomatic and is preferred to the use of a gerund in the genitive plus an object in the accusative (. . . *necandī Caesarem causā*), which could be used to achieve the same meaning.

The account of the apotheosis of Julius Caesar is the last story in the *Metamorphoses*. At the end of it, Ovid celebrates Augustus and says that he too will enter the heavens and listen to the prayers of mortals. He ends his poem with a statement about his own immortality as a poet, saying that he will be carried *super astra* (*beyond the stars*). Since he has just described Venus' release of Caesar's soul into the realm of the stars, Ovid seems to suggest at the end of the epic that his own literary immortality will outlast Caesar's (and perhaps Augustus'). Indeed, the last word of the entire epic is *vivam* (*I will live*).

Glossary

ā/ab: (prep. + abl.) from, away from

abdō, abdere, abdidī, abditum: to hide, conceal

abeō, abīre, abivī or abiī, abitum: to go away, pass into a state

abhorreō, abhorrēre, abhorruī: to shrink back from, shudder at

absum, abesse, abfuī, abfutūrum: to be away from, be absent

absūmō, absūmere, absumpsī, absumptum: to reduce, consume

accēdō, accēdere, accessī, accessum: to approach, come near

accessus, ūs m.: approach, entrance, access

accidō, accidere, accidī: to fall upon, happen, occur

accipiō, accipere, accēpī, acceptum: to receive, take, hear

accipiter, accipitris m.: hawk

acclīnātus, a, um: leaning on

Actaeōn, Actaeonis m.: Actaeon, a grandson of Cadmus

acūmen, acūminis n.: point, sharpness, cunning

acuō, acuere, acuī, acūtum: to sharpen

acūtus, a, um: sharp, pointed

ad: (prep. + acc.) to, towards

adambulō, adambulāre, adambulāvī, adambulātum: to walk near, walk about

addō, addere, addidī, additum: to add, join to

adeō, adīre, adiī, aditum: to go or come to, approach

adflō, adflāre, adflāvī, adflātum: to blow on

adfor, adfārī, adfātus sum: to speak to, address

adhūc: (adv.) still

adipiscor, adipiscī, adeptus sum: to arrive at, obtain, acquire

aditus, ūs m.: approach, entrance, access

adlevō, adlevāre, adlevāvī, adlevātum: to lift up, erect

admoneō, admonēre, admonuī, admonitum: to warn

admoveō, admovēre, admōvī, admōtum: to move towards

adnuō, adnuere, adnuī, adnūtum: to nod, give assent

adolescō, adolescere, adolēvī: to grow up

adōro, adōrāre, adōrāvī, adōrātum: to entreat, worship

adsevērō, adsevērāre, adsevērāvī, adsevērātum: to assert with confidence

adsimulō, adsimulāre, adsimulāvī, adsimulātum: to make like, imitate

adspiciō, adspicere, adspexī, adspectum: to look at, notice

adsuētus, a, um: customary, usual, familiar

adsum, adesse, adfuī, adfutūrum: to be at a place, be present

adulter, adulterī m.: adulterer

adulterium, ī n.: adultery

aduncus, a, um: hooked

advena, ae m. or f.: stranger

adventus, ūs m.: an arrival

adytum, ī n.: the innermost area of a temple

Aeētēs, Aeētae m.: Aeëtes, king of Colchis

aegis, aegidis f.: aegis, special chest-armor embellished with a Gorgon-head

aēneus, a, um: bronze

aēnum, ī n.: something made of bronze, bronze cauldron

Aeolia, ae f.: Aeolia, a region on the northwest coast of Asia Minor

aequē: (adv.) equally

aequō, aequāre, aequāvī, aequātum: to equal, make equal

aequor, aequoris n.: flat surface, plain, sea

aequoreus, a, um: surrounded by sea

āēr, āeris m.: air

aerātus, a, um: made of bronze

aereus, a, um: of bronze

aes, aeris n.: something made of bronze, bronze cymbal

Aesculāpius, ī m.: Aesculapius, god of healing

aesculeus, a, um: of oak

Aesōn, Aesonis m.: Aeson, father of Jason

Aestās, Aestātis f.: Summer, divine representation of the summertime

aetas, aetātis f.: age, period of life

aether, aetheris m.: the upper air (aethera = acc. sing.)

aetherius, a, um: heavenly

Aethiopicus, a, um: Ethiopian

Aetna, ae f.: Etna, a volcano in Sicily

aevum, ī n.: age, period of time

Agavē, Agavēs f.: Agave, mother of Pentheus

Agēnor, Agēnoris m.: Agenor, a king of Phoenicia

ager, agrī m.: field

agitō, agitāre, agitāvī, agitātus: to drive about, keep in movement, agitate

agmen, agminis n.: army, battle line

agnoscō, agnoscere agnōvī, agnītum: to recognize, know

agnus, ī m.: lamb

agō, agere, ēgī, actum: to drive, do, set in motion

agrestis, agrestis m.: rural person

agricola, ae m.: farmer

āla, ae f.: wing

albeō, albēre: to be white

albus, a, um: white

aliī ... aliī: some ... others

aliquis, aliquid: someone, something

aliud ... aliīs: one thing (nom.) ... the others (dat.)

alius, alia, aliud: (adj. and pron.) another, other, different

alō, alere, aluī, altum: to nourish, support

alter ... altera: the one ... the other

alter, altera, alterum: one of two

altissimus, a, um: highest

altius: (adv.) higher

altus, a, um: high, lofty

alveus, ī m.: a hollow, cavity, bed of a stream

alvus, ī f.: belly, womb

amans, amantis m. or f.: lover

ambiō, ambīre, ambīvī, ambītum: to go around, surround

ambō, ambae, ambo: (adj. and pron.) both

ambulō, ambulāre, ambulāvī, ambulātum: to walk

ambustus, a, um: burnt

amīcitia, ae f.: friendship

amictus, ūs m.: dress, garment

āmissus, a, um: lost

āmittō, āmittere, āmīsī, amissum: to send away, lose

amnis, amnis m.: river

amō, amāre, amāvī, amātum: to love

amor, amōris m.: love

amplector, amplectī, amplexus sum: to embrace, wrap around

amplexus, ūs m.: embrace

Anaxaretē, ēs f.: Anaxarete, a young woman from Cyprus

Andromeda, ae: Andromeda, an Ethiopian princess

anguigena, ae m.: snake-born man

anguilla, ae f.: eel

anguis, anguis m. or f.: serpent, snake

angustus, a, um: narrow, confined

anīlis, e: like an old woman, aged

anima, ae f.: life, breath, soul

animal, animālis n.: animal

animō, animāre, animāvī, animātum: to endow with life

animus, ī m.: spirit, mind

Annus, ī m.: Year, divine representation of a year

ante: (adv. and prep. + acc.) before

antequam: (conj.) before

Antiopa, ae f.: Antiope, mother of Amphion and Zethus

antīquus, a, um: old, ancient

antrum, ī n.: cave, grotto

anus, ūs f.: an old woman

anxius, a, um: anxious, nervous

Āonia, ae f.: Aonia, part of the region of Boeotia in Greece

aper, aprī m.: a wild boar

aperiō, aperīre, aperuī, apertum: to open, uncover, lay bare

Apollō, Apollinis m.: Apollo, god of music, athletics, and prophecy

appāreō, appārēre, appāruī, appāritum: to appear, become visible

appellō, appellāre, appellāvī, appellātum: to address, name

approperō, approperāre, approperāvī, approperātum: to hasten

appropinquō, appropinquāre, appropinquāvī, appropinquātum: to approach

aptus, a, um: fitted to, suited to (+ dat.)

aqua, ae f.: water

Aquārius, ī m.: Aquarius (zodiac sign), a water carrier

aquōsus, a, um: watery

āra, ae f.: altar

Arachnē, ēs f.: Arachne, a Maeonian weaver

arānea, ae f.: spider, web

arāneum, ī n.: spiderweb

arātrum, ī n.: plow

arbiter, arbitrī m.: judge

arbor, arboris f.: tree

arboreus, a, um: of a tree

Arcadius, a, um: of Arcadia, a region in central Greece

arceō, arcēre, arcuī, arctum: to shut in, hinder, keep at a distance

arcessō, arcessere, arcessīvī, arcessītum: to summon, call to a place

arcitenēns, arcitenentis: bow-holding, epithet of Apollo

Arctos, ī f.: the constellations known as Great and Little Bear, the north

arcus, ūs m.: bow, arch

ardeō, ardēre, arsī: to burn, glow

ārea, ae f.: open space, plain, threshing floor

Arethūsa, ae f.: Arethusa, a Sicilian nymph

argenteus, a, um: of silver

argentum, ī n.: silver

argūmentum, ī n.: tale, proof

Ariēs, Arietis m.: Aries (zodiac sign), a ram

arista, ae f.: stalk of grain

arma, ōrum n. pl.: arms, weapons

armātus, a, um: armed

armentum, ī n.: herd, flock

armus, ī m.: shoulder

arō, arāre, arāvī, arātum: to plow, till

ars, artis f.: skill, art, work of art

artus, ūs m.: joint, limb

arvum, ī n.: field

arx, arcis f.: citadel, stronghold

ascendō, ascendere, ascendī, ascensum: to ascend, climb

astrum, ī n.: star

at: (conj.) but, at least, moreover

āter, ātra, ātrum: black, dark

Athēnae, ārum f. pl.: Athens

Athēnaeus, a, um: of Athens

Athēniēnsis, e: of Athens

athlēta, ae m.: athlete, contender

Atlās, Atlantis m.: Atlas, the god who holds up the sky

atque: (conj.) and, and indeed

ātrium, ī n.: hall

attonō, attonāre, attonuī, attonitum: to strike with thunder, make senseless

attrahō, attrahere, attraxī, attractum: to drag, lead

auctor, auctōris m.: author, progenitor, founder

audācia, ae f.: boldness, courage

audāx, audācis: bold

audeō, audēre, ausus sum: to dare

audiō, audīre, audīvī, audītum: to hear, listen to

auferō, auferre, abstulī, ablātum: to carry away, remove

augeō, augēre, auxī, auctum: to make grow

augur, auguris m. or f.: augur, soothsayer

augustus, a, um: august, majestic

Augustus, ī m.: Augustus, the first Roman emperor

aura, ae f.: air, breeze, wind

aureus, a, um: golden

auris, auris f.: ear

Aurōra, ae f.: Dawn, divine representation of dawn

aurum, ī n.: gold

Auster, Austrī m.: Auster, the south wind

aut: (conj.) or

autem: (conj.) but, however

Autumnus, ī m.: Autumn, divine representation of the fall

auxilium, ī n.: help, assistance

aveō, avēre: to desire, long for

āvertō, āvertere, āvertī, āversum: to turn away, remove, avert

avis, avis f.: bird, omen

avus, ī m.: grandfather

axis, axis m.: axle, axis

bāca, ae f.: fruit

Baccha, ae f.: a Bacchante, female follower of Bacchus

Bacchantēs, Bacchantium f. pl.: followers of Bacchus

Bacchus, ī m.: Bacchus, the fertility god of wine and madness

baculus, ī m.: staff, walking stick

bālātus, ūs m.: a bleating

barba, ae f.: beard

barbaricus, a, um: barbarian

barbarus, ī m.: barbarian

bāsiō, bāsiāre, bāsiāvī, bāsiātum: to kiss

bāsium, ī n.: kiss

beātus, a, um: happy

bellissimus, a, um: most beautiful

bellum, ī n.: war

bellus, a, um: beautiful

bēlua, ae f.: beast, monster

bēstia, ae f.: beast, animal

bibulus, a, um: drinking freely, absorbing

bidens, bidentis: with two teeth (often used for sheep)

biformis, e: of double form

bīnī, bīnae, bīna: two, double, a pair

bis: (adv.) in two ways, double

blanditia, ae f.: gentleness, coaxing, flattery

blandus, a, um: flattering, coaxing

Boeōtia, ae f.: Boeotia, a region of Greece

bonus, a, um: good

Boreās, ae m.: Boreas, the north wind

bōs, bovis m. or f.: cow, ox

bracchium, ī n.: arm

brevis, e: brief

Britannī, ōrum m. pl.: the Britons

būbō, būbōnis m.: owl

cacūmen, cacūminis n.: top, point, summit

cacūminō, cacūmināre, cacūmināvī, cacūminātum: to make pointed, point

Cadmus, ī m.: Cadmus, the son of Agenor

cadō, cadere, cecidī, cāsum: to fall, sink, plunge

caecus, a, um: blind

caedēs, is f.: a cutting down, a killing

caedō, caedere, cecīdī, caesum: to cut, strike, kill

caelātus, a, um: carved, engraved

caelebs, caelibis: unmarried, uncoupled, single

caelestis, e: heavenly, celestial

caelum, ī n.: heaven, sky

caeruleus, a, um: greenish blue

Caesar, Caesaris m.: Julius Caesar, Roman general and dictator

caespis, caespitis m.: turf, sod, earthen mound

Calais, is m.: Calais, a son of Boreas and Orithyia

calathus, ī m.: wicker basket

calcātus, a, um: stamped down, crushed
caleō, calēre, caluī: to be hot
calescō, calescere: to grow warm
calidus, a, um: warm, hot
cālīgō, cālīginis f.: darkness, mist
callidus, a, um: skillful, crafty, cunning
calor, calōris m.: heat
campus, ī m.: field
Cancer, Cancrī m.: Cancer (zodiac sign), a crab
candidus, a, um: shining, bright, white
cāneō, cānēre, cānuī: to be gray
canis, canis m. or f.: dog
cantō, cantāre, cantāvī, cantātum: to sing
cantus, ūs m.: song, melody
cānus, a, um: white, grey
capāx, capācis: able to hold much material, capacious
capillus, ī m.: hair
capiō, capere, cēpī, captum: to seize, take
Capitōlium, ī n.: the temple of Jupiter on the Tarpeian Rock
capra, ae f.: goat
Capricornus, ī m.: Capricorn (zodiac sign), a goat
caput, capitis n.: head
carchēsium, ī n.: drinking cup
careō, carēre, caruī, caritum: to lack (+ abl.)
Cāria, ae f.: Caria, a district in Asia Minor
carīna, ae f.: keel, ship
carmen, carminis n.: song, poem
carnōsus, a, um: fleshy, meaty
carpō, carpere, carpsī, carptum: to pluck, choose, sieze
casa, ae f.: cottage, cabin, house
Cassiopē, ēs f.: Cassiopea, mother of Andromeda
cassis, cassidis f.: helmet
Castalius, a, um: of Castalia, a fountain on Mt. Parnassus
castīgō, castīgāre, castīgāvī, castīgātum: to punish
castra, ōrum n. pl.: military encampment
castus, a, um: clean, chaste, pious

catēna, ae f.: chain, bond
causa, ae f.: cause, reason
causā: (+ gen., always after its object) for the sake of
cautēs, cautis f.: crag, cliff
caverna, ae f.: cavern, cave
cavus, a, um: hollow, concave
Cecropius, a, um: of Cecrops, a legendary king of Athens
cēdo, cēdere, cessī, cessum: to depart, yield (+ dat.)
celeberrimus, a, um: very famous, most celebrated
cēlō, cēlāre, cēlāvī, cēlātum: to hide, conceal, cover
cēna, ae f.: dinner
Cephalus, ī m.: Cephalus, son of Pandion
Cēphēnus, a, um: of Cepheus, ruled by Cepheus
Cēphēus, a, um: of Cepheus, a king of Ethiopia
Cēpheus, ī m.: Cepheus, father of Andromeda
Cerēs, Cereris f.: Ceres, goddess of grain and agriculture
cernēns, cernentis: spying, looking upon
cernō, cernere, crēvī, crētum: to separate, distinguish, perceive
certāmen, certāminis n.: contest, competition
certē: (adv.) certainly
certō, certāre, certāvī, certātum: to compete
certus, a, um: determined, fixed, certain
cerva, ae f.: deer
cervus, ī m.: stag
cēterī, ae, a: others, rest
Chaos n.: Chaos, personified boundless empty space
cibus, ī m.: food
cicāda, ae f.: cicada
Cicones, um m. pl.: Ciconians, a people in Thrace
cinctus, a, um: circled, encompassed

cingō, cingere, cinxī, cinctum: to gird, surround

Cīpus, ī m.: Cipus, an early Roman praetor

circumdō, circumdare, circumdedī, circumdatum: to set around, surround

circumeō, circumīre, circumiī, or circum- īvī, circumitum: to go around

circumfluus, a, um: flowing around

circumfundō, circumfundere, circumfūdī, circumfūsum: to pour around, surround

circumspiciō, circumspicere, circumspexī, circumspectum: to look round, survey, consider

circumstō, circumstāre, circumstetī: to stand around, encircle

Cīris, Cīris f.: a colorful bird

Cithaerōn, Cithaerōnis m.: Cithaeron, a mountain near Thebes

citus, a, um: quick, speedy

cīvīlis, e: civil, relating to a citizen

cīvis, cīvis m. or f.: citizen

clāmō, clāmāre, clāmāvī, clāmātum: to shout, make a loud noise, call to or upon

clāmor, clāmōris m.: a loud shouting

clārissimus, a, um: brightest, clearest, most famous

clārus, a, um: clear, shining, brilliant

classis, classis f.: fleet

claudō, claudere, clausī, clausum: to close, make inaccessible

claustra, ōrum n. pl.: bar, bolt

clipeus, ī m.: shield

Clymenē, ēs f.: Clymene, a nymph

Cnōsiacus, a, um: of Knossos

Cnōsius, a, um: of Knossos, a city on Crete

coclea, ae f.: snail

coeō, coīre, coiī, coitum: come together, assemble

coepiō, coepere, coepī, coeptum: to begin, commence

coeptus, a, um: begun

cōgitō, cōgitāre, cōgitāvī, cōgitātum: to think, reflect, consider

cognoscō, cognoscere, cognōvī, cognitum: to become acquainted with, know, recognize

coiēns, coeuntis: coming together, mating

Colchicus, a, um: of Colchis, a region of the Black Sea

colligō, colligere, collēgī, collectum: to gather together, collect

collis, collis m.: hill

collocō, collocāre, collocāvī, collocātum: to place, locate

collum, ī n.: neck

colō, colere, coluī, cultum: to cultivate, tend, worship, inhabit

color, colōris m.: color, hue

columna, ae f.: column, pillar

coma, ae f.: hair

combibō, combibere, combibī: to drink

comes, comitis m. or f.: companion, comrade, partner

committō, committere, commīsī, commissum: to join, combine

commūnis, e: that which is shared, common

compāgo, compāginis f.: a joining together, structure

compellō, compellāre, compellāvī, compellātum: to address, accost

compescō, compescere, compescuī: to confine, check, restrain

compleō, complēre, complēvī, complētum: to fill up, fulfill

complexus, ūs m.: an embrace

compōnō, compōnere, composuī, composi- tum: to compose, put together, arrange

compos, compotis: having mastery of, possessed of (+gen.)

comprehendō, comprehendere, comprehendī, comprehēnsum: to grab, understand

concha, ae f.: sea-shell, shell-fish

concilium, ī n.: meeting, assembly, council

concipiō, concipere, concēpi, conceptum: to receive, take completely, conceive

conclāmō, conclāmāre, conclāmāvī, conclāmātum: to cry out loudly

concursus, ūs m.: collision, attack

concutiō, concutere, concussī, concussum: to beat, strike, shake violently

conditor, conditōris m.: founder

condō, condere, condidī, condītum: to found, hide, bury

conferō, conferre, contulī, conlātum: to bring together, collect, bring to a place

conficiō, conficere, confēcī, confectum: to accomplish, wear out

confiteor, confitērī, confessus sum: to acknowledge, confess

conflagrō, conflagrāre, conflagrāvī, conflagrātum: to catch fire, burn up

confugiō, confugere, confūgī: to flee to, take refuge with

confundō, confundere, confūdi, confūsum: to pour together, mix up

congelō, congelāre, congelāvī, congelātum: to freeze thoroughly

coniciō, conicere, coniēcī, coniectum: to throw, bring together, drive, force

coniugiālis, e: marital

coniunctior, ius: more connected, more joined

coniungō, coniungere, coniunxī, coniunctum: to join together, marry

coniunx, coniugis m. or f.: spouse, wife, husband

conscendō, conscendere, conscendī, conscensum: to mount, climb up, go up to

consīderō, consīderāre, consīderāvī, consīderātum: to look at closely, consider, reflect

consilium, ī n.: deliberation, counsel, plan, advice

consistō, consistere, constitī, constitum: to put oneself in a place, take a stand, be posted

consors, consortis m. or f.: one who has an equal share, partner, wife

conspiciō, conspicere, conspexī, conspectum: to look at, observe

constituō, constituere, constituī, constitūtum: to cause to stand, settle, decide

constō, constāre, constitī, constātum: to stand, stand firm, stand unchanging

consulō, consulere, consuluī, consultum: to consider, consult

consūmō, consūmere, consumpsī, consumptum: to consume, spend

consurgō, consurgere, consurrexī, consurrectum: to raise oneself, rise, stand up

contemnō, contemnere, contempsī, contemptum: to despise, think badly of

contemptor, contemptōris m.: a despiser

contentus, a, um: content, satisfied

contineō, continēre, continuī, contentum: to hold together, restrain

contingō, contingere, contigī, contactum: to touch, affect

contrā: (adv.) on the opposite side

contrārius, a, um: opposite

cōnūbium, ī n.: marriage

conveniō, convenīre, convēnī, conventum: to meet, come together

conversus, a, um: turned

convexus, a, um: arched, vaulted

convīvium, ī n.: banquet, feast

convocō, convocāre, convocāvī, convocātum: to call together, assemble

cor, cordis n.: heart

corbis, corbis m.: basket

Corinthius, a, um: of Corinth, a city in southern Greece

corium, ī n.: skin, hide

cornū, ūs n.: horn

corōna, ae f.: garland, wreath, crown

corōnō, corōnāre, corōnāvī, corōnātum: to wreathe, crown

corpus, corporis n.: a body

corpusculum, ī n.: a small body

corripiō, corripere, corripuī, correptum: to seize violently, attack, blame, rebuke

corrumpō, corrumpere, corrūpī, corruptum: to corrupt, destroy, spoil

cortīna, ae f.: cauldron, tripod

crāter, crāteris m.: mixing bowl, fissure in the earth

crēdo, crēdere, crēdidī, crēditum: to trust, believe (+ dat.)

creō, creāre, creāvī, creātum: to create, make

crepitō, crepitāre, crepitāvī, crepitātum: to rattle, crash, clatter

crepusculum, ī n.: the twilight

Crēs, Crētis m.: a Cretan

crescō, crescere, crēvī, crētum: to grow

Crēta, ae f.: Crete, an island in the Mediterranean Sea

crīmen, crīminis n.: accusation, crime

crīnis, crīnis m.: hair

crīnītus, a, um: hairy

crista, ae f.: crest

cristātus, a, um: crested, plumed

cruciātus, ūs m.: torture, torment

crucio, cruciāre, cruciāvī, cruciātum: to torture

crūdēlis, e: cruel

cruentātus, um: bloody, made bloody

cruentō, cruentāre, cruentāvī, cruentātum: to make bloody

cruor, cruōris m.: blood from a wound, gore

crūs, crūris n.: leg

cubiculum, ī n.: bedchamber

cubitum, ī n.: elbow

culmen, culminis n.: summit, rooftop

culpa, ae f.: fault, blame

culter, cultrī m.: knife

cultūra, ae f.: cultivation, tilling

cum: (conj.) when, since, although, (prep. + abl.) with

cūnae, ārum f. pl.: cradle

cunctus, a, um: all, collectively, the whole

cunīculus, ī m.: rabbit

Cupīdo, Cupidinis m.: Cupid, the god of love (**cupīdo, cupidinis** f.: desire)

cupiō, cupere, cupīvī, cupītum: to desire, yearn for

cupressus, ūs f.: cypress tree

cūr: (interrog. adv.) why

cūra, ae f.: care, attention

cūria, ae f.: the senate-house in Rome

currō, currere, cucurrī, cursum: to run

currus, ūs m.: chariot

cursō, cursāre, cursāvī, cursātum: to run to and fro

cursus, ūs m.: course, path, journey

curvus, a, um: curved, bent, arched

cuspis, cuspidis f.: a point, spear

custōdia, ae f.: watch, guard, protection

custos, custōdis m.: guard

cutis, cutis f.: skin

Cyanē, ēs f.: Cyane, a Sicilian nymph

Cythereus, a, um: of Cythera, epithet of Venus

damnō, damnāre, damnāvī, damnātum: to condemn, cause loss or injury to

Danaë, ēs f.: Danaë, daughter of Acrisius and mother of Perseus

Daphnē, ēs f.: Daphne, a nymph

dē: (prep. + abl.) from, down from, about

dea, ae f.: a goddess

dēbeō, dēbēre, dēbuī, dēbitum: to owe, ought

decet, decēre, decuit: (impers. verb) it is proper, seemly, fitting (+ acc. of thing fitted)

dēcido, dēcidere, dēcidī: to fall down, fall away

dēcrētum, ī m.: a decree

decus, decoris n.: honor, glory, charm

dēdecet, dēdecēre, dēdecuit: (impers. verb) it is unfitting, not suitable

dēdūcō, dēdūcere, dēdūxī, dēductum: to draw out, spin

dēfendo, dēfendere, dēfendī, dēfensum: to defend

dēficio, dēficere, dēfēcī, dēfectum: to fail, run short, become weak

dēfluō, dēfluere, dēflūxī, dēflūxum: to fall down, drop off, disappear

deinde: (adv.) from that place, next, then

dēlābor, dēlābī, dēlapsus sum: to glide down, fall down, sink

Dēlius, ī m.: of Delos, epithet of Apollo

Delphī, ōrum m. pl.: Delphi, a place famous for Apollo's oracle

delphīnus, ī m.: dolphin

dēmēns, dēmentis: out of one's mind, insane

dēmittō, dēmittere, dēmīsī, dēmissum: to send down, drop

dēmō, demere, dempsī, demptum: take away, withdraw, remove

dēnegō, dēnegāre, dēnegāvī, dēnegātum: to deny

dēnī, dēnae, dēna: by tens

dēnique: (adv.) finally, at last

dens, dentis m.: tooth

densus, a, um: thick, dense

dēpōnō, dēpōnere, dēposuī, dēpositum: to put down

dēprendō, dēprendere, dēprendī, dēprensum: to catch hold of, detect, discover

dēprensus, a, um: seized, caught up

dērīdeō, dērīdēre, dērīsī, dērīsum: to laugh at, mock

dērigēscō, dērigēscere, dēriguī: to stiffen

dēscendō, dēscendere, dēscendī, descensum: to go down, descend

dēserō, dēserere, dēseruī, dēsertum: to leave, abandon, forsake

dēsignō, dēsignāre, dēsignāvī, dēsignātum: to signify, indicate, mark out

dēsiliō, dēsilīre, dēsiluī, dēsultum: to leap down

dēsinō, dēsinere, dēsiī, dēsitum: to cease, desist, stop

dēsistō, dēsistere, dēstitī, dēstitum: to cease

dēsōlātus, a, um: desolate, forsaken

despectō, despectāre, despectāvī, despectātum: to look down

dēspiciō, dēspicere, dēspexī, dēspectum: to look down on, despise, disregard

dēsum, dēesse, dēfuī, dēfutūrum: to fail, be lacking

Deucaliōn, Deucaliōnis m.: Deucalion, a son of Prometheus

deus, ī m.: a god

dexter, dextra, dextrum (or dextera, dexterum): right, on the right

Diāna, ae f.: Diana, goddess of the hunt

dīcō, dīcere, dixī, dictum: to say, speak

dictum, ī n.: something said

Diēs, Diēī m. or f.: Day, divine representation of a day

digitus, ī m.: finger

dignior, ius: more worthy

dignissimus, a, um: most worthy

dignus, a, um: worthy, deserving of (+ abl.)

dīlābor, dīlābī, dīlapsus sum: to fall down, fall apart, perish

dīlacerō, dīlacerāre, dīlacerāvī, dīlacerātum: to tear in pieces

dīlaniō, dīlaniāre, dīlaniāvī, dīlaniātum: to tear to pieces

dīligō, dīligere, dīlēxī, dīlēctum: to have affection for, choose

dīluvium, ī n.: flood

dīmittō, dīmittere, dīmīsī, dīmissum: to send away, let go

dīrus, a, um: horrible, dire

Dīs, Dītis m.: Dis, another name for Pluto

discēdō, discēdere, discessī, discessum: to depart, go away, separate

discors, discordis: disagreeing, opposed, not harmonious

disiungō, disiungere, disiunxī, disiunctum: to disjoin, unyoke, separate

dispēnsō, dispēnsāre, dispēnsāvī, dispēnsātum: to distribute

dissideō, dissidēre, dissēdī, dissessum: to be different, disagree

diū: (adv.) for a long time

dīversus, a, um: separate, different, opposed

dīves, dīvitis: rich

dīvidō, dīvidere, dīvīsī, dīvīsum: to divide

dīvitior, ius: richer

dīvus, a, um: divine

dō, dare, dedī, datum: to give

doleō, dolēre, doluī, dolitum: to grieve, suffer pain, cause pain (+ dat.)

dolor, dolōris m.: pain, sorrow, distress
domina, ae f.: royal lady, wife
dominus, ī m.: master
domō, domāre, domuī, domitum: to tame, subdue
domus, ūs f.: house, home
dōnum, ī n.: gift
Dōris, Dōridos f.: Doris, a sea nymph
dormiō, dormīre, dormīvī, dormītum: to sleep
dōtālis, e: given as part of a dowry
draco, dracōnis m.: snake
dubitō, dubitāre, dubitāvī, dubitātum: to hesitate, be doubtful
dubius, a, um: doubtful, uncertain
dūcō, dūcere, duxī, ductum: to lead
dum: (conj.) while
duo, duae, duo: two
dūrātus, a, um: made hard, hard
durior, ius: harder, tougher
dūrus, a, um: hard
dux, ducis m.: leader

ē/ex: (prep. + abl.) out of, from
ebur, eboris n.: ivory
eburnus, a, um: made of ivory
ecce: (interj.) behold! look!
Echīon, Echīonis m.: Echion, one of the Thebans sprung from the serpent's teeth
ēdō, ēdere, ēdī, ēsum: to eat
ēdō, ēdere, ēdidī, ēditum: to put forth, give out, make known
ēdoceō, ēdocēre, ēdocuī, ēdoctum: to explain, inform fully
ēducō, ēducāre, ēducāvī, ēducātum: to rear, bring up
efferō, efferre, extulī, ēlātum: to carry off, carry away, bury, destroy
efficiō, efficere, effēcī, effectum: to bring about, cause to happen
effluō, effluere, effluxī: to flow out, run out
effodiō, effodere, effōdī, effossum: to dig out
effrēnātus, a, um: ungoverned, unrestrained
effugiō, effugere, effūgī: to flee

effundō, effundere, effūdī, effūsum: to pour out
ego, meī m. or f.: (first person sing. pron.) mihi (dat.), mē (acc./abl.), I, me
ēiciō, ēicere, ēiēcī, ēiectum: to throw out, expel
ēlīdō, ēlīdere, ēlīsī, ēlīsum: to squeeze out, strike
ēligo, ēligere, ēlēgī, ēlectum: to choose, pluck out
ēlīmō, ēlīmāre, ēlīmāvī, ēlīmātum: to polish, elaborate, perfect
ēlūdō, ēlūdere, ēlūsī, ēlūsum: to fool
ēmicō, ēmicāre, ēmicuī, ēmicātum: to spring out, break forth
ēmineō, ēminēre, ēminuī: to project, stand out
ēmittō, ēmittere, ēmīsī, ēmissum: to send out, send away
enim: (conj.) indeed, in fact
ēnītor, ēnītī, ēnīxus sum: to struggle, exert oneself, give birth to
ensis, ensis m.: sword
ēnūtriō, ēnūtrīre, ēnūtrīvī, ēnūtrītum: to nourish, bring up
eō, īre, īvī or iī, itum: to go
Epidaurius, a, um: of Epidaurus, a town in Greece
Epidaurus, ī f.: Epidaurus, a town famous for the sanctuary of Aesculapius
epops, epopis m.: hoopoe, a bird with a crown of feathers and a long beak
epulae, ārum f. pl.: food, feast
equus, ī m.: horse
Erechtheus, ī m.: Erechtheus, an early king of Athens
erēctus, a, um: raised up, erect
ērigo, ērigere, ērēxī, ērectum: to lift up, raise, excite
ēripiō, ēripere, ēripuī, ēreptum: to snatch away, tear out, rescue
errō, errāre, errāvī, errātum: to wander
error, errōris m.: a wandering about, mistake
ērubēscō, ērubēscere, ērubuī: to blush, grow red

et: (conj.) and

etiam: (adv.) also, too

Eumenidēs, um f. pl.: Furies, goddesses of vengeance

Eurōpa, ae f.: Europa, daughter of the Phoenician King Agenor

Eurus, ī m.: Eurus, the east wind

ēvolvō, ēvolvere, ēvolvī, ēvolūtum: to unroll

exanimis, e: lifeless

exardescō, exardescere, exarsī, exarsum: to burn, become excited

excelsus, a, um: lofty, high

excidō, excidere, excidī: to fall out, fall from, slip

excipiō, excipere, excēpī, exceptum: to take out, except, receive

exclāmō, exclāmare, exclāmāvī, exclāmātum: to cry aloud, call out

excōgitō, excōgitāre, excōgitāvī, excōgitātum: to devise, invent

excutiō, excutere, excussī, excussum: to shake out

exemplum, ī n.: example

exerceō, exercēre, exercuī, exercitum: to bother, work

exhaustus, a, um: empty, exhausted

exilium, ī n.: banishment, exile

exhibeō, exhibēre, exhibuī, exhibitum: to bring out, reveal, show

exigō, exigere, exēgī, exactum: to drive out

exiguus, a, um: scant, few, small, little

exitium, ī n.: destruction, ruin

experientia, ae f.: trial, testing

experior, experīrī, expertus sum: to try, test, attempt

explōrō, explōrāre, explōrāvī, explōrātum: to search out, investigate

exsiliō, exsilīre, exsiluī, exsultum: to jump out

exspectō, exspectāre, exspectāvī, exspectātum: to await, look for, expect

exstimulō, exstimulāre, exstimulāvī, exstimulātum: to spur on

exstinguō, exstinguere, exstinxī, exstinctum: to put out, extinguish

exstō, exstāre: to stand out, show oneself

exsul, exsulis m. or f.: an exile, banished person

exsultō, exsultāre, exsultāvī, exsultātum: to jump up, leap up, exult

exta, extōrum n. pl.: the entrails of an animal

extemplō: (adv.) immediately, straightway

externus, a, um: foreign, strange

extrēmus, a, um: extreme, last, farthest

exululō, exululāre, exululāvī, exululātum: to howl loudly

exuō, exuere, exuī, exūtum: to take off, lay aside

exūrō, exūrere, exussī, exustum: to burn out, burn up

fabricō, fabricāre, fabricāvī, fabricātum: to make, construct

fābula, ae f.: story, tale

faciēs, faciēī f.: form, shape, face

facinus, facinoris n.: deed, evil deed, crime

faciō, facere, fēcī, factum: to make, do

factum, ī n.: deed, act

fācundus, a, um: eloquent

fallax, fallācis: deceitful, deceptive

fallō, fallere, fefellī, falsum: to deceive, lead astray, disappoint

falsus, a, um: false, fake, deceitful

falx, falcis f.: pruning-hook, scythe

fāma, ae f.: fame, reputation, story

famēs, famis f.: hunger

famulāris, e: relating to slaves

famulus, ī m.: servant, attendant

fastīgium, ī n.: gable, pediment

fastus, ūs m.: haughtiness, arrogance, pride

fātālis, e: fated, destined

fateor, fatērī, fassus sum: to confess, acknowledge

fātidicus, a, um: speaking fate, prophetic

fātum, ī n.: something fated, destiny

faux, faucis f.: throat, narrow entrance

fax, facis f.: torch

fēcundus, a, um: fruitful, fertile

fēlix, fēlīcis: fortunate, happy

fēmina, ae f.: woman

fēmineus, a, um: feminine, of a woman

femur, femoris n.: thigh

fera, ae f.: wild animal, beast

ferē: (adv.) almost, nearly

feriēns, ferientis: beating, striking

feriō, ferīre: to strike, knock

ferō, ferre, tulī, lātum: to bear, carry, endure

ferox, ferōcis: courageous, wild, warlike

ferreus, a, um: made of iron

ferrum, ī n.: iron

fertilitās, fertilitātis f.: fruitfulness, fertility

ferus, a, um: untamed, wild, rough

ferveō, fervēre, ferbuī: to boil, burn

fessus, a, um: tired, exhausted

festīnō, festīnāre, festīnāvī, festīnātum: to hurry, make haste

fēstus, a, um: having to do with a holiday or festival

fētus, ūs m.: offspring, sapling, fruit

fibra, ae f.: fiber

fictus, a, um: formed, fashioned, feigned

fidēs, eī f.: trust, belief, faith

fīdūcia, ae f.: trust, confidence, security

fīgō, fīgere, fīxī, fīxum: to fix, fasten, thrust a weapon

figūra, ae f.: form, figure, shape

fīlia, ae f.: daughter

fīlius, fīliī m.: son

fīlum, ī n.: thread

fingō, fingere, finxī, fictum: to shape, fashion, form

fīniō, fīnīre, fīnīvī, fīnītum: to put an end to, limit

fīnis, fīnis m. or f.: border, limit

fīō, fierī, factus sum: to become, occur, be done

firmō, firmāre, firmāvī, firmātum: to make firm, strengthen, prove

fissus, a, um: split, divided

flagrō, flagrāre, flagrāvī, flagrātum: to blaze

flamma, ae f.: flame, fire

flammifer, flammifera, flammiferum: carrying flames

flāvus, a, um: blonde, yellow

flectō, flectere, flexī, flexum: to bend, turn

fleō, flēre, flēvī, flētum: to weep

flētus, ūs m.: tears, weeping

flōs, flōris m.: flower

flūmen, flūminis n.: a flowing, river

flūmineus, a, um: of a river

fluō, fluere, fluxī, fluxum: to flow

fodiō, fodere, fōdī, fossum: to dig, pierce, stab

foedō, foedāre, foedāvī, foedātus: to make foul, make filthy

fōns, fontis m.: spring, fountain

forāmen, forāminis n.: an opening, hole

forceps, forcipis f.: pair of tongs, pincers

foris, foris f.: door, gate

forma, ae f.: form, shape

formō, formāre, formāvī, formātum: to form, shape, fashion

formōsus, a, um: beautiful

fors, forte (abl.) f.: luck, chance

fortior, ius: stronger, more powerful

fortis, e: strong, powerful

fortissimus, a, um: strongest, bravest

fortūna, ae f.: luck, fortune

fortūnātus, a, um: blessed, happy

forum, ī n.: public space in Rome, center for business and politics

fossa, ae f.: ditch, trench

frangō, frangere, frēgī, fractum: to break, break into pieces

frāter, frātris m.: brother

fraus, fraudis f.: deceit, deception, fraud

fremō, fremere, fremuī, fremitum: to roar, murmur

frēnum, ī n.: bridle, reins

frequentō, frequentāre, frequentāvī, frequentātum: to crowd, flock to, attend

fretum, ī n.: strait

frīgus, frīgoris n.: cold, coolness
frondātor, frondātoris m.: one who prunes
frondōsus, a, um: leafy
frons, frondis f.: leaf, foliage
frons, frontis f.: forehead, brow
frūstrā: (adv.) in vain
frutex, fruticis m.: shrub, bush
fuga, ae f.: flight, escape
fugiō, fugere, fūgī, fugitum: to flee
fugō, fugāre, fugāvī, fugātum: to cause to flee, chase away
fulgeō, fulgēre, fulsī: to flash, shine
fulgur, fulguris n.: lightning
fulmen, fulminis n.: lightning, thunderbolt
fulvus, a, um: yellow, golden
fūmō, fūmāre, fūmāvī, fūmātum: to smoke, fume
funda, ae f.: sling
fundō, fundere, fūdī, fūsum: to pour
fūnestus, a, um: deadly, fatal, destructive
fūnus, fūneris n.: funeral, burial
furēns, furentis: raging
furor, furōris m.: raging, madness, fury
furtim: (adv.) secretly
furtum, ī n.: trick, deceit, secret love
fūsus, ī m.: spindle
futūrus, a, um: future, yet to come

galea, ae f.: helmet
gaudeō, gaudēre, gāvīsus sum: to rejoice, be glad
gaudium, ī n.: joy, gladness
gelidus, a, um: cold, frozen, icy
gemellus, a, um: twin
Geminī, ōrum m. pl.: Gemini (zodiac sign), twins
geminus, a, um: double, twin, two
gemitus, ūs m.: groan
gemma, ae f.: jewel, gem
gemmāns, gemmantis: set with jewels
gener, generī m.: son-in-law
genetīvus, a, um: innate, inborn
genetrix, genetrīcis f.: mother
genitor, genitōris m.: father

genus, generis n.: birth, origin, class, type
germāna, ae f.: sister
gerō, gerere, gessī, gestum: to bear, carry, carry out, display
gestus, ūs m.: gesture
gignō, gignere, genuī, genitum: to produce, give birth to
glaciālis, e: icy, frozen
gladius, ī m.: sword
glaeba, ae f.: a lump of earth, clod, ball
glāns, glandis f.: ball of lead, bullet
glomerō, glomerāre, glomerāvī, glomerātum: to gather into a ball
glōria, ae f.: glory, fame
glōriōsus, a, um: haughty, boastful, famous
Gorgō, Gorgonis f.: Gorgon, a mythical monster
Gorgoneus, a, um: of a Gorgon, belonging to a Gorgon
gracilis, e: thin, delicate
Grādīvus, ī m.: Gradivus, epithet of Mars meaning "He who walks in battle"
gradus, ūs m.: step, pace
Graius, a, um: of Greece
grandaevus, a, um: aged, old
grandior, grandius: bigger, greater
grandō, grandinis f.: hail, hailstorm
grānum, ī n.: grain, seed
grātēs, ium f. pl.: thanks
grātia, ae f.: favor, indulgence, service
grātor, grātārī, grātātus sum: to congratulate, wish joy to
gravidus, a, um: heavy, laden, pregnant
gravis, e: heavy, burdened, weighed down
gravitās, gravitātis f.: seriousness, solemnity, weight
grex, gregis m.: herd, flock
gurges, gurgitis m.: whirlpool, pool
gutta, ae f.: drop, spot
guttur, gutturis n.: throat

habēna, ae f.: strap, rein
habeō, habēre, habuī, habitum: to have, hold

habitus, ūs m.: condition, attire, dress, bearing
Haemonius, a, um: of Haemonia, of Thessaly
haereō, haerēre, haesī, haesum: to stick, get stuck
haliaeetus, ī m.: osprey, sea-eagle
hamadryas, hamadryadis f.: a wood nymph
harēna, ae f.: sand
harundo, harundinis f.: fishing rod
haruspex, haruspicis m.: a soothsayer who prophesies by looking at entrails
hasta, ae f.: a spear
hastīle, hastīlis n.: shaft of a spear, spear
haud: (adv.) not at all, by no means
hauriō, haurīre, hausī, haustum: to draw out, drink
Hecatē, ēs f.: Hecate, goddess of witchcraft
Hecatēius, a, um: of Hecate, goddess of witchcraft
hedera, ae f.: ivy
Helena, ae f.: Helen of Troy, queen of Sparta
Helicon, Helicōnis m.: Helicon, a mountain in Greece
Hennaeus, a, um: of Henna, a Sicilian city
herba, ae f.: herb, grass
herbōsus, a, um: grassy
herī: (adv.) yesterday
Hermaphrodītus, ī m.: Hermaphroditus, the son of Mercury and Venus
Hersilia, ae f.: Hersilia, wife of Romulus
Hesperia, ae f.: Hesperia, a western land
heu: (interj.) oh! alas!
hic, haec, hoc: (demonst. pron.) this, these
hīc: (adv.) here, in this place
Hiems, Hiemis f.: Winter, divine representation of the winter
hirsūtus, a, um: rough, shaggy, bristly
homō, hominis m.: man, human being
honor, honōris n.: honor, prize
honōrātus, a, um: honored, respected
honos, honōris n.: honor, distinction
Hora, ae f.: Hora, the name of deified Hersilia
Hōrae, ārum f.: Hours, goddessess of time and seasons

horrendus, a, um: dreadful, terrible, horrible
horridus, a, um: unkempt, rough, uncouth, horrible
hortātus, a, um: having urged
hortor, hortārī, hortātus sum: to encourage, urge on
hortus, ī m.: garden
hospes, hospitis m.: host, guest, stranger
hospitium, ī n.: hospitality
hostīlis, e: hostile, unfriendly
hostis, hostis m.: enemy
hūc: (adv.) to this place
hūmnānus, a, um: human
humus, ī f.: ground
hydrus, ī m.: water-snake
Hymēn, Hymenis m.: Hymen, a god of marriage
Hymenaeus, ī m.: Hymenaeus, a god of marriage

iaceō, iacēre, iacuī, iacitum: to lie
iaciō, iacere, iēcī, iactum: to throw
iactātus, ūs m.: a shaking, fluttering, moving quickly up and down
iactō, iactāre, iactāvī, iactātum: to throw, hurl
iaculum, ī n.: dart, javelin
iam: (adv.) now, already
iamque: (adv.) now, already
Īapetus, ī m.: Iapetus, the father of Atlas
Iāsōn, Iāsonis m.: Jason, leader of the Argonauts
ibi: (adv.) there, in that place
īciō, īcere, īcī, ictum: to strike, hit
ictus, ūs m.: blow, strike
Īdaeus, a, um: of Mt. Ida, a mountain near Troy
īdem, eadem, idem: the same
igitur: (conj.) therefore
ignescō, ignescere: to catch fire
ignis, ignis m.: fire
ignōtus, a, um: unknown
ille, illa, illud: (demonst. pron.) that, those
illīc: (adv.) there, in that place
illūc: (adv.) to that place

Illyricus, a, um: of Illyria, a region bordering the Adriatic Sea

imāgo, imāginis f.: image, likeness

immēnsus, a, um: huge

immergō, immergere, immersī, immersum: to dip, plunge, immerse

immeritus, a, um: undeserving

immisceō, immiscēre, immiscuī, immixtum: to mix in, blend, intermingle

immittō, immittere, immīsī, immissum: to send in

immōtus, a, um: unmoved

impellō, impellere, impulī, impulsum: to push, drive, set in motion

imperfectus, a, um: unfinished, incomplete

imperō, imperāre, imperāvī, imperātum: to command, order

impetus, ūs m.: impulse

impius, a, um: impious, disrespectful

impleō, implēre, implēvī, implētum: to fill up

implūmis, e: featherless

impōnō, impōnere, imposuī, impositum: to lay or place upon, impose on

improbus, a, um: wicked

īmus, a, um: lowest, deepest

in: (prep. + abl.) in, on; (prep. + acc.) into

inānis, e: empty, void

incertus, a, um: uncertain, doubtful

incestus, a, um: impure, defiled, sinful

incidium, ī n.: sign, evidence

incipiō, incipere, incēpī, inceptum: to begin

incitō, incitāre, incitāvī, incitātum: to urge, motivate, excite

inclūdō, inclūdere, inclūsī, inclūsum: to close in, enclose

incognitus, a, um: unknown

inconditus, a, um: disorderly, not clearly arranged, hidden in

inconsōlābilis, e: incurable, inconsolable

increpō, increpere, increpuī, increpitum: to make a noise, resound

incumbō, incumbere, incubuī, incubitum: to lie down on, lean on

incūnābula, ōrum n. pl.: cradle, birthplace

inde: (adv.) from there

index, indicis m.: informer, that which informs, sign

indicō, indicāre, indicāvī, indicātum: to make known, show

indīgestus, a, um: confused, unarranged

indignāns, indignantis: offended, impatient

indolescō, indolescere, indoluī: to be pained, grieve

indūcō, indūcere, induxī, inductum: to bring in, introduce, draw over a surface (+ dat.)

indūrō, indūrāre, indūrāvī, indūrātum: to harden, make hard

inermis, e: unarmed

iners, inertis: inactive, idle

īnfāmia, ae f.: negative report, dishonor

infāns, infantis m. or f.: speechless one, baby

infectus, a, um: (infaciō) undone, unfinished

infectus, a, um: (inficiō) stained, dyed

infēlix, infēlīcis: unhappy

inferior, ius: lower

infernus, a, um: lower, from below

infestus, a, um: unsafe, dangerous, infested

īnfirmus, a, um: feeble, weak

ingemō, ingemere, ingemuī: to groan

ingenium, ī n.: nature, genius, character

ingēns, ingentis: huge

ingredior, ingredī, ingressus sum: to step in, enter, walk

inhibeō, inhibēre, inhibuī, inhibitum: to hold in check, restrain

inhospitus, a, um: inhospitable, uninviting

inimīcus, a, um: hostile, unkind

iniūria, ae f.: injury, harm

inlaqueō, inlaqueāre, inlaqueāvī, inlaqueātum: to trap, ensnare

innātus, a, um: inborn

innectō, innectere, innexuī, innexum: to entwine

innītor, innītī, innixus sum: to lean upon, rest on

innumerus, a, um: innumerable, countless

Īnō, ūs f.: Ino, a daughter of Cadmus

inobservātus, a, um: unseen, unobserved

inops, inopis: lacking in (+ gen.)

inōrdinātus, a, um: disordered, confused

inquit, inquunt: he, she, it says, they say

inrideō, inridēre, inrīsī, inrīsum: to mock, jeer at

inritus, a, um: void, invalid

insculpō, insculpere, insculpsī, insculptum: to cut into, engrave

inserō, inserere, inseruī, insertum: put in, insert

insidiae, ārum f.: ambush, treachery

insigne, insignis n.: a distinguishing mark, sign

insignis, insigne: distinguished, remarkable

insiliō, insilīre, insiluī: to leap on, leap into

insonō, insonāre, insonuī: to resound

instituō, instituere, instituī, institūtum: to put in place, establish

instrūmentum, ī n.: tool, instrument

insula, ae f.: island

insuō, insuere, insuī, insūtum: to sew in, sew up

insuperābilis, e: insurmountable

intābescō, intābescere, intābuī: to melt away, dissolve

intendō, intendere, intendī, intentum: to direct, stretch

inter: (prep. + acc.) among, between

intereā: (adv.) meanwhile

interius: (adv.) inside

intermittō, intermittere, intermīsī, intermissum: to discontinue, interrupt, suspend

intertexō, intertexere, intertexuī, intertextum: to interweave

interveniō, intervenīre, intervēnī, interventum: to come between, intervene, interrupt

intexō, intexere, intexuī, intextum: to weave in

intrā: (prep. + acc.) inside, within

intremiscō, intremiscere: to tremble

intrō, intrāre, intrāvī, intrātum: to walk into, enter

inveniō, invenīre, invēnī, inventum: to find, discover

invergō, invergere: to pour upon

invidiōsus, a, um: envious, hateful, hostile

invītō, invītāre, invītāvī, invītātum: to invite

invītus, a, um: unwilling

iō: (interj.) the cry of the Bacchantes

iocōsus, a, um: jocular, playful

iocus, ī m.: joke

Iolcus, ī f.: Iolcus, a city in Thessaly and Jason's home

Īphis, Īphis m.: Iphis, a young man from Cyprus

ipse, ipsa, ipsum: himself, herself, itself

īra, ae f.: anger, rage

īrātus, a, um: angered, enraged

Īris, Īris f.: Iris, goddess of the rainbow and messenger of the gods

irrigō, irrigāre, irrigāvī, irrigātum: to water, irrigate, wet, moisten

irrītō, irrītāre, irrītāvī, irrītātum: to stir up, incite

irrumpō, irrumpere, irrūpī, irruptum: to break in, rush in

is, ea, id: (third person pron.) eius (gen.) he, she, it, this, that

Ismēnis, Ismēnidis f.: a Theban woman

Ismēnus, ī m.: Ismenus, one of Niobe's sons

Issē, ēs f.: Isse, a princess of Lesbos

iste, ista, istud: (demonst. pron.) that, those

iter, itineris n.: journey, way

Itys, Ityos m.: Itys, the son of Tereus and Procne

iubar, iubaris n.: light, brightness, sunshine

iubeō, iubēre, iūssī, iūssum: to order, command

iūdex, iūdicis m.: judge

iugulum, ī n.: throat

iugum, ī n.: yoke, team of draft animals, mountain ridge

Iūlius, ī m.: Julius Caesar

iungō, iungere, iunxī, iunctum: to join, unite

Iūnō, Iūnōnis f.: Juno, wife of Jupiter, goddess of marriage

Iūnōnigena, ae m.: son of Juno

Iuppiter, Iovis m.: Jupiter/Jove, ruler of the gods

iūrātus, a, um: sworn to

iurgium, ī n.: argument, quarrel

iūrō, iūrāre, iūrāvī, iūrātum: to swear

iūs, iūris n.: right, law

iustē: (adv.) justly

iustissimus, a, um: most just

iūstitia, ae f.: justice

iustius: (adv.) more justly

iūtus, a, um: helped, aided

iuvenālis, e: youthful

iuvenca, ae f.: cow

iuvencus, ī m.: young bull

iuvenis, iuvenis m. or f.: young person, youth

Iuventa, ae f.: Juventa, the goddess of youth

iuventus, iuventūtis f.: youth, prime of life

iuvō, iuvāre, iūvī, iūtum: to help, aid, please, delight

labia, ae f.: lip

labō, labāre, labāvī, labātum: to waver, totter

labor, labōris m.: work, labor

lābor, lābī, lapsus sum: to glide down, fall, slip

labōrātus, a, um: made, manufactured

labōrō, labōrāre, labōrāvī, labōrātum: to work at

lac, lactis n.: milk

lacerō, lacerāre, lacerāvī, lacerātum: to tear, lacerate

lacertus, ī m.: arm

lacrima, ae f.: tear

lactō, lactāre, lactāvī, lactātum: to give milk, contain milk

lacus, ūs m.: hollow, lake

laedō, laedere, laesī, laesum: to strike, injure

laetus, a, um: joyful, happy, delighted

laevus, a, um: left side

lambō, lambere, lambī, lambitum: to lick, lap

lāna, ae f.: wool

lancea, ae f.: lance, spear

lānificus, a, um: having to do with wool-working

lāniger, lānigerī m.: ram

laniō, laniāre, laniāvī, laniātum: to tear to pieces

lapillus, ī m.: little stone, pebble

lapis, lapidis m.: a stone

laqueus, ī m.: noose, snare, trap

lascīvus, a, um: playful, insolent

latebra, ae f.: retreat, hiding place

lateō, latēre, latuī: to lie concealed

latex, laticis m.: liquid, fluid

Latīnus, a, um: of Latium, the region which includes Rome

Latius, a, um: of Latium

Lātōna, ae f.: Latona, mother of Apollo and Diana

lātus, a, um: wide, broad

latus, lateris n.: side

laudō, laudāre, laudāvī, laudātum: to praise

laurea, ae f.: the laurel tree

laurus, ī f.: the laurel tree, laurels

laus, laudis f.: praise

lavō, lavāre, lāvī, lautum: to wash

lectus, ī m.: couch, marriage bed

Lēda, ae f.: Leda, mother of Helen of Troy

legō, legere, lēgī, lectum: to pick out, choose, read

Lemnius, ī m.: of Lemnos, epithet of Vulcan

lentē: (adv.) slowly

lentus, a, um: supple, malleable, slow

Leō, Leōnis m.: Leo (zodiac sign), a lion

lētātus, a, um: murdered

lētum, ī n.: death, ruin

levis, e: light, swift

levō, levāre, levāvī, levātum: to raise up, lift, make light, ease

lex, lēgis f.: a law, formal agreement

Līber, Līberī m.: Liber, an Italian deity associated with Bacchus

līberō, līberāre, līberāvī, līberātum: to free
libīdō, libīdinis f.: lust
Lībra, ae f.: Libra (zodiac sign), scales
Libycus, a, um: of Lybia
licet, licēre, licuit: (impers. verb) it is allowed (+ inf.)
ligātus, a, um: tied up, caught up
ligō, ligāre, ligāvī, ligātum: to tie
līlium, ī n.: lily
līmen, līminis n.: threshold
lingua, ae f.: tongue
līnum, ī n.: linen, thread, hunter's net
liquefaciō, liquefacere, liquefēcī, liquefactum: to melt, liquefy
liquescō, liquescere, licuī: to become liquid, dissolve, melt
liquidus, a, um: liquid, fluid
līs, lītis f.: legal controversy, suit, quarrel, contention
lītus, lītoris n.: the shore
Līvor, Līvōris f.: Envy, the goddess of jealousy
loca, ōrum, n.: region
locus, ī m.: place
longius: (adv.) farther
longus, a, um: long, extended
loquor, loquī, locūtus sum: to speak
lūbricus, a, um: slippery, smooth
lūcēns, lūcentis: shining, gleaning
lūceō, lūcēre, luxī: to be bright, gleam
luctor, luctārī, luctātus sum: to wrestle, struggle, contend
luctus, ūs m.: lamentation, grief
lūcus, ī m.: wood, grove
lūdō, lūdere, lūsī, lūsum: to play, frolic, trick
lūdus, ī m.: game
luēs, luis f.: disease, pestilence, plague
lūmen, lūminis n.: light, sight, eye
lūna, ae f.: the moon
lupus, ī m.: a wolf
lustrō, lustrāre, lustrāvī, lustrātum: to go place to place, traverse, purify
lustrum, ī n.: a den, lair, bog, woodland
lux, lūcis f.: light
luxuriēs, luxuriēī f.: extravagance, excess

luxuriō, luxuriāre, luxuriāvī, luxuriātum: to be abundant, enlarge, grow rapidly
Lycāōn, Lycāonis m.: Lycaon, mythical ruler of Arcadia
Lycius, a, um: of Lycia, a region of Asia Minor
Lȳdia, ae f.: Lydia, a region of Asia Minor
lympha, ae f.: clear water, spring water
lyra, ae f.: lyre

maciēs, maciēī f.: leanness
mactō, mactāre, mactāvī, mactātum: to slay, sacrifice
maculō, maculāre, maculāvī, maculātum: to stain, pollute
maculōsus, a, um: spotted
madeō, madēre, maduī: to be wet
madidus, a, um: wet
Maeonius, a, um: of Maeonia, the eastern part of Lydia in Asia Minor
maereō, maerēre: to mourn, grieve
maestissimus, a, um: very sad, very gloomy
maestus, a, um: sad, dejected
magicus, a, um: relating to magic
magis: (adv.) more, rather
magister, magistrī m.: master, teacher
magnus, a, um: big, great
maior, maius: greater
male: (adv.) badly
malus, a, um: bad, evil
mandātum, ī n.: instruction, demand
maneō, manēre, mansī, mansum: to remain, stay
mānes, mānium m. pl.: ghosts, souls of the departed
manifestus, a, um: clear, visible
mānō, mānāre, mānāvī, mānātum: to pour, shed
Mantō, Mantūs f.: Manto, a Theban prophetess
manus, ūs f.: hand, band
marceō, marcēre: to wither, be faint, be weak
mare, maris n.: the sea
marītus, ī m.: husband

marmor, marmoris n.: marble
marmoreus, a, um: of marble
Mars, Martis m.: Mars, the god of spring-time and war
Martius, a, um: sacred to Mars, god of war
massa, ae f.: a mass, lump
māter, mātris f.: mother
māteria, ae f.: matter, material
māternus, a, um: of the mother, maternal
mātrōna, ae f.: married woman, matron
Māvors, Māvortis m.: archaic name for the god Mars
Māvortius, a, um: of Mars, having to do with Mars
maximus, a, um: greatest
Mēdēa, ae f.: Medea, a princess of Colchis and a sorceress
medēns, medentis m.: a physician
medicāmen, medicāminis n.: drug, medicine, poison
medius, a, um: middle
Medūsa, ae f.: Medusa, a mortal Gorgon whose gaze causes petrification
Megara, ae f.: Megara, a city in Greece
mel, mellis n.: honey
membrum, ī n.: limb
meminī, meminisse: (defect. verb) to remember (+ gen.)
memor, memoris: mindful, remembering
memorābilis, e: memorable, remarkable
memoria, memoriae f.: memory
memorō, memorāre, memorāvī, memorātum: to recall, relate
mēns, mentis f.: mind, reason, intellect
mensa, ae f.: a table
Mensis, Mensis m.: Month, divine representation of a month
Mercurius, ī m.: Mercury, the god of messengers, thieves, and merchants
mereō, merēre, meruī, meritum: to deserve, earn
mergō, mergere, mersī, mersum: to sink, plunge, immerse

meritō: (adv.) deservedly, justly
mersus, a, um: sunk, overwhelmed
messor, messōris m.: reaper, mower
metuō, metuere, metuī, metūtum: to fear, be afraid of
metus, ūs m.: fear, dread
meus, a, um: (poss. adj.) my, mine
micō, micāre, micuī: to vibrate, move rapidly, flicker
mīles, mīlitis m.: soldier
mille: (indecl.) a thousand
mināx, minācis: threatening
minimē: (adv.) not at all
minimus, a, um: smallest, least
Mīnōs, Mīnōis m.: Minos, king of Crete
minuō, minuere, minuī, minūtum: to lessen, diminish
minus: (adv.) less
Minyae, ārum m. pl.: the Minyans, the Argonauts
mīrābiliter: (adv.) miraculously, wonderfully
mīror, mīrārī, mīrātus sum: to admire, wonder at
misceō, miscēre, miscuī, mixtum: to mingle, mix
miser, misera, miserum: poor, wretched, pitiable
miserābilis, e: pitiable, miserable, wretched
miserescō, miserescere: to pity, have compassion for (+ gen.)
miserrimus, a, um: very unhappy, very miserable
mittō, mittere, mīsī, missum: to send
mixtus, a, um: mixed
moderāmen, moderāminis n.: a means of guiding, government
modo: (adv.) only, just now, lately
moenia, ium n. pl.: walls
mōles, mōlis f.: weight, bulk
mōlīmen, mōlīminis n.: great effort, exertion
mōlior, mōlīrī, mōlītus sum: to set in motion, work at

molliō, mollīre, mollīvī, mollītum: to soften

mollis, e: soft, tender

mollitia, ae f.: softness

mōmentum, ī n.: movement

moneō, monēre, monuī, monitum: to warn, admonish

mōns, montis m.: mountain

monstrō, monstrāre, monstrāvī, monstrātum: to show, point out, indicate

monstrum, ī n.: monster, supernatural thing or event, wonder

mora, ae f.: delay, pause

morbus, ī m.: disease, illness

morior, morī, mortuus sum: to die

moror, morārī, morātus sum: to delay, linger

mors, mortis f.: death

mortālis, e: mortal, human

mortuus, a, um: dead

mōs, mōris m.: custom, habit

moveō, movēre, mōvī, mōtum: to move, set in motion

mox: (adv.) soon

Mulciber, Mulcibēris m.: epithet of Vulcan, god of craftsmanship

multum: (adv.) much, very much

multus, a, um: many

mundus, ī m.: world, universe

mūnus, mūneris n.: office, charge, favor, gift

murmur, mumuris n.: murmur, rumbling

mūrus, ī m.: city wall

Mūsa, ae f.: a Muse

musca, ae f.: a fly

mūtātus, a, um: changed, transformed

mūtō, mūtāre, mūtāvī, mūtātum: to change

mūtus, a, um: mute, silent, quiet

mūtuus, a, um: reciprocal, mutual

Nāias, Nāiadis f.: a Naiad, water nymph

nanciscor, nanciscī, nactus sum: to meet, light upon

narrō, narrāre, narrāvī, narrātum: to tell, relate

nāsus, ī m.: a nose

nāta, ae f.: daughter

nātūra, ae f.: nature

nātus, a, um: born

nātus, ī m.: son

nāvicula, ae f.: little ship, boat

nāvigō, nāvigāre, nāvigāvī, nāvigātum: to sail

nāvis, nāvis f.: ship

nē: (adv.) not

nebula, ae f.: cloud, mist

nec: (adv.) and not

necātus, a, um: having been killed

necō, necāre, necāvī, necātum: to kill, slay

nefandus, a, um: impious, heinous

nefas n.: (indecl.) a crime, abomination

negō, negāre, negāvī, negātum: to deny

nēmō, nēminis m. or f.: no one, nobody

nemorōsus, a, um: wooded

nemus, nemoris n.: wood, grove

nepos, nepōtis m.: grandson, descendant

Neptūnus, ī m.: Neptune, god of the sea

nēquīquam: (adv.) in vain, to no purpose

Nēreus, ī m.: Nereus, a god of the sea

nervus, ī m.: sinew, bowstring

neuter, neutra, neutrum: neither

nex, necis f.: death

nexilis, e: tied together

nexus, ūs m.: a joint, entwining, connection

niger, nigra, nigrum: black, dark

nihil n.: (indecl.) nothing

Nīlus, ī m.: Nile, a river in Egypt

nimbus, ī m.: vapor, cloud

nimis: (adv.) too much

nimium: (adv.) excessively, too much

Niobē, ēs f.: Niobe, a queen of Thebes born in Lydia

nisi: (conj.) unless, if not

Nīsus, ī m.: Nisus, king of Megara

nitidus, a, um: shining, bright

niveus, a, um: snowy, white

nix, nivis f.: snow

nō, nāre, nāvī: to swim

nōbilis, e: well-known

noceō, nocēre, nocuī, nocitum: to be harmful

nōdōsus, a, um: knotty

nōdus, ī m.: knot

nōlō, nōlle, nōluī: to be unwilling (nōlī = imperative)

nōmen, nōminis n.: name

nōn: (adv.) not

nōndum: (adv.) not yet

nōnus, a, um: ninth

nōs, nostrī/nostrum pl.: (first person pron.) nōbīs (dat./abl.), nōs (acc.), we, us

nōscō, nōscere, nōvī, nōtum: to become acquainted with, know

noster, nostra, nostrum: (poss. adj.) our

nota, ae f.: mark

nōtissimus, a, um: most known, best known

notō, notāre, notāvī, notātum: to mark

novus, a, um: new, young

nox, noctis f.: night

nūbes, nūbis f.: cloud

nūbilum, ī n.: cloud mass

nūbō, nūbere, nupsī, nuptum: to cover, veil, marry (+ dat.)

nūdō, nūdāre, nūdāvī, nūdātum: to strip, lay bare

nūdus, a, um: naked

nullus, a, um: none, not any

num: (interrog.) introduces a question expecting a negative answer

nūmen, nūminis n.: divinity, divine spirit

numerus, ī m.: a number

numquam: (adv.) never

nunc: (adv.) now

nūpta, ae f.: married woman, wife

nurus, ūs f.: daughter-in-law

nūtō, nūtāre, nūtāvī, nūtātum: to nod

nūtrix, nūtrīcis f.: nurse

nympha, ae f.: nymph

Nȳsaeus, a, um: of Nysa, a region in Asia Minor

ō: (interj.) oh!

oblīquus, a, um: indirect, on one side, slanting

observō, observāre, observāvī, observātum: to watch, regard, attend to

obstipescō, obstipescere, obstipuī: to be amazed

obstō, obstāre, obstitī, obstātum: to stand against, oppose (+ dat.)

obumbrō, obumbrāre, obumbrāvī, obumbrātum: to overshadow, cover

occulō, occulere, occuluī, occultum: to cover, hide

occupō, occupāre, occupāvī, occupātum: to take hold of, seize, master

occurrō, occurrere, occurrī, occursum: to meet, appear

octāvus, a, um: eighth

oculus, ī m.: eye

ōdī, ōdisse: (defect. verb) to hate

odiōsus, a, um: hateful, despised

odium, ī n.: hatred

odor, odōris m.: smell

odōrō, odōrāre, odōrāvī, odōrātum: to make odorous, make sweet-smelling

Oetaeus, a, um: of Oeta, the mountain range between Thessaly and Macedonia

officium, ī n.: duty, position, service

olīva, ae f.: olive

olōrīnus, a, um: belonging to a swan

Olympus, ī m.: Mt. Olympus, home of the gods

ōmen, ōminis n.: sign, omen

omnipotēns, omnipotentis: all powerful

omnis, e: every, all

onus, oneris n.: burden, load

opifer, opifera, opiferum: bringing aid, helpful

oppidum, ī n.: town

ops, opis f.: resource, help, assistance

optō, optāre, optāvī, optātum: to desire, wish for

opus, operis n.: work, art, workmanship

ōrāculum, ī n.: oracle, divine utterance, place of prophecy

orbis lacteus: Milky Way

orbis, orbis m.: circle, coil
orbus, a, um: orphaned, childless
ōrdinātus, a, um: ordered, organized
ordinō, ordināre, ordināvī, ordinātum: to put in order, arrange
ordo, ordinis m.: row, line, order
Ōrīthyia, ae f.: Orithyia, a daughter of Erechtheus
ōrnō, ōrnāre, ōrnāvī, ōrnātum: to decorate
ōrō, ōrāre, ōrāvī, ōrātum: to speak, beg, pray
ōs, ōris n.: mouth, face
os, ossis n.: bone
osculum, ī n.: lips, mouth, kiss
ostendō, ostendere, ostendī, ostentum: to show, hold out, display
ostentum, ī n.: marvel, portent
ostium, ī n.: door, entrance, mouth
ovis, ovis f.: sheep

pābulum, ī n.: food, nourishment
pācālis, e: peaceful
paene: (adv.) almost
Palātīnus, a, um: of the Palatine, one of the seven hills of Rome
palātum, ī n.: palate, roof of the mouth
palla, ae f.: long garment, cloak
Pallas, Palladis f.: epithet of Athena/Minerva, the goddess of weaving, wisdom, and battles
palleō, pallēre, palluī: to be pale, grow pale
pallidus, a, um: pale
pallor, pallōris m.: paleness
palma, ae f.: palm of the hand
Pandīōn, Pandīonis m.: Pandion, father of Procne and Philomela
pandō, pandere, pandī, passum: to spread out, extend
papȳrifer, papȳrifera, papȳriferum: papyrus-bearing
pār, paris: equal, like
parātus, ūs m.: preparation, apparel
parens, parentis m. or f.: parent
pāreō, pārēre, pāruī, pāritum: to be obedient to, submit to (+ dat.)

pariō, parere, peperī, partum: to bring forth, produce
pariter: (adv.) equally
Parnāsus, ī m.: Parnassus, a mountain in Phocis sacred to Apollo
parō, parāre, parāvī, parātum: to prepare
pars, partis f.: a part, portion
partim ... partim: (adv.) in part ... in part
partus, ūs m.: offspring, birth
parum: (adv.) too little, not enough
parvus, a, um: small, little
passus, ūs m.: step, pace
pastor, pastōris m.: shepherd, herdsman
patefaciō, patefacere, patefēcī, patefactum: to throw open, open, reveal
pateō, patēre, patuī: to lie open, be accessible
pater, patris m.: father
patera, ae f.: a shallow dish, saucer
paternus, a, um: fatherly, paternal
patior, patī, passus sum: to suffer, allow, experience, tolerate
patria, ae f.: fatherland, native country
pātrius, a, um: fatherly, paternal
patulus, a, um: open, wide, broad
paucus, a, um: few, small in number
paulātim: (adv.) little by little, gradually
pavefactus, a, um: terrified
paveō, pavēre, pāvī: to be afraid, quake
pax, pācis f.: peace, tranquility
pectus, pectoris n.: breast, chest
Pēgasus, ī m.: Pegasus, flying horse born from Medusa
Peliās, Peliae m.: Pelias, king of Thessaly
pellis, pellis f.: skin, hide
pellō, pellere, pepulī, pulsum: to beat, strike, drive away
Penātēs, Penātium m. pl.: household gods
pendēns, pendentis: hanging
pendeō, pendēre, pependī: to hang suspended, suspend
Pēnēius, a, um: of Peneus, a river-god
penetrō, penetrāre, penetrāvī, penetrātum: to pass through, sink deep into
penna, ae f.: a feather, wing

pennātus, a, um: winged, feathered
Penthēus, ī m.: Pentheus, a grandson of Cadmus
per: (prep. + acc.) by, through, because of
percalescō, percalescere, percaluī: to become warm
percutiō, percutere, percussī, percussum: to strike, beat
perdō, perdere, perdidī, perditum: to ruin, destroy
pererrō, pererrāre, pererrāvī, pererrātum: to wander through
perferō, perferre, pertulī, perlātum: to carry all the way
perficiō, perficere, perfēcī, perfectum: to complete, perfect
perfundō, perfundere, perfūdī, perfūsum: to steep, pour over, fill, spread
perhorrēscō, perhorrēscere, perhorruī: to shudder, be terrified at
perīculum, ī n.: danger, risk
perlūcidus, a, um: shining, bright, transparent
permulceō, permulcēre, permulsī, permulsum: to stroke, soften
perpetuus, a, um: continuous, unending
Perseus, ī m.: Perseus, a son of Jupiter
perspiciō, perspicere, perspexī, perspectum: to see through, observe closely
perstō, perstāre, perstitī, perstātum: to stand firm
perterritus, a, um: frightened, terrified
perveniō, pervenīre, pervēnī, perventum: to come to, reach
pēs, pedis m.: the foot
petō, petere, petīvi, petītum: to seek, demand, beg
Phaethōn, Phaethōntis m.: Phaethon, son of Clymene and Sōl
pharetra, ae f.: quiver
pharetrātus, a, um: wearing a quiver
Philomēla, ae f.: Philomela, daughter of Pandion
Phōcis, Phōcidis f.: Phocis, a district in central Greece

Phoebēius, a, um: of Phoebus, of Apollo
Phoebeus, a, um: of Phoebus, of Apollo
Phoebus, ī m.: Phoebus, epithet of Apollo
Phoenīcēs, um m. pl.: Phoenicians
Phrygia, ae f.: Phrygia, a region of Asia Minor
Phrygius, a, um: of Phrygia
picea, ae f.: spruce-fir tree
pietās, pietātis f.: sense of duty, piety
pignus, pignoris n.: pledge, assurance
pingō, pingere, pinxī, pictum: to paint, depict
piscātor, piscātōris m.: fisherman
Piscēs, Piscium m. pl.: Pisces (zodiac sign), fish
piscīna, ae f.: a fishpond, reservoir
pius, a, um: dutiful, devoted to the gods
plācātus, a, um: quiet, peaceful, calm
placeō, placēre, placuī, placitum: to please, be agreeable to (+ dat.)
placidus, a, um: quiet, gentle
plācō, plācāre, plācāvī, plācātum: to soothe, calm
plāga, ae f.: a blow, wound
Plēias, Plēiadis f.: one of the Pleiades
plēnus, a, um: full
plūma, ae f.: feather, plumage
plumbeus, a, um: made of lead
plūrimus, a, um: very much, very many
plūs, plūris: more
Plūto, Plūtōnis m.: Pluto, god of the Underworld
pluvia, ae f.: rain
pluvius, a, um: rainy
poena, ae f.: punishment
poēta, ae m.: poet
pollex, pollicis m.: thumb
polliceor, pollicērī, pollicitus sum: to promise, offer
pōmārium, ī n.: orchard, garden for fruit
Pōmōna, ae f.: Pomona, the goddess of fruit-trees
pōmum, ī n.: fruit
pōnō, pōnere, posuī, positum: to place, put, put aside

pontifex, pontificis m.: a priest
pontus, ī m.: sea, ocean
populus, ī m.: people
porrectus, a, um: stretched out
porrigō, porrigere, porrexī, porrectum: to lay low, stretch out, extend
porta, ae f.: a gate, door
portendō, portendere, portendī, portentum: to indicate, predict
portō, portāre, portāvī, portātum: to bring, carry
portus, ūs m.: port
poscō, poscere, poposcī: to request, ask for, demand
possideō, possidēre, possēdī, possessum: to possess, hold
possum, posse, potuī: to be able, have in one's power
post: (prep. + acc.) behind, after
posteā: (adv.) afterwards
postis, postis m.: a door post
postquam: (conj.) after
postulō, postulāre, postulāvī, postulātum: to demand, claim, request
potentia, ae f.: power, ability
potior, potīrī, potītus sum: to obtain, possess (+ acc. or abl.)
praecipuus, a, um: peculiar, excellent, distinguished
praecutiō, praecutere, praecussī, praecussum: to shake in front
praeda, ae f.: spoil, plunder
praedīcō, praedīcere, praedixī, praedictum: to prophesy, foretell
praemium, ī n.: profit, reward
praemoneō, praemonēre, praemonuī, praemonitum: to warn beforehand
praemonitus, ūs m.: prediction, warning
praenuntius, a, um: foretelling
praepōnō, praepōnere, praeposuī, praepositum: to put before
praesāgus, a, um: foreboding, predicting
praescius, a, um: having foreknowledge, prescient

praesignis, e: remarkable, illustrious
praestāns, praestantis: standing before, excelling (+ dat.)
praeter: (prep. + acc.) besides, except
precor, precarī, precātus sum: to beg, entreat, pray
premō, premere, pressī, pressum: to press, pursue closely
pretiōsior, ius: more precious, more valuable
prex, precis f.: prayer, plea
prīmum: (adv.) at first, first
prīmus, a, um: first, foremost
prior, ius: former, previous
priscus, a, um: old, ancient
pristinus, a, um: former, earlier, of yesterday
prō: (prep. + abl.) in place of, on behalf of
probō, probāre, probāvī, probātum: to approve
Proca, ae m.: Proca, a king of the Italian city of Alba
procer, proceris m.: a chief, prince, noble
Procnē, ēs f.: Procne, daughter of Pandion
Procris, Procris f.: Procris, a daughter of Erechtheus
procul: (adv.) far away, at a distance, from afar
profānus, a, um: not sacred, uninitiated, ordinary
prōfero, prōferre, prōtulī, prōlātum: to carry forward, bring forth, offer
prōgeniēs, ēī f.: offspring
prohibeō, prohibēre, prohibuī, prohibitum: to hold back, restrain, prevent
prōicio, prōicere, prōiēcī, prōiectum: to throw forward, fling away
prōles, prōlis f.: offspring, descendants
prōmittō, prōmittere, prōmīsī, prōmissum: to promise
prōmō, prōmere, prompsī, promptum: to bring forth, produce
prōnus, a, um: stooped forward, leaning forward
prope: (adv.) nearby, near

**propero, properāre, properāvī, proper-
ātum:** to hasten

Prōserpina, ae f.: Proserpina, goddess of
springtime

**prospectō, prospectāre, prospectāvī, pros-
pectātum:** to gaze out at, look out on

prōtinus: (adv.) further, immediately

pudendus, a, um: deserving of shame,
shameful

pudīcus, a, um: chaste, modest

pudor, pudōris m.: modesty, shame

puella, ae f.: girl

puellāris, e: girlish

puer, puerī m.: boy

pugnō, pugnāre, pugnāvī, pugnātum: to
fight

pugnus, ī m.: the fist

pulcher, pulchra, pulchrum: beautiful

pulcherrimus, a, um: most beautiful

pulsō, pulsāre, pulsāvī, pulsātum: to beat

pulvereus, a, um: dusty

pulverulentus, a, um: dusty

pulvīnar, pulvīnāris n.: cushioned seat, seat
of honor

pūniceus, a, um: red, purple

pūniō, pūnīre, pūnīvī, pūnītum: to punish

puppis, puppis f.: stern of a ship

purpura, ae f.: purple

purpureus, a, um: purple, crimson

pūrus, a, um: pure, clean, simple, bare

putātor, putātoris m.: pruner of trees

putō, putāre, putāvī, putātum: to think

pyropus, ī m.: bronze

Pyrrha, ae f.: Pyrrha, a daughter of
Epimetheus

Pȳthia, Pȳthiōrum n.: the Pythian Games

Pȳthōn, Pȳthōnis m.: Python, a huge serpent

quā: (adv.) where

quācumque: (adv.) wherever

quadrīgae, ārum f. pl.: four-horse chariot

quaerō, quaerere, quaesīvī, quaesītum: to
search for, seek

quālis, e: of what sort, like

quam: (adv.) than, as, how

quamquam: (conj.) although

quamvīs: (conj.) although

quandō: (adv.) when

quantus, a, um: of what size, how great,
how much

quasi: (conj. and adv.) as if

quater: (adv.) four times

questus, ūs m.: complaining, complaint

quia: (conj.) because

quī, quae, quod: (interrog. adj.) which?
what? what kind of?

quī, quae, quod: (rel. pron.) who, which,
what, that

quid: (interrog. adv.) why

quidem: (adv.) surely, in fact, indeed

quinque: (indecl. numer.) five

quinquennium, ī n.: a period of five years

Quirīnus, ī m.: Quirinus, a god with whom
the deified Romulus was identified

quis, quid: (interrog. pron.) who, what

**quisquam, quaequam, quidquam or
quicquam:** anyone, anything

quisque, quaeque, quidque: (pron.) each,
every

quisquis, quaequae, quidquid: whoever,
whichever, whatever

quod: (conj.) because

quōmodo: (adv.) in what manner, how

quondam: (adv.) once, formerly

quoniam: (conj.) since, because

quoque: (conj.) also, too

quotiens: (adv.) how often, how many

quotiēscumque: (conj.) however often

radiāns, radiantis: shining, gleaming

radiō, radiāre, radiāvī, radiātum: shine,
radiate

radius, ī m.: ray, spoke, shuttle for weaving

rādix, rādīcis f.: root

rāmus, ī m.: branch

rapidus, a, um: swift, hurrying

rapiō, rapere, rapuī, raptum: to seize, take,
rape

raptor, raptōris m.: robber, kidnapper, rapist

rāstrum, ī n.: rake, hoe

ratis, ratis f.: raft, boat

recidō, recidere, reccidī, recāsūrum: to fall back

recessus, ūs m.: a recess

recipiō, recipere, recēpī, receptum: to take back, recover

reclūdō, reclūdere, reclūsī, reclūsum: to open, reveal, disclose

rēctor, rēctōris m.: ruler

recubō, recubāre, recubāvī, recubātum: to lie back, incline

recurvus, a, um: turned back, bent

recūsō, recūsāre, recūsāvī, recūsātum: to reject, refuse

redditus, a, um: given back, restored

reddō, reddere, reddidī, redditum: to give back, restore, return to

redeō, redīre, rediī, reditum: to come back, return

redūcō, redūcere, reduxī, reductum: to draw backwards, lead back

referō, referre, rettulī, relātum: to bring back, carry back, return, report

reflectō, reflectere, reflexī, reflectum: to turn back, reflect

refringō, refrigere, refrēgī, refrāctum: to break open

refugiō, refugere, refugī: to flee, escape

rēgālis, e: royal

rēgia, ae f.: palace, royal house

rēgīna, ae f.: queen

regnum, ī n.: rule, kingship, kingdom

regō, regere, rēxī, rēctum: to rule, control

relegō, relegere, relēgī, relectum: to gather again, go over again

religō, religāre, religāvī, religātum: to tie again

relinquō, relinquere, relīquī, relictum: to leave behind

remedium, ī n.: remedy, relief

remeō, remeāre, remeāvī, remeātum: to return, go back

rēmex, rēmigis m.: bench of oarsmen, rower

rēmigium, ī n.: rowing, the oars, oarsmen

reminiscor, reminiscī: to recollect, remember

remittō, remittere, remīsī, remissum: to send back, let go back

removeō, removēre, remōvī, remōtum: to move back, withdraw

reor, rērī, ratus sum: to calculate, judge, reckon

repellō, repellere, reppulī, repulsum: to drive back, drive away

repente: (adv.) suddenly

repetō, repetere, repetīvī, repetītum: to seek again, begin again, repeat

repleō, replēre, replēvī, replētum: to refill, fill up

requiēs, requiētis f.: rest

requiescō, requiescere, requiēvī, requiētum: to rest

rēs Rōmāna, reī Rōmānae f.: Roman state

rēs, reī f.: a thing, affair, matter

reserātus, a, um: unbarred, opened

resideō, residēre, resēdi, resessum: to sit back

resolvō, resolvere, resolvī, resolūtum: to untie, release, open

resonō, resonāre, resonāvī, resonātum: to resound, echo

respondeō, respondēre, respondī, responsum: to answer to, reply

restō, restāre, restitī: to remain, stand against, oppose (+ dat.)

rēsūmō, rēsūmere, rēsumpsī, rēsumptum: to take again, resume

resurgō, resurgere, resurrexī, resurrectum: to rise again, appear again

rēte, rētis n.: net

retinācula, ōrum n. pl.: rope, cable

retractō, retractāre, retractāvī, retractātum: to undertake again, recall

retrō: (adv.) backwards

reveniō, revenīre, revēnī, reventum: to come back, return

revirescō, revirescere, revirescuī: to grow
strong again
revocō, revocāre, revocāvī, revocātum: to
call back, recall
rēx, rēgis m.: king
Rhēa Silvia, Rhēae Silviae f.: Rhea Silvia,
the mother of Romulus and Remus
rīdeō, rīdēre, rīsī, rīsum: to smile,
laugh at
rigeō, rigēre: to be stiff, to be hard
rīpa, ae f.: river bank, shore
rītus, ūs m.: religious ceremony, rite
rōbur, rōboris n.: oak
rogō, rogāre, rogāvī, rogātum: to ask
Rōma, ae f.: Rome
Rōmānus, a, um: of Rome
Rōmuleus, a, um: of Romulus
Rōmulus, ī m.: Romulus, the first king of
Rome
rōrāns, rōrantis: causing dew, dripping,
being moist
rostrum, ī n.: beak, snout, muzzle
rota, ae f.: wheel
rubens, rubentis: red
rubor, rubōris m.: redness
rudis, e: unworked, crude
rūga, ae f.: wrinkle
rūmor, rūmōris m.: a rumor, report
rumpō, rumpere, rūpī, ruptum: to break,
shatter, burst
ruō, ruere, ruī, rutum: to rush
rursus: (adv.) again
rūs, rūris n.: country, land

saburra, ae f.: sand, ballast
sacer, sacra, sacrum: sacred
sacerdōs, sacerdōtis m. or f.: priest, priestess
sacra, sacrōrum n. pl.: sacred rites
sacrificō, sacrificāre, sacrificāvī,
sacrificātum: to offer sacrifice
Saeculum, ī n.: Generation, divine representation of a generation
saepe: (adv.) often
saepes, is f.: a hedge

saepius: (adv.) more often
saevior, ius: more savage
saevitia, ae f.: ferocity, savagery
saevus, a, um: savage, fierce
sagitta, ae f.: arrow
Sagittārius, ī m.: Sagittarius (zodiac sign),
an archer
salamandra, ae f.: salamander
Salmacis, Salmacidis f.: Salmacis, a nymph
in Caria
salus, salūtis f.: health, welfare, safety
salūtifer, salūtiferī m.: bringer of health
salūtō, salūtāre, salūtāvī, salūtātum: to
greet, say goodbye to
sanctus, a, um: holy, sacred
sanguineus, a, um: bloody
sanguis, sanguinis m.: blood, vigor, strength
saniēs, salieī f.: diseased blood, poison
sānō, sānāre, sānāvī, sānātum: to cure,
restore to health
sānus, a, um: healthy, sound
satiātus, a, um: satisfied, sated
satiō, satiāre, satiāvī, satiātum: to satisfy, fill
satis: (indecl. adj. and adv.) enough
Sāturnia, ae f.: Saturnia, epithet of Juno,
daughter of Saturn
satus, a, um: sprung, born, sown
satyrus, ī m.: a satyr, goat-man
saxum, ī n.: rock, crag
scāla, ae f.: ladder, flight of stairs
scelerātus, a, um: wicked, profane
scelus, sceleris n.: crime, wicked deed, evil
scēptrum, ī n.: scepter, royal staff
scindō, scindere, scidī, scissum: to cut, tear
asunder
sciō, scīre, scīvī, scītum: to know
scopulus, ī m.: boulder
Scorpiō, Scorpiōnis m.: Scorpio (zodiac
sign), a scorpion
scrobis, scrobis m.: ditch, trench
Scylla, ae f.: Scylla, daughter of Nisus
secō, secāre, secuī, sectum: to cut
secūris, is f.: an axe, hatchet
secus: (adv.) otherwise

sed: (conj.) but

sedeō, sedēre, sēdī, sessum: to sit

sēdes, sēdis f.: seat

sēligō, sēligere, sēlēgī, sēlectum: to choose, select

sella, ae f.: seat

semel: (adv.) once

Semelē, Semelēs f.: Semele, a daughter of Cadmus

sēmen, sēminis n.: seed, child

sēmilacer, sēmilacera, sēmilacerum: half-mangled

sēmivir, sēmivirī m.: a half-man, effeminate man

semper: (adv.) always

senātus, ūs m.: the senate

senecta, ae f.: old age

senectus, senectūtis f.: old age

senex, senis m.: old man

senīlis, e: aged, old

sententia, ae f.: opinion, thought

sentiō, sentīre, sensī, sensum: to feel, experience, perceive

sēparātio, sēparātiōnis f.: severance, separation

sēparō, sēparāre, sēparāvī, sēparātum: to disjoin, sever, separate

septem: (indecl. numer.) seven

septemfluus, a, um: flowing sevenfold, seven-mouthed

sequor, sequī, secūtus sum: to follow, pursue

sermo, sermōnis m.: talk, conversation

serō, serere, seruī, sertum: to connect, bind together, weave

serpēns, serpentis f. or m.: creeping thing, snake

serpō, serpere, serpsī, serptum: to crawl, creep

sertum, ī n.: wreath, woven garland

sērus, a, um: late, advanced

serva, ae f.: slave

servātor, servātōris m.: savior

servō, servāre, servāvī, servātum: to keep, save, preserve

sex: (indecl. numer.) six

sī: (conj.) if

sībilō, sībilāre, sībilāvī, sībilātum: to hiss

sībilus, a, um: hissing, whistling

sīc: (adv.) thus

siccō, siccāre, siccāvī, siccātum: to dry, dry up

Sīcelis, Sicelidis: of Sicily

sīdereus, a, um: belonging to the stars

sīdus, sīderis n.: star, constellation

signum, ī n.: sign, mark, statue

silentium, ī n.: silence

sileō, silēre, siluī: to be silent

silex, silicis m.: stone

silva, ae f.: wood, forest

similis, e: like, similar to (+ dat.)

simul atque: (conj.) as soon as

simul: (adv.) at the same time

simulācrum, ī n.: image, likeness

simulō, simulāre, simulāvī, simulātum: to make like

sine: (prep. + abl.) without

sinister, sinistra, sinistrum: left, on the left

sinō, sinere, sīvī, situs: to let alone, allow, permit

sinus, ūs m.: a bending, fold, pocket, lap

sistō, sistere, stitī: to stand, cause to stand still, stop

sitis, sitis f.: thirst

situs, a, um: situated, buried

situs, ūs m.: decay, neglect

sīve/seu ... sīve/seu: (conj.) whether ... or

smaragdus, ī m.: emerald

socer, socerī m.: father-in-law

socius, a, um: sharing, companion

sōl, sōlis m.: sun

soleō, solēre, solitus sum: to be accustomed

solidus, a, um: solid

solitus, a, um: accustomed, usual

solium, ī n.: seat

sollertia, ae f.: cleverness

sollertius: (adv.) more skillfully

sollicitō, sollicitāre, sollicitāvī, sollicitātum: to move violently, incite, seek to obtain by bribery

solum, ī n.: floor, bottom
sōlus, a, um: alone, only
solūtus, a, um: loose, loosened, unbound
solvō, solvere, solvī, solūtum: to loosen, dissolve, set free
somnium, ī n.: dream
somnus, ī m.: sleep
sonō, sonāre, sonuī, sonitum: to make a noise, sound
sonus, ī m.: a sound, noise
sordidus, a, um: dirty, foul, sordid
soror, sorōris f.: sister
sors, sortis f.: a lot, fortune, oracular response
spargō, spargere, sparsī, sparsum: to sprinkle, strew, scatter
sparsus, a, um: strewn, scattered
spatior, spatiārī, spatiātus sum: to spread out, expand
spatium, ī n.: space, extent
speciēs, speciēī f.: view, sight, appearance
speciōsus, a, um: beautiful, splendid
spectābilis, e: visible, worth looking at
spectō, spectāre, spectāvī, spectātum: to look at, observe, behold
spēlunca, ae f.: cave
spērātus, a, um: hoped for
spernō, spernere, sprēvī, sprētum: to put away, reject, scorn, despise
spēs, eī f.: hope
sphaera, ae f.: globe, sphere
spīceus, a, um: of corn
splendidus, a, um: splendid, bright, distinguished
spoliō, spoliāre, spoliāvī, spoliātum: strip, despoil, rob
spolium, ī n.: spoil, booty
spūma, ae f.: foam
spūmō, spūmāre, spūmāvī, spūmātum: to foam
squāleō, squālēre, squāluī: to be stiff, be dirty
squāma, ae f.: scale
squāmōsus, a, um: scaly
stabulum, ī n.: quarters, stable, brothel

stagnum, ī n.: standing water, pond
stāmen, stāminis n.: the vertical warp on a loom, woven web, wool threads
statim: (adv.) immediately
statua, ae f.: statue, image
statuō, statuere, statuī, statūtum: to set up, fix upright
stella comans, stellae comantis f.: a hairy star, a comet
stēlla, ae f.: star
sternō, sternere, strāvī, strātum: to spread, make (a bed)
stillō, stillāre, stillāvi, stillātum: to drip
stimulus, ī m.: spur, cattle prod
stīpō, stīpāre, stīpāvī, stīpātum: to press around, crowd
stipula, ae f.: stalk of grain, grain-stubble
stō, stāre, stetī, statum: to stand
strātum, ī n.: coverlet, horsecloth
strīdēns, strīdentis: hissing, vibrating
strīdō, strīdere, strīdī: to make a harsh noise, creak, hiss
stringō, stringere, strixī, strictum: to pull out (a weapon), tighten
studiōsior, ius: more diligent about, more eager for (+ gen.)
studium, ī n.: eagerness, pursuit
stultus, a, um: foolish, silly
stupeō, stupēre, stupuī: to be struck dumb, be stunned
Stygius, a, um: Stygian, of Styx
Styx, Stygis f.: Styx, a river in the Underworld
suādeō, suādēre, suāsī, suāsum: to advise, recommend, persuade
sub: (prep. + abl.) under
subeō, subīre, subiī or subīvī, subitum: to go under, pass under
subigō, subigere, subēgī, subāctum: to work up, work into a smooth thread
subitō: (adv.) suddenly
sublīmis, e: lofty, exalted, elevated
successus, ūs m.: outcome, success
sūcus, ī m.: juice, sap

suī (gen.): (reflex. pron. sing. or pl.) **sibi** (dat.), **sē** (acc.) himself, herself, itself, themselves

sulcō, sulcāre, sulcāvī, sulcātum: to furrow, wrinkle

sulfur, sulfuris n.: brimstone, sulfur

sum, esse, fuī, futūrum: to be

summa, ae f.: a summary, most important point, sum total

summoveō, summovēre, summōvī, summōtum: to move up from below, drive off, remove

summus, a, um: highest

sūmō, sūmere, sumpsī, sumptum: to take up, assume, select

super: (prep. + acc.) over, above

superbus, a, um: arrogant

superēmineō, superēminēre, superēminuī: to overtop, stand above

superō, superāre, superāvī, superātum: to overcome, prevail, be greater than

supersum, superesse, superfuī, superfutūrum: to be above, remain

superus, a, um: high, supreme, situated above

supervolō, supervolāre, supervolāvī, supervolātum: to fly above

supplex, supplicis m.: a suppliant, petitioner

supplicō, supplicāre, supplicāvī, supplicātum: to worship, entreat (+ dat.)

suppōnō, suppōnere, supposuī, suppositum: to place under, bury, sow

surgō, surgere, surrexī, surrectum: to elevate, rise, arise

supprimō, supprimere, suppressī, suppressum: to block, check, push down

suspendō, suspendere, suspendī, suspensum: to hang, hang up, suspend

suspīrō, suspīrāre, suspīrāvī, suspīrātum: to take a deep breath, sigh

sustineō, sustinēre, sustenuī, sustentum: to hold up, carry, sustain

suus, a, um: (reflex. poss. adj.) his, her, its own

tābēs, tābis f.: a wasting away, melting, pestilence

taciturnus, a, um: quiet, silent

tacitus, a, um: silent

tactus, ūs m.: touch

taeda, ae f.: torch

tālis, e: such, of such a kind

tam: (adv.) so, to such a degree

tamen: (conj.) however, nevertheless

tangō, tangere, tetigī, tactum: to touch, reach, arrive at

Tantalus, ī: Tantalus, a king of Lydia

tantum: (adv.) only, to such a degree

tantus, a, um: so much, so great

Tartara, ōrum n. pl.: Tartarus, the infernal regions

Tartareus, a, um: of Tartarus, a region in the Underworld

Taurus, ī m.: Taurus (zodiac sign), a bull

tectum, ī n.: roof, building

tegō, tegere, texī, tectum: to cover, surround

tegumen, teguminis n.: a covering

tēla, ae f.: that which is woven, web, warp, loom

tellūs, tellūris f.: earth, ground

tēlum, ī n.: dart, arrow, spear

tēmō, tēmōnis m.: beam, yoke

temperō, temperāre, temperāvī, temperātum: to govern, manage

templum, ī n.: temple

temptāmentum, ī n.: a trial, attempt

temptō, temptāre, temptāvī, temptātum: to attempt, try

tempus, temporis n.: temple, brow, time

tenax, tenācis: holding fast, clinging

tendō, tendere, tetendī, tentum and tensum: to stretch out, extend

tenebrae, ārum f. pl.: shadows, shade, darkness

teneō, tenēre, tenuī, tentum: to hold

tener, tenera, tenerum: soft, delicate, youthful

tentōrium, ī n.: tent

tenuis, e: thin, fine

tenuissimus, a, um: very fine, most delicate

tepidus, a, um: lukewarm, tepid

ter: (adv.) three times

teres, teretis: rounded, polished, smooth

Tēreus, ī m.: Tereus, husband of Procne

tergum, ī n.: back

terra, ae f.: land

terrēnus, a, um: earthen, of the earth

terreō, terrēre, terruī, territum: to terrify, alarm

terribilis, e: dreadful, frightful

territus, a, um: thoroughly scared

terror, terrōris m.: fright, dread, object which causes fear

tertius, a, um: third

texō, texere, texuī, textum: to weave

thalamus, ī m.: bedroom, marriage bed

Thēbae, ārum f. pl.: Thebes, a city in Boeotia

Thēbāis, Thēbāidis f.: a Theban woman

Thēbānus, a, um: of Thebes, Theban

Themis, Themis f.: Themis, a Greek goddess of the earth and justice

Thrācia, ae f.: Thrace

Thrācius, a, um: of Thrace

Thrax, Thrācis m.: of Thrace

Thrēicius, a, um: of Thrace, a region north of Greece

Tiberīnus, a, um: of the Tiber River

tībia, ae f.: flute, pipe

tignum, ī n.: beam, ceiling beam

timeō, timēre, timuī: to fear

timor, timōris m.: fear, dread

tingō, tingere, tinxī, tinctum: to wet, moisten, dye, imbue

Tīresiās, ae m.: Tiresias, a man known for wisdom

titulus, ī m.: glory, title, honor

toga, ae f.: the toga, garment worn by Roman men

tolerō, tolerāre, tolerāvī, tolerātum: to endure, withstand

tollō, tollere, sustulī, sublātum: to raise, lift up, remove, destroy

tondeō, tondēre, totondī, tonsum: to shear, clip, shave

tonitrus, ūs m.: thunder

tonō, tonāre, tonuī, tonitum: to thunder

torpor, torpōris m.: sluggishness, dullness

torqueō, torquēre, torsī, tortum: to twist, turn

torreō, torrēre, torruī, tostum: to burn, roast

torus, ī m.: couch, bed, marriage bed

torvus, a, um: fierce

tot: (adv.) so many

totidem: (indecl. adj.) just as many

tōtus, a, um: whole

tractus, ūs m.: a pulling

trādō, trādere, trādidī, trāditum: to hand over

trahō, trahere, traxī, tractum: to draw, drag, take

trāiciō, trāicere, trāiēcī, trāiectum: to throw, pierce, penetrate

transcrībō, transcrībere, transcrīpsī, transcrīptum: to write over, transfer, convey

translūceō, translūcēre: to shine across, shine through

tremō, tremere, tremuī: to shake, quiver, tremble

tremor, tremōris m.: shaking, quivering, tremor

trepidō, trepidāre, trepidāvī, trepidātum: to be agitated

trēs, tria: three

triplex, triplicis: triple

tristis, e: sad

triumphō, triumphāre, triumphāvī, triumphātum: to celebrate a triumph, gain victory

triumphus, ī m.: a triumphal procession, victory

trucīdo, trucīdāre, trucīdāvī, trucīdātum: to slaughter

trūdō, trūdere, trūsī, trūsum: to thrust, push forth

truncus, ī m.: trunk of a tree

tū, tuī: (second person sing. pron.) **tibi** (dat.), **tē** (acc./abl.), you

tuba, ae f.: military horn

tum: (adv.) then, at that time

tumeō, tumēre, tumuī: to swell, be puffed up

tumulus, ī m.: hill, burial mound

tunc: (adv.) then

turba, ae f.: crowd, mob

turbātus, a, um: troubled, disturbed, agitated

turbō, turbinis m.: whirlwind

turpis, e: ugly, foul, shameful

turpiter: (adv.) in shame

turris, turris f.: a tower, citadel

tūs, tūris n.: frankincense

tūtus, a, um: safe

tuus, a, um: (poss. adj.) your

tyrannis, tyrannidis f.: tyranny, despotic rule

tyrannus, ī m.: an absolute ruler, tyrant

Tyrius, a, um: of Tyre, a Phoenician city, purple

Tyrrhēnus, a, um: of Etruria, Etruscan

ūber, ūberis n.: udder

ubi: (adv.) when, where

ubīque: (adv.) everywhere

Ulixes, Ulixis m.: Ulysses, the Greek hero Odysseus

ullus, a, um: any, anyone

ulmus, ī f.: elm

ulterius: (adv.) further, for a longer time

ultimus, a, um: last, final

ultrā: (adv.) beyond, further

ululāns, ululantis: producing howls, yelling loudly

ululātus, ūs f.: a howling, shrieking

ululō, ululāre, ululāvī, ululātum: to howl

umbra, ae f.: shade, shadow, dead spirit

umerus, ī m.: upper arm, shoulder

ūmidus, a, um: moist

ūmor, ūmōris m.: moisture, fluid

ūnā: (adv.) together

unda, ae f.: water, wave

unde: (adv.) from where

undique: (adv.) from everywhere

ūnus, a, um: one, single

urbs, urbis f.: city

urna, ae f.: water jar, urn

ursa, ae f.: bear

usque: (adv.) as far as, all the way to, continuously

ūsus, ūs m.: practical experience, use

ut: (adv.) as, just as

uterque, utraque, utrumque: each of two, both

uterus, ī m.: belly, womb

ūtilis, e: useful, beneficial, profitable

ūtor, ūtī, ūsus sum: to use (+ abl.)

ūva, ae f.: grape

uxor, uxōris f.: wife

vacō, vacāre, vacāvī, vacātum: to be empty

vacuus, a, um: empty, void

vādō, vādere: to go, hasten

vāgīna, ae f.: sheath

vagō, vagāre, vagāvī, vagātum: to wander, ramble

valdē: (adv.) intensely, greatly

valeō, valēre, valuī, valitum: to be strong, be healthy

vallis (valles), vallis f.: valley

valvae, ārum f. pl.: doors

variō, variāre, variāvī, variātum: to change, alter, diversify

varius, a, um: diverse, manifold

vastō, vastāre, vastāvī, vastātum: to devastate, ravage, make empty

vastus, a, um: empty, desolate, enormous

vātes, vātis m. or f.: seer, prophet

vel: (conj.) or

vēlātus, a, um: wrapped, covered, concealed

vellus, velleris n.: fleece, hide

vēlō, vēlāre, vēlāvī, vēlātum: to cover, hide

velox, vēlōcis: swift, quick

vēlum, ī n.: sail, covering

vēna, ae f.: blood vessel, vein

vēnātor, vēnātōris m.: a hunter, sportsman

vēnātus, ūs m.: the chase, hunting

venēficus, a, um: magical, poisonous

venēnum, ī n.: poison, venom

venerō, venerāre, venerāvī, venerātum: to worship, entreat

veneror, venerārī, venerātus sum: to ask, entreat with reverence, worship

venia, ae f.: pardon

veniō, venīre, vēnī, ventum: to come

venter, ventris m.: belly

ventus, ī m.: wind

Venus, Veneris f.: Venus, the Roman goddess of love and sexuality

Vēr, Vēris n.: Spring, divine representation of the springtime

verber, verberis n.: lash, whip

verbum, ī n.: word

veritus, a, um: fearful, fearing

vernō, vernāre, vernāvī, vernātum: to flourish, bloom

vērō: (adv.) truly

verrō, verrere, verrī, versum: to sweep

versus, a, um: turned, turned over

vertex, verticis m.: whirlpool, crown of head, summit

vertō, vertere, vertī, vertus: to turn, turn around

Vertumnus, ī m.: Vertumnus, god of the cycle of the seasons

veru, ūs n.: a spit

vērum, ī n.: the truth

vērus, a, um: true

Vesta, ae f.: Vesta, goddess of the hearth

vester, vestra, vestrum: (poss. adj.) your

vestīgium, ī n.: footprint, trace

vestīgō, vestīgāre, vestīgāvī, vestīgātum: to track down, trace out

vestīmentum, ī n.: garment

vestis, vestis f.: garment, clothing

vetō, vetāre, vetuī, vetitum: to forbid, prohibit

vetus, veteris: old, ancient

vetustus, a, um: old

via, ae f.: road, way, journey

viātor, viātōris m.: a traveler

vibrō, vibrāre, vibrāvī, vibrātum: to shake, quiver, vibrate

victima, ae f.: a sacrificial victim

victor, victōris m.: victor, winner

victōria, ae f.: victory

victrix, victrīcis f.: female victor

victus, a, um: conquered

videō, vidēre, vīdī, vīsum: to see

villus, ī m.: shaggy hair

vīmen, vīminis n.: branch, twig

vinclum, ī n.: bond, binding, sandal strap

vincō, vincere, vīcī, victum: to conquer

vinculum, ī n.: chain, bond

vindicō, vindicāre, vindicāvī, vindicātum: avenge

vīnum, ī n.: wine

viola, ae f.: a violet

violātus, a, um: broken, injured

violō, violāre, violāvī, violatum: to treat with violence, outrage, rape

vīpereus, a, um: of a snake

vir, virī m.: a man

vireō, virēre, viruī: to be green

virga, ae f.: branch, twig

virgineus, a, um: maiden, virgin

virginitās, virginitātis f.: virginity

Virgō, Virginis f.: Virgo (zodiac sign), a virgin

viridis, e: green

virīlis, e: manly, masculine

virtūs, virtūtis f.: manliness, excellence, virtue

vīs, vis f.: strength, power, force

viscera, viscerum n. pl.: the flesh, inner organs, entrails

vīsitō, vīsitāre, vīsitāvī, vīsitātum: to see, visit

vīsus, a, um: seen, looked upon

vīsus, ūs f.: a sight, appearance

vīta, ae f.: life

vitiō, vitiāre, vitiāvī, vitiātum: to injure, damage, rape

vītis, vītis f.: vine

vītō, vītāre, vītāvī, vītātum: to escape, avoid

vīvō, vīvere, vixī, victum: to live

vīvus, a, um: living

vix: (adv.) with difficulty, scarcely

vōcālis, e: uttering sounds, singing, vocal, sonorous

vocō, vocāre, vocāvī, vocātum: to call, summon

volō, volāre, volāvī, volātum: to fly, move quickly

volūbilis, e: turning, spinning, whirling

volucris, volucris f.: a bird, flying thing

voluptās, voluptātis f.: pleasure, enjoyment

volvō, volvere, volvī, volūtum: to roll, twist, turn round

vōs, vestrī/vestrum pl.: (second person pron.) vōbīs (dat./abl.), vōs (acc.), you all

vōtum, ī n.: prayer, wish

vōx, vōcis f.: voice

Vulcānus, ī m.: Vulcan, the god of craftsmen and fire

vulgus, ī m.: common people, crowd

vulnerō, vulnerāre, vulnerāvī, vulnerātum: to wound

vulnus, vulneris n.: a wound

vultus, ūs m.: face, expression, appearance

Zephyrus, ī m.: Zephyr, the west wind

Zētēs, ae m.: Zetes, a son of Boreas and Orithyia

zōna, ae f.: zone, region, girdle

Index